# LEFTWARD JOURNEY

# LEFTWARD JOURNEY

The Education
of Vietnamese Students
in France
1919–1939

## Scott McConnell

Transaction Publishers
New Brunswick (U.S.A.) and Oxford (U.K.)

Library of Congress Catalog Number: 88-4771
ISBN: 0-88738-238-X
Printed in the United States of America

**Library of Congress Cataloging-in-Publication Data**

McConnell, Scott.
  Leftward journey.

  Revision of thesis (doctoral)—Columbia University.
  Bibliography: p.
  Includes index.
  1.Vietnamese students—France—History—20th
century.  2. France—Politics and government—1914-1940.
3. Returned students—Vietnam—History—20th century.
4. Communists—Vietnam—History—20th century.  I. Title.
LC3501.V53M34  1988      371.97′9592′044      88-4771
ISBN 0-88738-238-X

# Contents

# List of Abbreviations

| | |
|---|---|
| AEMNA | Association des Étudiants Musulmans Nord Africains (North African Muslim Students' Association) |
| AGEI | Association Générale des Etudiants Indochinois (General Association of Indochinese Students) |
| AN | Archives nationales, Paris |
| ANSOM: NFI | Archives nationales, Section d'outre-mer, Nouveau Fonds Indochine |
| AOM- Indochine | Archives du governement generale de l'Indochine, |
| ARUP | Archives of the Rector of the University of Paris |
| CAI | Service de Contrôle et d'Assistance aux Indigènes (Service of Supervision and Aid to French Colonial Subjects) |
| ICP | Indochinese Communist party |
| JO | *Journal officiel de la République française* |
| JP | Jeunesses Patriotes (Patriotic Youth) |
| PAI | Parti Annamite de l'Indépendance (Independence Party of Annam) |
| PCF | Parti Communiste Francais (French Communist Party) |
| SAMI | Service d'Assistance Morale et Intellectuelle (Service of Moral and Intellectual Aid) |
| SFIO | Section Française de L'Internationale Ouvrière (French Socialist Party) |
| Slotfom | Service de liaison entre les originaires de la France d'outre mer |
| VNQDD | Viet Nam Quoc Dan Dang (Vietnamese Nationalist party) |

# Acknowledgments

I owe thanks to many people for helping me to complete this project. In France, staff members of the Archives Nationales and other libraries and archives were unfailingly courteous and helpful. During my research Daniel Hémery and Gail Kelly were generous with their time and knowledge. Patrick Fridenson offered me useful advice on sources. Benjamin Stora, Claude Liauzu, and Charles-Robert Ageron took time to answer some of my questions, and made helpful suggestions.

This book originated as a doctoral dissertation at Columbia University, under the deft supervision of Professor Robert Paxton. I am grateful for his patience with an often wavering graduate student, and for his wise commentary on earlier drafts. I am also thankful for the advice and admonishment I have received over the years from Professor Fritz Stern, about this project and much else.

I also express thanks to Professor Samuel Popkin, who was kind enough to read and comment upon the manuscript at a late date.

Many friends and family members willed the completion of this work. I am particularly thankful to Jerry Muller, who provided significant counsel and much needed encouragement. Above all I am grateful to my wife Margaret and children Neil and Kristen, who goaded me in subtle ways to bring this book to completion.

# Introduction

This is a study of the interaction between France and those Vietnamese students who left their colony in the decade after World War I to pursue their education in France. It is an examination of a particular example of one of the broader dilemmas faced by all of the European colonial powers. Simply put, in order to sustain and strengthen their empires, Europe's colonialists needed to create an educated class of colonial subjects imbued with colonial loyalties. But the more education the colonial subjects were exposed to, the more likely they were to oppose European rule. This study is the story of how France tried and failed to resolve this dilemma.

The history of the Vietnamese student migration is not only a story of French failure, but is also a significant chapter in the development of Vietnamese anticolonialist nationalism. The political consequences of the student migration to France involved not only the strengthening of those Vietnamese movements most opposed to French rule, but the turning of Vietnamese nationalism leftward. This book is an effort at explaining how and why this happened.

Prior to 1900, few Frenchmen with colonial responsibilities doubted that the spreading of French schools and French ideas among the peoples of her empire was a good and necessary thing. In 1847, the young Duc d'Aumale, the second French Governor General to rule Algeria, stated that "the opening of a school in the native milieu is worth as much as a battalion for the pacification of the country."[1] This comment expressed a state of mind common among the men who ruled the French empire, and statements like it would be repeated thousands of times throughout the nineteenth century. There were some notable dissenters from this view, who argued that the spread of French ideas to the peoples of the South and East would have lamentable consequences. But, when France was building her empire, such arguments were well outside the mainstream of French colonial thought and practice.[2]

France's great imperial surge in the nineteenth century was the work of men intent, above all else, on enhancing the power of France. The desire for naval stations, markets for French goods, access to resources, and all the intangible elements of international prestige and power were never absent from their calculations. But they were also convinced that along with the French flag, they brought to torrid and inhospitable parts of the world the spirit of progress and enlightenment, science and rationality, freedom from superstition and disease. And they believed that the more colonial subjects were exposed to French learning, the more they would see the benefits of French rule. The Third Republic politicians who oversaw the completion of France's conquest of Vietnam, for example, were the same men who created the French public school system and brought the rationalist catechisms of the Third Republic into French hamlets where the patterns of life had not changed for centuries. Those men most responsible, in France, for the transformation of "peasants into Frenchmen" at least entertained the idea of making Vietnamese, Algerians, and Africans into Frenchmen too.[3]

In Vietnam, as elsewhere in her empire, French conquest brought with it social upheaval. In order to rule, the French had to bend the colony's traditional elites to their will, or else strip them of their power and humiliate them. In one characteristic incident, French officers, trying to persuade Vietnam's emperor to make further concessions to France, gathered a crowd of Vietnamese spectators, sent three of the emperor's envoys up in a dirigible, and brought them down terrorized and groveling. This was a demonstration of mastery far more telling then mere brute force. It was the kind of action, backed up by military power, that helped bring about a collapse of traditional authority throughout the French colonial domain.[4]

Yet the weakening of the old order left a void which the French would find extremely difficult to fill. One part of traditional Vietnam that passed into history was the educational system—a complex structure of Chinese character schools and Confucian examinations that socialized almost every Vietnamese child. It disappeared almost immediately in the first area of French conquest, the southern region known as Cochinchina, and was more gradually eroded in the North. Replacing it was a difficult project. For Frenchmen would discover, first in Vietnam, and later in North Africa and Africa, that there was a paradox at the heart of their colonial educational policies. Simply stated, they found that the more they exposed their subjects to French education, the more frequently would arise men who would oppose French rule, using ideas borrowed from the traditions of French republicanism or learned in France. These men would prove to be far more effective opponents of colonialism than their traditionalist predecessors.

There was a social component to the paradox as well. The French presence in the colonies spurred the creation of new social classes, new cultural styles, and created men with expectations of a new sort. By early in the twentieth century, no French official would write on the subject of colonial education without at least mentioning the danger of the *déclassé*—a new type of marginal man who, because of his exposure to French education, would not fit easily into any social role available to him in the colony.

Before World War I this problem was still of modest scope. But one consequence of the Great War was to make the world smaller. From Vietnam, France recruited one hundred thousand workers and soldiers, and brought them to France; those who returned sensed French vulnerability in a way that their fathers never did. In the wake of the war, a new type of Vietnamese nationalism, more knowledgeable about France and the world, began to make its presence felt. Within a half dozen years of the war's end, several thousand young Vietnamese were clamoring to go to France—a development that was largely a reflection of the new nationalist spirit.

This student migration—where it came from, what happened to it in France, how French officials tried to contend with it, shape it, and eventually failed to master it—is the subject of this study. The number of Vietnamese students who came to France in the interwar period, perhaps three thousand overall, was not large in comparison with the student migrations after World War II. But it was dramatic for a colony whose university graduates during the previous sixty years of French rule numbered no more than several hundred, and would have a considerable impact on the complexion of Vietnamese anticolonialism. These Vietnamese were, as well, the first group of colonial students to come to France in significant numbers, the largest group by a considerable margin, and the group that most worried French authorities; to a considerable extent, the path they took shaped French expectations about the Africans and North Africans who followed in their footsteps.

The phenomenon of young, often rebellious, and often disaffected young men coming to the *métropole* from the distant colony was unique neither to France nor to Vietnam. Indian students had been coming to England since the middle of the nineteenth century; they paved the way for an African migration that began after World War I. During the interwar period London was the place where men who would inherit power over what was formerly the British empire were most often educated. Following the Vietnamese to Paris would come students from Tunisia, Morocco, Algeria and Senegal, and later still from Cambodia. How many future heads of state, how many ministers, how many authors, and editors, and leaders of political factions emerged from the groups of students educated in Paris and London between the wars?

Or, a darker question, how many of these students acquired in Europe not only the organizational and intellectual skills to lead, but the ideological motivation to carry out, amongst their own people, political murders by the thousands? This too is a consideration of this study. The explosion in intellectual contact between Europe and her colonial subjects between the wars—which far exceeded all previous educational interaction—coincided with a large scale disaffection from the ideals of bourgeois liberalism within Europe. The Europe encountered by these contingents of colonial students was a continent in which communism and fascism were vital, growing, and dynamic faiths—a circumstance that could not help but have an enduring influence on the political attitudes of the students, and, eventually, on the societies to which they returned.

Three main themes are woven into this study of the Vietnamese students in France. At one level this is a book concerned with the history of the French government, the ideas it had about its empire, and the way these ideas helped shape the actual policies of French colonialism. A second theme is the students' own story: how young Vietnamese encountered the West and responded to it. And finally, this is an account of the leftward journey of a decisive minority among the students, and an analysis of the relationship between anticolonial nationalism and the world Communist movement.

Regarding French governmental policies, the most striking point that emerges from the study of the Vietnamese student migration is how little the French prepared for it and how poorly they managed it. Lack of intellectual acuity and foresight is seldom prominent on the list of negative traits that have been attributed to Frenchmen. The worst consequences of the Vietnamese student migration were, long before they occurred, analyzed and anticipated by French officials. And yet France neither stemmed the student migration nor made any serious effort to control it and turn it to French advantage. Thus France's inability to master the students can be viewed as part of France's failure to make timely choices about the political shape and future of her empire. Stanley Hoffmann's well known conception of the Third Republic as the "stalemate society" is so strikingly apt as to be relevant to an almost limitless number of social and political issues on which one French government after another was unable to enforce a political decision. French policies towards her empire fall easily under its heuristic domain.[5]

Unlike the British, who knew, by the interwar period, that they were preparing their colonial subjects for eventual self-government, the French made no such choice. They vacillated between the unrealistic notion that they were preparing to "assimilate" their colonies and make them more fully part of France, and equally futile efforts to freeze the social status quo so that French rule in the colonies might endure as easily as it had in the nineteenth century. Successive French governments of Indochina thus swung back and forth between liberalizing reform and harsh repression. This inconsistency permeated the making of French policy towards the Vietnamese students; as its consequence France exerted little influence over the sociological shape of the Vietnamese student migration, over its educational experience in France, and over the migration's political implications for the future of Vietnam.

In exploring how the Vietnamese students' experience in France shaped their political views, this study proceeds from the premise that there was a wide menu of political choices open to them. The young Vietnamese could choose the government-encouraged route of "Franco-Vietnamese collaboration." They could become the partisans of various reformist or more radical factions of Vietnamese nationalism. Or they could become Communists, of either the Stalinist or Trotskyite variety. Young Vietnamese encountered all of these choices while they were residing far from home, in the main cities of the colonizing power—an experience that could not help but be the source of a great deal of personal uncertainty and alienation.

One possible type of alienation, experienced by Vietnamese and many other colonials who studied in the West, was rooted in the students attraction to France. For Vietnamese students, study in France meant liberation from parental constraint, the opportunity for intellectual growth outside the confines of Vietnamese society, and relief from the racism that was prevalent in colonial Vietnam. France could seduce. But that was the problem—for those Vietnamese who grew to love France gradually became estranged from many aspects of life in Vietnam, at great emotional cost to themselves. To become more French meant a certain burning of bridges to one's own people, to one's parents. This kind of estrangement produced tremendous psychic burdens, and sapped the will; the more French they became, the less effective they would be once they returned to Vietnam. This proved to be a decisive reason why France found it so difficult to create a self-confident, assertive, pro-French political elite, why so many of the Franco-Vietnamese collaborators seemed self-divided and politically neutered.

One way a Vietnamese could overcome these conflicts of allegiance and this sense of self-division was to teach himself to hate the French, and to nurture the anti-French resentments that inevitably existed in the Vietnamese consciousness. Through the cultivation of hatred could be developed a certain kind of strength—one reason, perhaps, why the most intransigent Vietnamese nationalists seemed to be more willful and politically effective men than their Vietnamese opponents. This study attempts to illuminate some of the emotional foundations of the political choices made by this generation of Vietnamese.

Finally, this book is an examination of one area in which the Communist perspective triumphed over its competitors within the broader context of Vietnamese nationalism. When the French first conquered Vietnam, Republican France was part of a larger European bourgeois and democratic culture that was thought of as embodying the world's future. Even Western socialism, which challenged it, was not integrally hostile to the achievements of that culture. Colonial officials or army officers who had to contend with the early manifestations of Vietnamese resistance could feel confident in their belief that the spirit of the rebels came from the past, not the future.

The Russian Revolution instantly punctured this satisfying conceit. Leninism was immediately perceived as an alternative to the world of bourgeois republics and colonial administrations that was not in the least reactionary; it was linked to a philosophy of history that "scientifically" pointed the way to the world's future. Thus Communist anticolonialism, which began to stir in Africa and Asia by the mid-1920s, was, on an intellectual level, anticolonialism of an entirely new type. It is both curious and revealing that, in their internal documents, French bureaucrats began to designate students who were Communist as having political conceptions that were "advanced." This would seem to be a large and probably unconscious concession to the Marxist theory of history, and reveals much about the effect the Russian Revolution had, for everyone involved in colonial issues, on the sense of where the future lay.

The encounter of the Vietnamese students in France with communism was not, of course, primarily a matter of political theory; it was a political and emotional relationship with a living political organization. The tie forged in France between the French Communist party and some Vietnamese students suffered from many of the uneasy aspects that characterized all relationships between the white colonists and their colonial subjects. Nevertheless these hurdles were usually overcome, and the result was a political alliance that served as a springboard for Vietnamese Communists to win a hegemonic position in the movement for Vietnamese national self-determination.

Vietnamese students were, moreso than others from the French empire, receptive to communism. There were of course colonial students from throughout the French empire who flirted with communism—and among colonial students schooled in London some sort of fellow traveling with Communist movements was commonplace. Yet out of all the French and British colonies during the interwar period, only in Vietnam did solid Communist allegiance deeply penetrate the Western-educated intelligentsia. This Communist achievement is one central reason why Saigon, in 1935, emerged as one of the few places in the world where Communists were able to win a contested election.

In an effort to explain this success, this book examines not only how the Third International succeeded, but how communism's ideological and organizational competitors in France failed. For instance, one can very nearly write the history of the Vietnamese students in France without referring to the French Socialists. Even ties between the Vietnamese and the Catholic Church were thin compared to the links created between Moscow and the Vietnamese in Paris. The hegemony of Communist attitudes within the Vietnamese student migration is the one striking distinction between the Vietnamese and the North African and African students who followed after them. In contrast to the experience of the Vietnamese, one cannot describe the North African experience in France without reference to a diverse array of influences, which include Pan-Arabism and an enhanced interest on the part of the French Socialists. By the 1930s, when students from throughout the French empire were converging in Paris, the Third Republic was under fire, at various times, from the Left, the far Right, from Catholics, from intellectuals of all stripes. But these influences counted for far less with the Vietnamese, who came to France earlier. Viewing the Vietnamese experience in comparative perspective leads to the hypothesis that the France of the 1930s left a much different imprint on colonial students than the France of the 1920s.

This book had its beginnings as a doctoral dissertation that sought to focus on French attitudes and policies towards the Vietnamese students. It remains in great part an exploration of how official France tried and failed to create a moderate, non-Communist, and possibly collaborating Vietnamese elite between the wars—certainly its last opportunity to do so. In seeking answers to this question, I have relied on the writings of Frenchmen who observed Vietnamese students, wrote rules for them, administered them, and worried about them. I also explored the writings of the French journalists and professors who examined France's colonial educational dilemmas, and tried to conceive how France might escape them.

But in analyzing France's political failure with those Vietnamese who attended French schools, I found it impossible not to trespass into the territory properly belonging to historians of Vietnam. I have done so with some trepidation, for I do not read Vietnamese, nor do I have a deep scholarly background in Vietnamese history or culture.

Nevertheless it became clear during my research that an interesting and neglected part of the history of Vietnamese nationalism existed in the archives of those French agencies that dealt with the student migration. There could be found newspapers, leaflets, and even letters Vietnamese students sent home. More often than not these sources were written in French, the language which Vietnamese in France during this time usually used to express political ideas. Other material has been translated by French officials. These sources provide a fragmentary but fascinating glimpse into the consciousness of the young men in France whose political development would, generations later, loom so large in the perceptions of

Americans. The sections of this book that treat these materials are the most speculative and the most susceptible to the characteristic difficulties of writing history "from below." In many cases I have inferred conclusions from sources that are fragmentary, and can only speculate as to how representative they are. Nevertheless the freshness of some of the material produced by Vietnamese students made the temptation to use it impossible to resist.

In so doing I have been conscious of my own cultural distance from the Vietnamese experience. Many questions that emerge from this subject might be explored more deeply or treated differently by a trained Asia scholar. There are surely source materials in Vietnam, or Vietnamese language materials in the West, inaccessible to me, which would throw more light on them. One issue I have explored only tangentially is whether the fact that the Vietnamese came from a Confucian culture made them more receptive to Marxism than other peoples—a theory which, during the Vietnam war, assumed a certain political life of its own.[6] In the text I argue that Vietnam's Confucian residue was not an important element in the political consciousness of the students. However I don't discount the possibility that I would see the matter differently if I had a greater sense of the Confucian mind, or a greater feel for the extent to which a Vietnamese from the generation in question was influenced by Confucian concepts.

One of the few positive consequences of the Vietnamese-American war has been the development, in the United States, of a number of first-rate scholars of Vietnam, whose work does much to illuminate the Vietnamese experience. Of course their books give an outsider like myself the feeling that there is a great deal about Vietnam that he will never know. But readers of this book will recognize the extent to which their scholarship, as well as that of several French specialists on Vietnam, has been indispensable to me.

## Notes

1. As quoted in Charles-Robert Ageron, *Les Algériens Musulmans et la France, 1871-1919* (Paris: Presses Universitaires de France, 1968), 319.
2. The racist theorist Arthur de Gobineau was one intellectual who rejected the idea that Western education would bring Asian people closer to France; his arguments represented the first expression of an anti-assimilationist tendency that would appear in the next century in the writings of colonial writers like Jules Harmand and Louis Vignon. In *Les Réligions et les Philosophies dans l'Asie Centrale* (Paris: 1866), 135, cited by Elie Kedourie, *Nationalism in Asia and Africa* (New York: New American Library, 1970), 26, de Gobineau speculates on the effect European ideas will have on the Asian consciousness: "I am inclined to think that the dangers for us will not be negligible. Not physical dangers: on this score we may rest easy, for the Asiatics have no swords which can offer resistance

to our bayonets. It is to moral dangers that I refer. In this great intellectual swamp some new combustion of principles, of ideas, of pestilential theories will take place, and the poison which it will produce will be transmitted by contact more or less quickly, but surely." The sociologist Gustave Le Bon also felt that French education would only create trouble in the French empire. For his assessment see "De l'Influence de l'Education et des Institutions Européenes sur les Populations Indigènes des Colonies," *Congrès Colonial International de Paris,* 1889.

3. See Raoul Girardet, *L'Idée Coloniale en France de 1871 à 1962* (Paris: La Table Ronde, 1972), 137-138 for a discussion of the relationship between domestic educational expansion and France's imperial surge.

4. Alexander Woodside, *Community and Revolution in Modern Vietnam* (Boston: Houghton Mifflin, 1976), 9.

5. See Stanley Hoffman, "Paradoxes of the French Political Community" in *In Search of France* (New York: Harper and Row, 1965).

6. See particularly Frances FitzGerald, *Fire in the Lake: the Vietnamese and the Americans in Vietnam* (Boston: Little Brown, 1972); and Nguyen Khac Vien, "Confucianism and Marxism in Vietnam" in Nguyen Khac Vien, *Tradition and Revolution in Vietnam* (Berkeley: Indochina Resource Center, 1974).

# 1

# Prelude to Migration:
# The Indochinese Background

By the early 1920s, there were, for the first time, enough Vietnamese students in Paris to be noticed by the popular press. Though they did not arouse so much curiosity as other foreign students, particularly the much larger contingent from China, the Vietnamese were the subject of occasional human interest stories, which usually stressed their seriousness of scholarly purpose, and their gratitude to France. Had a curious French journalist chosen to ask how the Vietnamese students got to France, by what criteria they were chosen, what was their social and academic background, and, more pointedly, what was the French policy for education in her Indochinese colony and what role did educating students in France play in it, he would have had a difficult time finding someone who could give him a comprehensive answer. For the Vietnamese student presence in Paris after the war was not so much the consequence of any particular program as it was the outcome of a tangled interplay of French policies, French compromises, Vietnamese aspirations and Vietnamese social movements. The Vietnamese presence in France was not something planned by the French. Instead it was the result of France's long term failure to create an educational policy in the colony that would satisfy both Vietnamese aspirations and her own needs as the colonizing power.

## Albert Sarraut's Legacy

The term of Albert Sarraut as Indochina's Governor General is a suitable point to begin unraveling this tangle. A rising young Radical Socialist politician from l'Aude, Sarraut arrived in Hanoi, the administrative capital of Indochina, in 1911 and proceeded to make a name for himself. He was the only French Governor-General to serve two terms in the colony, and when he returned to France after the war he was named minister of colo-

1

nies—a post he held longer than any figure of the interwar period. The Radical Socialist politician was a master of political rhetoric and a talented writer; in numerous speeches and in two influential books, Sarraut, more than any other of his contemporaries, shaped the language in which Frenchmen talked about their empire. If he was not the first French official to claim that humanitarianism and altruism were the main forces driving the French colonial enterprise, he was first to place such claims at the heart of his political discourse.

Sarraut's rhetorical skills served him well in Indochina. He arrived in the wake of a renewed period of social turbulence, whose root cause was identical with that of the many resistance movements the French had faced ever since their conquest of Cochinchina, the southernmost third of the Indochina peninsula in 1867: the fact that there would always be Vietnamese unreconciled to French rule. With much more success than his predecessors, Sarraut sought to tame the nationalist passions by promising the Vietnamese elite that reforms in French rule were forthcoming, and convinced large numbers of them that France was now truly in touch with their aspirations.[1]

We begin with Sarraut not only because of his general importance to French colonial policy, but because he was the figure most responsible for the design of the educational system in Vietnam during the remaining decades of French rule. The young Vietnamese who began to flow into France in the interwar period were both the products and the castoffs of the *franco-indigène* system that Sarraut had put in place. Indeed Sarraut's contribution to building the educational system of Indochina was the most lasting part of his legacy. It was also an essential component of his effort to convince the Vietnamese that France was ruling them in their interest; more importantly, it was an effort to remove education from the realm of political agitation, where it had been ever since the French began their rule of the colony.

In building the so called *franco-indigène* school system in Indochina, Sarraut was trying to settle a problem that had troubled the French since their arrival in Vietnam. The simple fact was that, though the French had largely succeeded in destroying the traditional educational system of Vietnam, after two generations of rule they had not succeeded in creating an adequate system to replace it. Adding to the dilemma was the fact that education had, once again, become a political rallying cry for Vietnamese nationalists. Finally, Sarraut, like all French officials in the colony, had to contend with the fact that the French *colons* who resided in Vietnam considered that educating the Vietnamese was asking for trouble. Moreover, there was a growing and influential body of literature written by some of French colonialism's most experienced and intellectual defenders which warned that giving France's colonial subjects a French education was a bad idea.

When Sarraut took the post in Hanoi, the French were facing a renewal of political unrest, which was sometimes violent. To be sure, the French had contended with Vietnamese hostile to their rule ever since they first arrived in Vietnam. They had not conquered the central and northern provinces of Vietnam (Annam and Tonkin) until 1883, and had faced nearly continuous guerrilla warfare until the turn of the century. The first generation of rebels fought under the banner of Vietnam's emperor, and were led by Vietnam's mandarin ruling class, its scholar gentry.[2] The fact that traditional elites rallied to fight against the colonizers was not unique to Vietnam—though it is fair to say that Vietnam was more difficult to pacify than France's other colonies.[3] In the case of Vietnam, however, the old ruling class was a mandarin scholar gentry which owed its position to its education—specifically its accomplishments in the examinations of the Sino-Confucian system. Because education had always been directly linked to political power in Vietnam, educational issues, to a greater degree than in other French colonies, carried a highly charged political connotation.

### The Old Regime and the French Conquest

Nearly all those who have studied precolonial Vietnam have admired aspects of the traditional educational system. In principle, and, to a great extent, in practice, it was exceedingly democratic; as the historian Joseph Buttinger has described it: "All of the country's officials were scholars, and all scholars, whether in government service or not, were morally obliged to teach the young. No village was without its school, no school without its qualified teachers, and no gifted pupil was denied the chance to attend an institution of higher learning."[4]

The schools taught Confucian classics in Chinese characters. Like the Chinese system it was modeled upon, Vietnamese education at its lower levels involved rote learning by repetition, for the purpose of indoctrinating the student with moral maxims on how to accept and correctly fulfill his role within society. At higher levels talented students trained in poetry composition and literary exegis of the Confucian classics. Every three years competitive examinations in these fields were held in the imperial capital at Hue, and the small number of scholars who passed became mandarins— servants of the emperor, Vietnam's ruling class. Democratic as Vietnamese education was (obviously the children of the existing mandarin elite had a better chance to receive the kind of tutoring that would enable them to excel in exams) the system did little to prepare the Vietnamese elite to understand and confront successfully the Western challenge.[5]

Twentieth century scholars have found more virtues in the traditional system than did the French officers who took control of Cochinchina in the 1860s. When the Vietnamese emperor, under duress, ceded Cochinchina to France, the old education system collapsed almost immediately. Mandarin scholars who taught there either fled to the North, tried to organize armed resistance, or simply stopped teaching. This troubled the French not at all; most French officers considered the old mandarin elite nothing but a class of pedants and parasites who had stultified the development of Vietnamese society. Acting with tremendous self-assurance, they set about to train interpreters and collaborators who could speak French, and with equal rapidity set out to eliminate the Chinese language—which had heretofore appeared on every official and legal document in Cochinchina—from the life of the colony. The French rationale for doing this was in great part political: by eliminating Chinese characters they were beginning to sever their subjects from any Vietnamese tradition that still counseled armed resistance. But the proclamations of Cochinchina's first French rulers make it clear that they were profoundly convinced that the establishment of French rule was a humane and progressive act, which promised a more moral and civilized life for the Vietnamese people. Admiral Bonard, Cochinchina's first French governor, wrote in 1862 that the official language of Chinese was "incompatible with all progress," and that "The development of Franco-Annamite schools which will substitute alphabetic writing for characters is the surest way at arriving at change: after a generation it must be hoped that one will be able to communicate ideas of progress and humanity in a language that all the Franco-Annamite people will understand."[6]

The French found it easier to disband the old system than to build another to put in its place. They succeeded in establishing a school for interpreters in Saigon, but encountered difficulty with all their other educational programs. The first French schools sought to instruct students in the French language or in *quoc ngu,* the romanized transcription of the Vietnamese language that had been developed by Catholic missionaries centuries before. But they had few teachers, and hardly any books. Furthermore, they found it difficult to entice Vietnamese parents to send their children to the newly created schools. The graduates of the interpreters school, meanwhile, found themselves in the powerful position of helping the French authorities dispense justice to their compatriots, and became known as the most venal and disreputable class of people in Vietnam. Repeated efforts by the French to expand the number of Vietnamese going to school invariably ran into unanticipated difficulties, which included the nearly complete absence of qualified teachers.[7]

Nor did the French have much success with sending students to France.

A small number of children from "influential families" were sent to Catholic schools in the South of France as early as 1865. After a year or two of language training, they went to primary school; by 1870 there were ninety young men studying in such circumstances. When they returned, it was found that no more than a quarter of them could be gainfully employed by the French colonial administration and after 1879 the number of Vietnamese encouraged and subsidized to go to France was reduced to a trickle for the rest of the century.[8]

After two generations of French rule of Cochinchina, no honest observer could assert that their educational accomplishments were impressive. In 1907, the former lieutenant-governor of the colony, M. Rodier, gave a precise indictment of the lack of progress before a parliamentary commission in Paris:

> Some hundred Annamites speak French, and some thousand murder the language—domestic servants, cooks, coolies, and rickshaw bearers. As for the rest of the population, it knows neither Annamite nor French. That is to say that while the Annamites continue to speak their language, they no longer know how to read or write it. That is why I maintain that we have turned them into illiterates.[9]

Amidst this aura of failure, however, there were glimmers which the French could point to as the possible portents of future success. French policies had in fact worked a dramatic change in the intellectual and educational culture of their subjects in Cochinchina. In a period of thirty years, the French had gradually eliminated the Sino-Confucian system of education, and had created a potentially successful substitute, based on an alphabetized written language—*quoc-ngu*—that could be learned much more easily by common people. After their initial failures in the school system, they had by the turn of the century established several French language schools in Saigon where the children of Vietnamese notables could receive a French language secondary education, and had finally started to train teachers who could teach in *quoc-ngu* in the village schools.[10]

What might have given the French the most gratifying sense of their cultural accomplishment was the gradual emergence, towards the end of the nineteenth century, of a collaborating elite of talented and energetic Vietnamese—scholars, administrators, soldiers—who worked tirelessly to help the French consolidate their rule in Cochinchina. This elite was small but, by the early years of the twentieth century it consisted of more than a few isolated individuals. In Saigon, it was a recognizable social group, whose members intermarried with one another, and, at least to some extent. with the French. Early collaborators, like the scholar Petrus Ky, were Catholic, but by the turn of the century, a considerable number of Vietnamese with mandarin backgrounds had joined in with the French. The first Vietnamese who were willing to work with the French had come to think of Vietnam as, in the words of Petrus Ky, a "poor disinherited country." Because of its long enforced association with China, they felt, Vietnam had lagged in social and intellectual development. France represented science, rationality, a way for Vietnamese to catch up and become a modern nation; collaboration had a definite "progressive" aspect to it in the early colonial period. There is a great deal of continuity between the thought of Petrus Ky, who was one of the first Vietnamese to help the French in the nineteenth century, and later twentieth century collaborators such as Pham Quynh and Bui Quang Chieu, who will be discussed in more detail in chapter 3. But the first collaborators had one notable advantage over their successors: they chose to side with France when the French were the principal cultural force in Vietnam that was identified with progress. Thus, in comparison with their successors, they seem to have been a self-assured class of men. Later collaborators who had to uphold their choice once the new Vietnamese nationalist ideologies, including Marxism, were shaking the world, had a much more difficult time justifying their positions, to themselves as much as to others.[11]

During the first years of the twentieth century, Paul Beau, one of Sarraut's predecessors, had proclaimed his intention to achieve a "moral conquest" of Indochina, an idea based on the hope that collaboration with France could become more widespread and rooted in Vietnamese society. The educational component of Beau's policies involved the raising of teachers' salaries to attract more able men into the profession, and the increase in the number of scholarships available for talented Vietnamese to study in France. Had the French empire in Indochina existed in a vacuum, and had the French the ability to control what ideological currents afloat in the world reached the Vietnamese, there is a chance that, in another generation, efforts such as Beau's might have born fruit.

### Japan Lights a Spark

But unfortunately for the French, a new chapter in the history of the activities of Vietnamese unreconciled to French rule was opened by the dramatic victory of the Japanese over the Russian fleet in 1905. For the first time an Asian power had inflicted a defeat on Europeans. The reasons for Japan's success were instantly clear to many of the Vietnamese who were politically coming of age in 1905. Japan had borrowed from the West, had absorbed lessons of Western science, industrial technique and even political organization. The most important political leader among those stirred by Japan's victory was the dissident Phan Boi Chau. After having placed first in the mandarinal examinations at Hue, Phan Boi Chau had refused to take a governmental post and gone into exile in China. In 1905, inspired by the Japanese victory, he traveled to Japan. There he poured out a series of nationalist pamphlets which analyzed the reasons for his country's submission to the French and exhorted the youth of Vietnam to study Western methods in order to regain their independence. Since the French had, by this time, made almost no provision for their subjects to learn science, Phan Boi Chau encouraged parents to send their children to Japan for education. More than one hundred students came, supported by donations of wealthier Vietnamese when their own parents could not afford it.

While this "Exodus to the East" movement, as the Vietnamese called it, was not large, in both its size and its political impact it far surpassed the regular trickle of students who were then receiving scholarships for study in France. Small as its initial numbers were, there was every indication that the movement would accelerate. More tellingly, it was financed and organized by the Vietnamese themselves, for the obvious purpose of training Vietnamese to undermine French rule. The Japanese were ambivalent about this last aspect, and carefully sequestered the students in their own schools. When Japan found it in its interest to make a treaty with France in 1907, recognizing one another's "territorial rights" on the Asian continent, the days of the "Exodus to the East" movement were numbered. The following year, French authorities asked the Japanese to expel most of the students. While the Japanese hesitated, they did require the students to send letters home via the French postal service, facilitating the identification of their families. Soon enough the students began to receive letters from their parents entreating them to return so that they could avoid trouble from the colonial regime.[12]

Equally alarming to the French was the development of the Dong Kinh Free School, a private school in Hanoi run by activist scholar gentry, which the French permitted to open in 1907. Though it was not the first of its kind, the school soon acquired a political notoriety that the French were unable to ignore. Indeed this modest institution of four-to five hundred students immediately emerged as a staging ground for nationalist agitation.

Classes at the school were taught in Chinese, French, and *quoc ngu,* and an effort was made to teach some rudimentary science courses.[13] The school acquired a printing press and printed pamphlets calling for nationalist regeneration, as well as Chinese translations of the works of Rousseau and Montesquieu. Teachers developed didactic slogans and chants to spread the message of modernization into the countryside; the hair-cutting chant "Snip, snip, clip, clip/Drop stupid practices/Study Western customs . . ." was soon being repeated throughout Vietnam. Within a few months it had become clear to the French authorities that the leaders of the school enjoyed a reputation among the Vietnamese that far surpassed that of those mandarins of the Imperial court who were collaborating with the French. And while much of the school's message was consistent with the message of modernization and Western learning that the French themselves were encouraging, the school was also printing the pamphlets of Phan Boi Chau calling for the renewal of armed struggle against the French. Efforts by Paul Beau's administration to dampen enthusiasm for the school by offering comparable instruction elsewhere, or encouraging Vietnamese students to go to France, did little to weaken the Free School's attraction to young Vietnamese, and in 1908, ten months after the French permitted the school to open, they closed it. Some months later, when there was a wave of mass protests against French tax measures in central Vietnam, the French arrested the Free School's principal and most important teachers and deposited them in Poulo Condor, the island prison off the coast of Vietnam.[14]

The effervescence in Vietnam's cities which gave rise to the Exodus to the East and the Dong Kinh Free School signaled to the French that they now were forced to contend with a new type of national resistance, which would prove far more difficult to deal with than movements inspired by traditional Vietnamese allegiances to their emperor and the Sino-Confucian tradition. For from that point on, it was no longer possible for Frenchmen to assure themselves that as Chinese characters disappeared and the French began to make progress in the spreading of literacy in French and in *quoc ngu* in the primary schools, Vietnamese resistance to their rule would fade away. By 1910 it was apparent that Vietnamese desire for higher modern education was bringing the Vietnamese not closer to France, but further away.

The question of how to meet such demands became a vexing one for French officials and an issue of contention between the colonial government and representatives of the roughly 40,000 French *colons* who lived in the colony. About half of the *colons* were women and children and about 10,000 were military personnel. But the remaining 10,000 held the dominant posts in the colony's bureaucracy, its professions, trading firms, mining companies, and banks. They would, over the next thirty years, consistently resist French governmental efforts to increase educational and professional opportunities for the Vietnamese, which they saw, quite correctly, as a threat to their positions. Thus their attitude towards the issue of colonial education came into direct conflict with that stressed by the administrators sent from France. When Paul Beau pointed out that Vietnamese youth could not be shielded from the wave of assertive national renewal that was sweeping over Asia, and that "Vietnam will instruct itself by us and with us, or by others and against us,"[15] the *colons* replied that every educated Vietnamese not only meant "one coolie less" but in all likelihood would produce one more rebel.[16]

The *colon* reaction, however crudely expressed, did at least signal a perception of a visceral truth about education and colonial rule: that the likely effect on France's colonial subjects of the advance of literacy, the knowledge of science, and, above all, knowledge of French political traditions was to render them less, rather than more amenable to French rule. In the wake of political events such as the Exodus to the East and the activities of Dong Kinh Free school, observations of this sort began to influence the colonial administration as well, particularly after they were reiterated and expounded upon by a number of talented colonial writers and theorists in France.

### Jules Harmand and the Perils of Native Education

The first vigorous exposition of the dangers of allowing the Vietnamese access to higher education appeared in Jules Harmand's widely read volume, *Domination et Colonisation,* which was published in 1910. Trained as a doctor, Harmand had served the French government in various posts in Indochina and elsewhere in Asia for more than thirty years, rising eventually to the rank of ambassador. He argued in the tradition of such men as Gustave Le Bon and Leopold de Saussure, opponents of colonial assimilation, who, before the turn of the century, had ridiculed the French pretension of making natives into Frenchmen; his arguments would, in turn, be repeated and amplified after World War I.[17] Harmand maintained that the French were deceiving themselves if they imagined that the Vietnamese would ever willingly accept their rule. French policy, therefore should strive to reduce the tensions betwen their administration and those they governed—not by substituting their social and administrative institutions for native ones, but by maintaining the indigenous institutions wherever possible. His aim was the pragmatic one of rendering French rule more tolerable, and while he had no qualm about stating that his recommended policy "resolutely and firmly reserves all the rights of domination," he hoped to "reduce the frictions and the hatred."[18]

Harmand insisted that exposing the natives to French education would only increase the pressures on French rule. He pointed out that in all of Europe's colonies, those subjects who had received the most European education became the most active opponents of European rule. At the time Harmand wrote, this was, so far as Vietnam was concerned, still a debatable proposition—no matter how much it was stressed by the French *colons.* But like so many Frenchmen who warned of the dangers of educating the natives, Harmand pulled out the British experience with educated Indians to make his case. The "babous"—that sneering word which the French often used to describe educated Indians—had been the principal source of resistance to British rule in the colony for more than a generation. Buttressing his argument with quotations from Lord Curzon and Sir John Strachey, Harmand maintained that British education had sapped the morality of their most gifted subjects, depriving them of the virtues of their forefathers, for which they substituted only the vices of the British.[19]

Harmand mocked the notion that natives who studied humanistic subjects in French schools were learning anything of value to them or to their compatriots. "Learned parrots" was his term for those students who had learned enough French to write schoolboy "compositions" on French literary subjects—for nothing, he asserted, came more easily to primitive peoples than the repetition of phrases and sentences learned by rote memory.[20]

Though this sort of caricature of the learning capacities of France's colonial subjects can easily enough be described as simply racist, there was much in Harmand's treatment of the subject that was written with such a lack of cant that it seemed infused with an uncommon realism. He forthrightly stated that France's Vietnamese and North African subjects were separated from her by " a moral abyss that is more unfathomable than the oceans"—which no amount of philosophical or moral instruction could bridge. What they did want from the French was not moral or political teachings, which they in fact detested, but knowledge of Western industrial technique—the one area in which Western superiority was beyond debate. According to Harmand, the colonial peoples wanted only the material benefits of European civilization, and he argued that it was quite possible for French instruction to concentrate on giving it to them. By this line of reasoning, the Japanese experience became one that the French could study, and in some ways emulate—for Japan's rulers had demonstrated how a people could take what was wanted from Europe in administrative, financial, and industrial techniques, while maintaining a separate identity.[21] Thus the conservative French colonial theorist had arrived at a position remarkably similar to that of the most vociferous Vietnamese rebel-nationalist of the time, Phan Boi Chau.

Harmand thought that young natives should be taken on as closely supervised apprentices in public works, mines, and banks rather than sent to school; he preferred that native education be entrusted to French army corporals, navy mechanics, and colonial doctors rather than school teachers or professors steeped in the French classics. He vigorously argued against sending any students to study in France: the French-educated Vietnamese, he noted, were "moral and intellectual half-breeds . . . the most irreconcilable opponents of our civilization." There were, he acknowledged, some exceptions, which, in the quasi-scientific Darwinian language that was so often used to discuss colonial matters, he described as "mutations" of the sort that led to evolution in the animal kingdom; a small number of carefully screened and highly talented students could be sent to France without danger to French rule or themselves. But in general it was a practice that France should avoid.[22]

Harmand's recommendations quickly found an audience among the French officials who dealt with education in the colony. Since the exodus to Japan had been shut off, the only avenue for Vietnamese pursuing higher education was travel to France. Nevertheless, in the years prior to World War I, French officials in the colony were already lamenting that granting scholarships to the Vietnamese to study in France was a profound waste of the administration's money. In one analysis, the Resident Superior of Tonkin presciently raised the issue of what the colony would do with the students when they returned. They would, he feared, demand jobs in the colonial administration, which happened to be filled by Frenchmen. Furthermore, they were not likely to be "full of admiration before the spectacle of our strength and riches and the marvels of our science" but would more likely to be jealous and embittered, with a highly inflated sense of their own worth. Those from prominent families tended to readapt, but the sons of poor families who had received scholarships returned "unprepared to live in the social milieu which nature and birth had imposed . . . *déclassé, déraciné,* and if it might be permitted, *déracé.*"[23]

Though the colonial government never got around to implementing them, the recommendations proposed by the Resident Superior were hardly dramatic; he suggested a severe examination system to screen out all but the best students—to be supplemented by a board of inquiry to ensure that those who passed the exam were "excellent subjects" as well. Such a modest policy seemed feasible so long as the students trying to go to France numbered only in the dozens, as they did in the prewar period.[24]

## Sarraut's School System

This then was the situation Sarraut encountered when he arrived in the colony in 1911. The dilemmas of education were connected to all of the colony's vexing political problems. France's unbroken string of victories over the rebel bands of previous decades had left her in full military control of the colony, but the disturbances of 1908 were still a fresh memory, and a perceptive observer could discern rumblings of a new generation of nationalists. Sarraut faced the nearly impossible task of satisfying the growing Vietnamese demand for educational access without alienating the French *colons* or opening up gates to Western instruction in such a manner that would make the Vietnamese more difficult to rule.

With few exceptions, historians have judged Sarraut's accomplishments in Indochina favorably. A great number of histories of French rule in Vietnam treat Sarraut as a successful reformer, who, as one admirer put it, "killed nationalism with kindness." Another described him as the "first Governor General to win native devotion." A Vietnamese who was prominent in Saigon's politics described how Sarraut "nursed the dreams" and "magnified the hopes" of Vietnam's notables.[25]

Education was a subject about which Sarraut spoke frequently to the Vietnamese—indeed his policies were one of the main elements of his efforts to reconcile the Vietnamese to French rule. Characteristically, he used uplifting progressive language to describe policies that were modest, even conservative. Soon after arriving at his post he asked the Vietnamese who had "entrusted themselves to our tutelage" to "recognize the white school house that smiles on your children where you formerly wallowed in miserable ignorance."[26] In view of the dire effects the French conquest had on Vietnam's traditional educational system and its once literate populace, such language was not devoid of fatuousness. Nevertheless, by the end of his tenure as Governor-General, even a Vietnamese skeptical of French intentions would have been forced to admit that Sarraut had done more than his predecessors to put something in place of what had been destroyed.

In his final speech as Governor-General before returning to France, Sarraut described his accomplishments. He had, he told his Vietnamese audience, been severely criticized by his compatriots for building too many schools; he could not deny the charge: had not Danton, "our grand ancestor," proclaimed that after bread, education was the first need of all peoples? He proclaimed that France would assert no limits to how far her students could advance, would never say "You will go no further; you will learn no more." It was true, he admitted, that he had received precisely that kind of advice—to give the Vietnamese "a professional education, manual training, to turn you into specialists, good workers and artisans, but that and only that." But he had rejected it: "No! I want more. For you," he told his audience, "I want more than that." "France" he continued, "cannot go half-way with the races it has adopted. And when fortune has designated to her, among her children, a people as supple in their aptitudes as the Annamites, she knows if it is her duty to harmonize the favors of her instruction to the progressive rhythm of normal evolution, it means she must not spread out her learning too hastily, and create *déclassés.*"[27]

Yet these final phrases, about the dangers of spreading French learning "too hastily" and the need to follow the rhythms of "normal" evolution tell as much about Sarraut's educational legacy as his grandiloquent presentation of France as teacher of the world's peoples. As we have seen, Sarraut's program had to respond to conflicting political pressures. He could not help but recognize that the Vietnamese were serious enough about acquiring Western education to organize it themselves; both the Exodus to the East movement and the Dong Kinh Free school had demonstrated this. But he was equally constrained by his own perception and that of other Frenchman that French education was potentially subversive to French rule.

Sarraut formulated three principal measures in education. First he ordered that those Vietnamese who were able to pass the entrance examinations and afford the tuition be admitted to the French *lycées* in Saigon and Hanoi. Though Vietnamese could compete for only those places that remained open after the children of the French *colons* had been admitted, it was this kind of reform that gave Sarraut a reputation as a dangerous radical among the conservative *colons*—a reputation he used skillfully with the Vietnamese. More significantly, he was the main figure in setting up the guidelines of the *franco-indigène* school system, which remained largely unchanged throughout the interwar period, and was the main place in which large numbers of Vietnamese encountered French instruction. Finally Sarraut was the French official most responsible for the shaping of the University of Hanoi—which was France's notably unsuccessful effort to give Vietnamese access to higher French education without exposing them to the perceived dangers of the *métropole*.

Under Sarraut's leadership, all of the various rules of education policy in Indochina were brought together and codified in one document, the 1917 Code of Public Instruction, and all of the diverse administrative tasks were centralized in one office in Hanoi. The 1917 code, the fruit of lengthy consultations among French political authorities, experts in native education, and Vietnamese notables, decreed that there would be one cohesive system for educating Vietnamese—the *franco-indigène* or Franco-Vietnamese system. This meant there was one centrally controlled school system that was totally separate from both the French schools and the remaining, privately funded, traditional Chinese character schools. Students would find it difficult to pass from one system into another. Sarraut's code initially decreed that all Franco-Vietnamese instruction would be in French, while the curriculum should stress practical and utilitarian teaching. It soon proved impossible to begin teaching Vietnamese children in a foreign language as soon as they started school, and a few years after Sarraut's departure, the *franco-indigène* schools began to use *quoc-ngu* for instruction in the early grades, while introducing French gradually, as a second language, in grades 4 and beyond. The Franco-Vietnamese system gradually superseded the remaining private schools in Annam and Tonkin that still taught in Chinese characters. The teachers of the old tradition were dying out, and in 1915 the French eliminated the triennial mandarin exams held in the imperial capital of Hue, thus severing the last links of the old written language to state service and political power.[28]

The most widely voiced complaint about the *franco-indigène* educational system, leveled at the government by both French and Vietnamese critics of the colonial regime, was that the French did not build enough schools to educate more than a small percentage of Vietnam's school-age children. While the number of Vietnamese children attending class in the Franco-Vietnamese system rose from 125,688 in 1920 to 287,037 by 1938, it never amounted to more than ten percent of the school-age population. Moreover, very few of the students who entered the *franco-indigène* system continued past primary school, or grade 6; so called "upper-primary" schools (grades 7-10) were far fewer in number, usually located in urban areas, and required the student to pass a French language examination for admission. Thus during the interwar period the percentage of Vietnamese students who completed "upper primary" was never more than 2 percent of the student population, which meant that during the interwar period something on the order of one in six hundred school-age Vietnamese received an education up to the tenth grade level.[29] Despite the fact, then, that the number of schools and students more than doubled during the interwar period, the school system the French created in Vietnam probably touched a smaller percentage of the populace than the Confucian system it gradually replaced. This gave credence to the biting slogan raised by the opponents of French rule, accusing the French of having constructed "three prisons for every school."[30]

Some critics of the *franco-indigène* system have made the provocative charge that the French were guilty not so much of educating an insufficient number of Vietnamese as they were of creating a school system explicitly designed to foster social and intellectual passivity. Indeed one contemporary American scholar, Gail Kelly, has observed that the French educational budget—roughly fifteen percent of the total budget of the colony—represented a much higher portion than that alloted to education by independent developing countries, and from this has concluded that France viewed education as an important tool of political control and indoctrination. Kelly notes that the textbooks used to teach Vietnamese children how to read and write depicted occupations such as rice farming and artisan production favorably and made the city appear like a threatening and frightful place. Their purpose, she argues, was the consciously obscurantist one of keeping the Vietnamese ignorant of the modern world.[31]

It is of course true that political factors were never absent from French consideration when they formulated their educational programs. Sarraut, when he introduced the education code of 1917, wrote that a government was always more exposed to rebellion if its population was ignorant, and that French policy should render the populace able to "discern the call of the true patriot from that of the rash fanatic." But the available historical sources do not seem to provide convincing documentation of a French grand design for obscurantism in the Vietnamese primary schools.[32]

### The University of Hanoi

There is, however, ample evidence that the French were conscious that higher education had the potential to cause trouble. While this can be demonstrated by the writings of French officials and colonial theorists, it is also reflected in the organization of what some Frenchmen perceived as Sarraut's crowning legacy to education in Indochina: the University of Hanoi. While there were some in the French community who condemned the University, which opened its doors in 1917, as a pretentious grouping of "grandes écoles," it was in fact a much less ambitious undertaking. The modesty of its conception was amply illustrated by Edmond Chassigneux, a high official in the Indochinese education bureaucracy, who described the structure and purposes of the new school before an audience at the influential Committee for French Asia in the spring of 1921. Chassigneux said the school could be likened to the technical training institutes that grew up around universities in France proper, drawing on the intellectual resources—the professors, the libraries—of the *faculté* at the center. Indeed the University of Hanoi was a series of such training institutes: a medical and pharmaceutical school that prepared "native auxiliary doctors and pharmacists," a school of law and administration whose graduates could become "native clerks," and schools of agriculture, a veterinary school, a teachers school, and schools of commerce and applied science. In one decisive sense, however, the "university" differed dramatically from the sort of technical schools that existed in France: unlike their metropolitan counterparts, the schools of the University of Hanoi had no real *faculté* at the center; indeed the Indochinese administration had, for its university, managed to hire practically no full-time faculty members.[33] It is perhaps not surprising that since its opening in 1917, student enrollments at the new university had declined steadily over the first eight years of its existence (from 516 in 1917 to 390 in 1925).[34]

There is little sign that the French officials who constructed and operated such educational institutions as the University of Hanoi were conscious of the glaring discrepancy between what Sarraut had promised the Vietnamese in terms of educational opportunity, and what the French administration was willing to deliver. Officials such as Chassigneux acknowledged the intense desire of the Vietnamese for higher education; in speaking of the students at the new university he said most were hampered by an insufficient background in the French language, but had "great abilities of assimilation and a large capacity for work"—capacities, indeed, which made them the "unique exception among the peoples of our colonial empire."[35] The French were happy to convince themselves that the Vietnamese desire for education in some way meshed with the need of the colonial administration for trained manpower to staff, at lower salaries, low level posts in the government—the posts that had heretofore been filled by what was called the "European proletariat." Sarraut was one in a series of French governor-generals who advocated giving the Vietnamese more access to the lower level government jobs—as an important cost-saving measure, while reserving the "positions of direction and control" for French citizens.

Of course it cannot be denied that the several hundred Vietnamese who received training in forestry, surveying and road building, or rudimentary medical training during the early years of the university's existence, used that training to benefit both themselves and their nation. But French officials made a grievous error in assuming that the kind of school they had created—without real professors, and without the facilities or intent to train young Vietnamese to become real doctors, engineers, lawyers, or administrators—could satisfy the aspirations of Vietnam's restless elites for very long. French officials like Chassigneux could tell interested audiences how the "great prestige" of the new university was felt in the most remote provinces of Indochina, or how Albert Sarraut was venerated throughout the colony as "founder of the university." But within a decade of its founding, no French official could still deny that this institution, which the Vietnamese derisively labeled a "nursery for bureaucrats" was coming nowhere near to fulfilling its function as the summit of the educational achievement for a knowledge-hungry people.

To understand how Frenchmen thought to be informed about the colonies could consider the University of Hanoi something to take pride in one must return to the broader perspective that prevailed in Paris on colonial questions after World War I, and to the general debate over what should be the proper relationship between education and empire.

### War and the Anxiety of Empire

The University of Hanoi opened its doors at a time when Frenchmen were full of self congratulation about the empire. As was repeated again and again, during the war, France had discovered that she had colonies.

Over 700,000 workers and soldiers had been recruited from French colonies in the Caribbean, North Africa, Africa, and Indochina, including 100,000 Vietnamese. Most Frenchmen were ignorant of the fact that these soldiers were recruited by unsavory and often vicious methods; the memory of them that Frenchmen kept was that they had fought bravely for France at the time of her greatest need. The *force noire* from Senegal and the other colonial units became, for the French, an enduring symbol of the emotional ties between France and her colonies. A memorandum on their demobilization at the Ministry of War, signed by Clemenceau, commented on France's colonial soldiers: "One could demand anything from these men, and obtain everything from them."[36]

It is noteworthy, however, that this renewed French sense of her empire's importance did not encourage the French to greater efforts to make the colonial bond closer by exposing more of her colonial subjects to French culture and education. French caution in this regard had, indeed, increased since the war. One indication of this was the prominence of the work of a conservative colonial writer, Louis Vignon. A well-known professor at the *École Coloniale,* France's training school for colonial administrators, and the son-in-law of a former prime minister, Vignon's post-war influence was symptomatic of increased French skepticism about colonial education. In 1919 he published an important volume, *Un Programme de Politique Coloniale.* This book was similar in many ways to the volume Jules Harmand had published nearly a decade before, but it was more scholarly, systematic, and above all timed to influence French policies for the whole of the inter-war period. Vignon's work was in fact a broadside attack on many of the notions that guided French policies until that time, though, as we shall see, its central arguments were quickly assimilated by colonial decision makers.

Vignon's central target was the idea that France should try to make her colonial subjects more French, through changing the institutions that ruled them or giving them French education. For years he had been professing that French colonial rulers should leave the structures of indigenous rule as intact as possible in the colonies they governed. They should leave in place the traditional rulers, chiefs and notables and concentrate their efforts on such practical issues as the modernization of agriculture and the building of education systems.[37] It was ridiculous and presumptuous to want to make them into Frenchmen, for African, Asians, Muslims were not "backward" but simply "other men."[38] Thus Vignon attacked what he took to be the guiding spirit of French educational policy in the colonies, what he labeled the *"fureur scolaire"*—the notion that the peoples France had colonized differed from the French "only because they haven't yet received European instruction."[39]

Unlike most procolonial writers, Vignon did not shy away from realistic depiction of both the brutality of the colonizing process, and the terrors that had been involved in wartime conscription. But he thought the greatest hurt the French had inflicted was more psychological: the damage done by the French "language, books, and ideas." Instructing her subjects in the French language was already a fault, for it brought with it "ideas altogether different from their own, elaborated over centuries bit by bit by brains which are differently constructed, and which work differently from their own." The Muslims, Asiatics, or Blacks who had acquired enough education to read some Montesquieu or Rousseau, or the history of the English or French revolutions or European political journals and debates had suffered a terrible injury:

> All of that, badly understood, and poorly digested, retained only in the memory by (people) whose forebears did not and could not conceive of anything of the kind, has more or less poisoned them. Ideas in the intellectual realm can be likened to medicines in the physiological realm: some of them, when absorbed by an organism which is ill-suited to receive them . . . produce fever, disequilibrium, or death. Similarly, European and particularly French conceptions of liberty, equality, the rights of peoples and individuals inevitably produce, in peoples whose ideas and social structures are profoundly different from our own, a permanent state of fever and disequilibrium.[40]

In making a *tour d'horizon* of what he described as the abysmal results of French educational policies in all of the colonies, Vignon criticized all of the measures that Sarraut had undertaken to reorganize education in Indochina: the opening of French *lycées* to the children of Vietnamese notables, the "cruel" elimination of the Chinese language mandarinal exams, the emphasis on French language teaching in the lower grades, the opening of a group of "grandes écoles" at the University of Hanoi.[41] The emphasis on French language teaching, and the official hostility to education in the Chinese tradition had, Vignon, argued, severed the Vietnamese from their own past; but nothing useful had been substituted. When one asked, for example, a Vietnamese mandarin what he thought of a book that one had loaned him, at his own request, one was "struck by the emptiness or the polite evasiveness of the response." Vignon concluded "This is not to deny the intelligence of our Indochinese subjects, but, because it is different from our own, European books and ideas are unintelligible to it."[42] Vignon recommended that the French scale down the ambitions of the *fureur scolaire* and concentrate on technical and agricultural education, given in the Vietnamese language.

While Vignon had written a polemic against the practice of the French colonial establishment, the establishment responded, very nearly, by acknowledging that he was right. In its publication *L'Asie Française,* the

Committee of French Asia devoted three issues to a careful discussion of Vignon's work.[43] Their reviewer did not disagree with Vignon's assertion that native education should be utilitarian, and avoid inflaming French subjects with French ideas. He simply pointed out that Vignon had failed to take into account the political pressures that the Indochina government had to contend with. The issue of "political utility" required that France defend herself against the charge that she was witholding education from people who desperately wanted it. Furthermore, French measures to expand educational facilities in the colony were designed to discourage Vietnamese from seeking their education in France, where they would be all the more exposed to the dangers Vignon perceived.[44]

Those who were responsible for making policy, aware of desire for modern education on the part of France's subjects, could not state their views as bluntly as Vignon. But the plans France made for her empire in the first years after World War I indicated that conclusions of the Harmand-Vignon sort had replaced the notion that greater immersion in French education and French ideas would make the peoples in the colonies more easy to rule and more useful to France.

### Sarraut as Colonial Minister

A sense of how influential the Vignon type of critique had become can be had by returning to Albert Sarraut's conceptions. Named as minister of colonies in 1920, shortly after his return from Indochina, Sarraut presented detailed programs for the economic development of the colonies to the French Senate. In April of the following year he submitted his program to the Chamber. By then it had become clear that German reparations were not going to be forthcoming to pay the capital costs of Sarraut's program. Thus, although widely discussed and admired, and referred to the appropriate parliamentary finance committee, the program died. Sarraut's design, which would be published in 1923 as *La Mise en Valeur des Colonies Françaises* is therefore more revealing of France's intentions than its practice; nevertheless it was constantly cited over the next decade as the kind of detailed analysis that could guide French policy in the appropriate direction.[45]

Presented as a guide to colonial economic development, *La Mise en Valeur* made it very clear that the appropriate economic function of the empire was to provide France with raw materials—cotton, wool, silk, rubber, fats, minerals—so that she would not deplete her currency reserves buying these goods on the world market.[46] Development of these resources required the creation of an infrastructure of ports, roads, systems for public hygiene and the like in the colonies. Significantly, Sarraut made no provision to start industrial production in the colonies. The training of the labor force was an essential part of his plan, and Sarraut sharply differentiated his proposed policies from those of an exploitative imperialism which did nothing to "instruct, raise, and perfect" the colonial population.[47] In what may have been a veiled reference to Vignon, he took pains to differentiate his own position from the views of those who thought there was an unbridgeable gap between Frenchman and their native subjects.[48]

But Sarraut's actual view of the purposes of colonial education was not, when all was said, very different from Vignon's. Education, he exclaimed, was a central part of a systematic development strategy, and, as he put it, a moral duty as well. But it should be designed in harmony with French interests, and should have a "practical and realistic character." These last phrases meant that education should be primary and technical, designed to train the inhabitants of the colonies to collaborate with—work under—the French in the colonial administration and the extractive economy.[49] Unlike Vignon, Sarraut did admit the possibility that a carefully selected colonial "elite" might progress beyond technical education; he foresaw that there was political danger in forcing this elite to seek higher education in other countries if France seemed unwilling to provide it. But he carefully asserted that this elite would be limited to those who had proved themselves by a process of formal selection—a vague formula that implied political as well as academic discrimination.[50]

Thus, at the opening of the interwar period, the main distinction between a conservative gadfly critic and a prominent mainstream exponent of French colonial policy was in the type of language used to describe French policies. There was, in effect, no one of importance in the French colonial establishment who thought exposing France's colonial subjects to French higher education in France would tighten the bonds of the empire. What remained was a good deal of sentimental assimilationist rhetoric, which implied that France sought such closeness. As the most influential producer of such language during the interwar period, Sarraut never failed to describe the tie between France and her colonies as a moral and familial one. His more ambitious programs, particularly in the economic realm, were never enacted, but the language he used to frame them persisted for decades. About the relationship between France and her colonial subjects, he wrote:

> The secret of our colonial peace resides less in the reality of our force than in the sign of our authority. The sign is the heart and the native knows it. We are for him friends, beings of the same family, the great family of human beings. Less generous perhaps than other nations in the verbal liberalism of the constitution granted, we compensate for the parsimony of our colonial franchise by sincere feeling . . . we know, as a father knows, how to let the humble

visage of our black or yellow brother rest against our breast, so that he might hear our heart beating to the rhythms of his own.[51]

One might speculate that the ability to produce such hyperbole somehow shielded Sarraut, and the Frenchmen who listened to him, from recognizing their colonial dilemmas and choices. For the ultimate effect of such language was to render the French deaf to the demands then being raised throughout their empire. In the Vietnamese case, in so far as education policy was concerned, it meant that Sarraut was failing to recognize that the heirs of an old and literate civilization would not long be content with an educational system that promised them little more than the chance to become clerks and engineering assistants. It meant, in the aftermath of the Great War, that the French were willing to base their policy on the belief that the same people who more than a decade before had organized their own exodus to Japan, and who had founded their own schools for the study of Western thought, could be persuaded to ignore the realm of knowledge that concerned the laws and ideas that shape communities. And it meant that no French scholar or official stepped forth to wonder if, by discouraging the Vietnamese from acquiring anything but the most utilitarian aspects of Western learning, the French were preparing to raise a Vietnamese generation in a sort of moral and ethical void, which would be filled up in ways official France could not control.

In the World War's aftermath, such objections were not raised, and had they been, they probably would not have pierced the complacency and satisfaction France then felt about her colonial domain. The empire had held fast during its time of greatest trial, and contributed mightily to France's victory. Given this undeniable fact, it is not surprising that in 1920 no influential voice complained about the lack of a French policy that could hope to satisfy Vietnamese demands for higher education. On the other hand, what French colonial official, unable to arrive at a satisfactory policy for the dozens of Vietnamese students who went abroad before 1918, could anticipate that France could solve the problem when the number of such students had increased twenty-fold, and the idea of *La Plus Grande France* had to contend with all the hopes and aspirations that had been unleashed world-wide by the Russian Revolution?

## Notes

1. Joseph Buttinger, *Vietnam: A Dragon Embattled* vol. 1 (New York: Praeger, 1967), 87-100.
2. David Marr, *Vietnamese Anticolonialism: 1885-1925* (Berkeley, University of California Press, 1971), 77-83.
3. Only Algeria, among the French colonies, posed comparable difficulties of mili-

tary pacification. But after the major insurrection of 1871, and the lesser skirmishes of the next decades, the French did not face violent rebellion in their colonial province until after World War II. See Vincent Confer, *France and Algeria: the Problem of Civil and Political Reform, 1870-1920* (Syracuse: Syracuse University Press, 1966), 8-12.

4. Buttinger, *Vietnam,* 46.
5. See Alexander Woodside, *Vietnam and the Chinese Model* (Cambridge: Harvard University Press, 1971), 171-234 for a rich discussion of the traditional system.
6. Quoted in Milton Osborne, *The French Presence in Cochinchina and Cambodia: Rule and Response (1859-1905)* (Ithaca: Cornell University Press, 1969), 38.
7. Osborne discusses the striking inadequacies of the early schools in *The French Presence,* 98-108. Virginia Thompson, *French Indochina* (New York: Macmillan, 1937), 456, describes the noxious role played by the interpreters.
8. See Osborne, 103-104 for an account of the first, failed efforts. I am uncertain how small the trickle which followed the first French attempt to bring students to France actually was. Osborne writes that after 1879 there were no more than three or four students a year who received scholarships for study at *lycées* in France or Algeria, or at the *École Coloniale* in Paris. They were all the sons of Vietnamese who were working for the French administration. See Osborne, 159 and 325. But William Cohen, in *Rulers of Empire: The French Colonial Service in Africa* (Stanford: Hoover Institution Press, 1971), 39-40, writes that twenty Indochinese a year attended the *École Coloniale* from 1889 to 1914, training as telegraph operators, clerks, accountants, and the like.
9. Jean Chesneaux, *Contribution à l' Histoire de la Nation Vietnamienne* (Paris: Editions Sociales, 1955), 197.
10. Osborne, 156-171, describes the French inculcation of *quoc-ngu* education as a "qualified triumph."
11. See Osborne, 95-98, and 131-144, for a depiction of the nineteenth century collaborators.
12. Marr, *Vietnamese Anticolonialism,* 120-155 has the most thorough discussion of the "Exodus to the East" episode.
13. Any efforts by the Vietnamese to begin to learn the sciences themselves were always hindered by the lack of qualified teachers and instructional materials. At Dong Kinh, the science teaching was done by a man whose experience was that he had read Chinese translations of some English science texts. Marr, *Vietnamese Anticolonialism,* 164-165. Most students flocked to the courses in modern literature and history; within months Dong Kinh became a magnet for scholars from all over Vietnam who opposed the French regime.
14. The most thorough discussion of the school can be found in Marr, 156-184. See also Buttinger, *Vietnam,* 50-54, who claims the school taught more than a thousand students.
15. M. Prêtre, "L'Enseignement Indigène en Indochine," *L'Asie Française,* August 1912.
16. For a discussion of the *colons* see Buttinger, *Vietnam,* 17-19 and 48. See also David Marr, *Vietnamese Tradition on Trial* (Berkeley: University of California Press, 1981), 23-24.
17. Raymond F. Betts, *Assimilation and Association in French Colonial Theory, 1890-1914* (New York: Columbia University Press, 1961), 59-89.

18. Jules Harmand, *Domination et Colonisation* (Paris: Ernest Flammarion, 1910), 160.
19. Ibid., 263.
20. Ibid., 261.
21. Ibid., 268-271.
22. Ibid., 269-274.
23. AOM-Indochine, 51537.
24. At the time this official was writing there were about 95 Vietnamese students in France. The most precise figure I have found for the period prior to 1920 comes from 1916, which relates that there were 95 students from Vietnam in France, two-thirds of whom came from Cochinchina. Only 23 of these received scholarships from the colony, while the rest, including 57 students from Cochinchina, were paid for by their families. AOM-Indochine 51537.
25. About Sarraut, Virginia Thompson writes, "His first governorship remains green in Annamite memory as that of the most popular man France ever sent to the colony." Virginia Thompson, *French Indochina,* 88. Others who portray Sarraut's reign in Indochina as liberal and enlightened are such critics of French colonial policy as Thomas Ennis, *French Policy and Developments in Indochina* (Chicago, University of Chicago Press, 1936), 102-103, and Phillipe Devillers, *Histoire du Vietnam de 1940 à 1952* (Paris: Editions du Seuil, 1952), 38. One of the few critics of Sarraut is Joseph Buttinger, who summed up Sarraut's policy as "to deny in practice what for reasons of expediency was admitted in principle." See Buttinger, *Vietnam, vol. I,* 87-100 and 481-492. Nguyen Phan Long, a Vietnamese active in Saigon politics of the period, described Sarraut's effect on the Vietnamese elite as follows: "He nursed their dreams, magnified their hopes . . . alas when the magician of the word fell silent, the grand illusion dissipated." Quoted in Charles-Robert Ageron, *France Coloniale ou Parti Colonial?* (Paris: Presses Universitaires de France, 1978) 229.
26. quoted in Buttinger, *Vietnam* I, 482.
27. The speech, given on April 27, 1919, is reprinted in *L'Asie Française,* Feb.-July 1919.
28. Thompson, *French Indochina,* 291-292 and Gail P. Kelly, "Colonial Schools in Vietnam: Policy and Practice," *Proceedings of the 2nd Annual Meeting of the French Colonial Historical Society* (March 1977).
29. Figures on the number of students attending *Franco-indigene* elementary, primary, and upper-primary schools are taken from Gail P. Kelly, "Schooling and National Integration: the Case of Interwar Vietnam," *Comparative Education,* vol. 18, no. 2 (1982) 180-186. David Marr in *Vietnamese Tradition,* 37-38, uses Kelly's and other statistics for estimates of the size of the population with upper-primary education.
30. Chesneaux, *Le Viet-Nam* 196 refers to the three prisons for every school formula as a "celebrated" but somewhat "simplistic" slogan. Buttinger, *Vietnam,* 484 quotes from the Trotskyist publication *Mouvements Nationaux et Luttes de Classes au Viet-Nam* by Anh-Van and Jacqueline Roussel: "In 1930, there were in all of Indochina 4,806 schools . . . Between 1930 and 1941, the administration opened . . . 850 more. But if the number of schools is still very small, the number of prisons, on the contrary, has grown rapidly . . . 20,852 in 1941, as against 14, 350 in 1939. During that same period, 186 schools were opened. Thus in 1941 there was one school for 3,245 inhabitants, and one prison for less than 1,000 persons."

31. Gail P. Kelly, "Colonial Schools in Vietnam: Policy and Practice," *Proceedings of the 2nd Annual Meeting of the French Colonial Historical Society* (March 1977) and Gail P. Kelly, "Franco-Vietnamese Schools, 1918 to 1938" (Ph.D. diss., University of Wisconsin, 1975). An early publication of the Democratic Republic of Vietnam (North Vietnam) about French education argued, along lines similar to Kelly, that French education was systematically and consciously obscurantist. See *Deux Victoires de la Revolution Vietnamienne* Hanoi, 1946, as cited in Johanne Marie Coyle, "*Indochinese Administration and Education: French Policy and Practice, 1917-1945*" (Ph.D. diss., Fletcher School of Law and Diplomacy, Tufts University, 1963). This was not always the perspective of the Vietnamese Communist movement. Truong Chinh, a prominent Vietnamese Communist, wrote in 1954: "During the entire period of the French occupation, Vietnamese were able to learn how to think and act according to scientific methods. Our painting, our literature, our music, our architecture are marked by the progressive influence of French culture." Quoted in Paul Isoart, *Phénomène National Vietnamien* (Paris: Librarie Générale de Droit et de Jurisprudence, 1961) 279. Kelly does make the case convincingly that teaching in the *franco-indigène* schools was deficient in comparison with the standards of metropolitan France. But she does not persuade me, through reference to either internal memoranda or public pronouncements, that there is evidence to support the view that France tried consciously to keep the Vietnamese backward.

32. As cited in *l'Asie Française,* Feb.-July 1919. It is interesting that by the late 1920s some French educational officials in the colony were advocating, without success, that France try to reintroduce Confucian thought and models of discipline into the schools in order to make the Vietnamese less rebellious. See chapter 4.

33. This speech was reprinted in *L'Asie Française,* November, 1921. About the lack of full-time faculty members, Chassigneux said the following: "Except for a very small number of exceptions (in particular at the school of medicine) the University of Hanoi does not have any professors as such, who specialize in teaching. Its teachers are guest lecturers (*'chargé de cours'*) . . . government functionaries who are contracted to teach several times a week . . . they change often: a given functionary sometimes abandons his course because he leaves for France, or is called into service in another part of the colony. Changes and vacations introduce into the curriculum a regrettable instability . . ."

34. Coyle, "Indochinese Administration and Education," 187-188.

35. *L'Asie Française*, November, 1921.

36. See Albertini, *Decolonization,* 265-267, and Christopher Andrew and A.S. Kanya-Forster, *France Overseas: The Great War and the Climax of French Imperial Expansion* (London: Thames & Hudson, Ltd., 1981), 209-211. For Clemenceau's estimation of the colonial soldiers, see Slotfom I, 4.

37. William Cohen, in *Rulers of Empire,* 49 quotes from a summary of one of Vignon's courses at the *École Coloniale,* in 1904: "The policy to follow toward native societies: necessity of studying the religion, customs, traditions, laws and administrative organizations of conquered societies. Profound differences between the mentality of Europeans and that of Asians and Africans . . . opposition between the principles of 1789 and the conservatism of non-european populations. The advantage gained by respecting their ideas and social forms."

38. Louis Vignon, *Un Programme de Politique Coloniale: les Questions Indigènes* (Paris: Librarie Plon, 1919), 467. His views on a broader range of colonial questions are concisely summarized by Albertini, *Decolonization,* 293-296.

39. Vignon, 466.
40. Ibid., 468.
41. Ibid., 505-507.
42. Ibid., 491.
43. Charles Fournier Vailly, "Un Programme de Politique Indochinoise," *L'Asie Francaise,* May, November and December, 1920.
44. *L'Asie Française* December, 1920.
45. Albertini, 272.
46. Albert Sarraut, *La Mise en Valeur des Colonies Française* (Paris: Payot, 1923), 17.
47. Ibid., 85-86.
48. Ibid., 100-101.
49. Ibid., 95-98. Sarraut's "Circulaire sur le dévelloppement de l'enseignement indigène" of October 1920, sent to the Governor Generals of the various colonies, also stressed that instruction should have a "practical and realistic" character. Cited in *L'Asie Française,* January, 1921.
50. In *Mise en Valeur,* 98 Sarraut writes "The organization of our instruction in the colonies must not hesitate to furnish to a native elite, *which will have been formally chosen by the proof of its capacities* the possibilities of access to higher domains of science and to the full flourishing of the personality." (Emphasis in original).
51. Ibid., 122-123.

# 2

# Half an Education:
# French Policies and the Vietnamese
# Students, 1920-1925

When World War I ended, no Frenchman could yet say what increasing the exposure of the Vietnamese to French higher education would lead to: more talented Vietnamese collaborators or more committed rebels. The consensus among France's colonial specialists and administrators held that higher French education, particularly education in France proper, should be doled out to the Vietnamese and other colonial subjects in carefully regulated doses. Jules Harmand and other influential colonial writers pointed to Great Britain's dismal experience with the new class of London-educated Indians as a warning to be heeded by France. By the war's end, this line of reasoning—embellished with anthropological speculations about the dangerous effects of Western thought on those raised in different geographical and cultural milieus—had led to acceptance of the idea that the thrust of France's colonial educational efforts should be narrowly utilitarian and technical. This was the belief of nearly all Frenchmen who had anything to do with the colonies.[1]

Yet despite the frequency with which this view was expressed in official documents, in public speeches, in the writings of colonial theorists, or in the opinions of Indochina's anxious and defensive *colon* community, the decade of the 1920s saw an accelerating migration of Vietnamese students to France. Within six years of the armistice there may have been as many as five hundred young Vietnamese studying in France—over five times the number who had been studying there a decade earlier. During the latter half of the 1920s, the size of the Vietnamese student contingent would double and double again.[2]

On balance, the impact that France had on the students was destructive to the maintenance of French rule in Indochina. Some students did go on to work in the colonial administration, become professionals in Saigon, or

27

participate in those political groups that were willing to collaborate with France in ruling Vietnam. But a majority of those students who would become politically engaged returned to Vietnam as anticolonial radicals, and often as Communists. They fulfilled, in other words, nearly all the pessimistic predictions made by Frenchmen who had previously stressed the undesirability of exposing France's colonial subjects to education and life in the *métropole*.

The question arises as to what extent this radicalization of the young Vietnamese was the product of French influences, and to what extent it was simply the outgrowth of a process well underway in Vietnam, which France could do nothing to change. Were the young Vietnamese malleable when they first came to France? Was it their experience in France that taught them to be rebels? Could official France have behaved differently, and set the students on an alternate political course? If so, when were the decisions made, and when did radicalization assume a momentum that France was powerless to thwart? Was the embrace of Marxism by many of Vietnam's most talented and energetic students due to factors indigenous to the political cal culture of Vietnam? Did Confucianism predispose the Vietnamese to Marxism? What was the role played by the French Communist Party? Of the Socialists? The Catholic Church? What unofficial institutions in France paid attention to the Vietnamese, and could they have acted differently, more effectively? What efforts were made to imbue the Vietnamese with the spirit of collaboration with France? What about non-Communist nationalism—what were its strengths, weaknesses, the reasons for its ultimate failure? What was the fate, among the Vietnamese, of such ideas as political pluralism and democracy, practiced doctrines of the French Third Republic? Finally, in what way was the Vietnamese experience different from that of Tunisians and Moroccans and Senegalese, and the many other colonial students who also came into France during the interwar period?

These are some of the questions this study will address. None, considered separately, provides a comprehensive explanation of the political story of the students. Taken together, however, they do open up perspectives about a group that would become a central and politically decisive part of the Vietnamese intelligentsia.

## The Calm Years

This chapter treats the first wave of students in the postwar period. In terms of the development of the Vietnamese student movement these years, roughly 1920 to 1925, represented a sort of grace period for France. In retrospect these first few years can be seen as a calm before the storm of rising student radicalism, and they may well have been the time in which the French could have developed policies to win over incoming students before they turned to radical nationalism. But this would have required a degree of foresight given to few governments, and, at least so far as colonial matters were concerned, not given to post World War I France.

In examining the initial French policies towards the students, it is necessary first of all to explore why Vietnamese students were coming to France in the first place, when almost all colonial officials who thought about the matter considered it a bad policy. How, in other words, did actual French policies towards the students evolve in directions both more liberal and haphazard than colonial officials intended? What factors in the postwar climate of politics and opinion combined to work against the original French consensus to limit the access of young Vietnamese to higher education in France?

First, the theory according to which greater exposure to French ideas would lead to greater hostility to French rule was, at the opening of the postwar period, unproven by actual French experience. The Indochina colony had been relatively calm since the protests of 1908. There had been some sporadic and isolated acts of terrorism since then, easily suppressed by the French authorities. But, as French officials occasionally pointed out, the perpetrators of such actions were men cut in the mold of the traditional Vietnamese patriots, who had not been reached by French education and Western ideas. As the educational system that inspired such traditional loyalties was dying out there was some reason for Frenchmen to believe that a growing number of Vietnamese would show themselves grateful for French rule.[3]

Another element that contributed to France's willingness to allow Vietnamese students to study in French schools was France's own pride in her role as a nation that had much to teach other peoples. This sentiment, at once cultural and political, permeated France's political rhetoric, journals and educational establishments. Buttressing it was the fact that France's previous experience with students from abroad was a positive one; France's natural and official posture in the 1920s was to welcome them. Edouard Herriot, a quintessential Third Republic politician and France's premier from 1924-1925, was expressing a commonly held opinion when he exclaimed before the French Chamber of Deputies in 1922: "(O)f all the possible forms of propaganda, the best is that which consists of favoring the stay in France of students who live among us, who assimilate our customs, who read our great authors, who are familiar with our professors and our teaching establishments."[4]

In 1921 there were over 3000 foreign students at the University of Paris—over 20 percent of the university's enrollment. Most were Europeans. The greatest number came from Poland and Rumania—nations where the idea that Paris was the artistic and intellectual capital of the world may have been more deeply rooted than anywhere else.[5]

But no group of foreign students who came to France after the war interested and pleased their hosts more than the Chinese. Indeed the government of China had first arranged for 200 young Chinese to come to France as early as 1902; many more "student workers" arrived with the large (140,000) contingent of Chinese workers that France had hired to aid her during the war, and in 1919 the Chinese delegation to the Versailles peace conference suggested that the two governments jointly finance a still larger contingent.[6] This consultation resulted in the establishment of the *Institut Franco-Chinois* at Toulon, which opened its doors in 1921; its purpose was to receive Chinese students, lodge them, give them additional language training, and place them in the *lycées*, technical schools, and universities of the area. By 1921 there were more than 1600 Chinese students and "worker-students" in Paris, in Lyon, and in scattered *lycées* and technical schools throughout France.

Governmental encouragement was certainly not the only factor that made France attractive to young Chinese. France's prestige as a victor in the Great War counted for something. So too did France's reputation as a militantly secular nation, which appealed to a generation of young Chinese who had railed against the mission colleges established in China by England and the United States. Perhaps most important of all—and this remained true so long as Russia was wracked by civil war, and unreachable—France was preeminently the nation with the reputation of Revolution.[7] Thus the voyage to France was made by a generation of China's radical youth. Not until historians began to explore the backgrounds of the leaders of Chinese communism was it noticed that a large number of important Communist leaders had spent time there.[8]

The accounts of contemporaries give no indication that Chinese came by their radicalism through contact with members of the French Communist party. Some commented favorably on the élan of the French workers movement—having witnessed the giant railroad strikes of 1920; others may have been in contact with emissaries of the Third International, such as Ho Chi Minh.[9] But their political activity was so discreet that their French hosts hardly noticed it; the conservative and procolonial press had little but praise for the young Chinese who showed such good taste in coming to France for their education.[10]

While the French seemed happy with the influx of *foreign* students they had, before the arrival of the Vietnamese, almost no experience with the arrival of students from their own empire. In French West Africa, few students received more than elementary instruction; before 1900 education had been entrusted entirely to missionaries, and not until 1920 was a single *lycée* constructed in the territory. Some dozen Africans were given scholarships to attend a teacher training course in Aix-en-Provence between 1920 and 1924; they were kept separated from the French students and their studies and outside activities were carefully surveyed. One was sent home for "anti-French" sentiments.[11] In 1924 the Ministry of Colonies recorded the presence of only five African students in the Paris region, none of whom attended the university.[12]

Nor, during the early 1920s, did many students come from the French protectorates of Tunisia and Morocco, or from Algeria—administered by the French as a province. In the 1930s, North African students would come to France in large numbers, and become the object of much French attention and debate; during the 1920s, however, there were not more than one or two dozen Moroccans and Algerian students in France, and only slightly more Tunisians.[13]

Actual experience with foreign students, then, did not predispose the French to restrict the coming of Vietnamese. Recognition of a political danger would have had to come from particular knowledge about the people of Vietnam, or from the British experience with Indians. But it would have been difficult for the French to assert that France should heed the bitter British experience with her Indian subjects. For nearly any Frenchman who cared about the colonies was willing to believe that France could inspire genuine devotion in her subjects. By contrast, the sole British colonial purpose, as readers of *L'Asie Française* were often reminded, was the making of profit.

The belief that the French could do better than the English at winning the loyalty of their colonial subjects was not held only by procolonial journalists, or political figures like Albert Sarraut. It was the sort of national conceit that could be expounded even by such a prolific expert on Asian affairs as the University of Paris professor René Grousset. In a 1924 essay combining both sound insights and a large dose of this characteristic political blindness, Grousset analyzed how European ideas, rhetoric, and military technique had "Europeanised" Asia, awakened the continent from a slumber of centuries, and provoked the "revolt of Asia against Europe."[14] Much of what Grousset wrote was a diatribe against the British—the people "more closed than any other to the spirit of other races," who were, because of their clumsiness and the brutality of their policies, the principal instigators of this Asian revolt. They certainly would suffer the consequences.[15] But with a striking lack of foresight, Grousset predicted that French rule in Indochina would be spared the storm of vengeance that European rule elsewhere had stirred up: Frenchmen could await the future "without anxiety." His reasoning was here no more subtle than that of any less-celebrated propagandist for French colonialism: Vietnam, which Grousset, expressing a not uncommon view, referred to as "France's pupil," understood that it needed France's guidance and protection until it had "attained its majority."[16] While this description undoubtedly left the French satisfied with their role in Indochina, once the Vietnamese were referred to as France's "pupils" it became even less evident that France should prevent them from attending schools in France.

### The Policy of Least Resistance

The policy towards Vietnamese students that emerged after the war can best be described as a compromise forged on the path of least resistance. It represented an attempt to satisfy both those officials and intellectuals who feared that French education offered too freely would create politically restive *déclassés* and those who were against any strict limitation on what and where Vietnamese could study. Actual French policy could be stated in three points: the French expanded the limited school system initiated by Sarraut in Vietnam, funded a handful of scholarships for Vietnamese study in France,[17] and, most significantly, decided to allow those Vietnamese who could pay for their transportation, tuition, and living expenses the liberty to make their own arrangements for French education.

Permission to come was not, to be sure, granted automatically. Until 1925, a student wishing to leave the colony for France required the authorization of the Governor General, which would be granted only after a review of an educational passbook, the *livret universitaire*, which contained his photograph, information about his parents, and his scholastic record, and the permission of the French colonial official responsible for his province. These requirements, considered odiously constraining by many Vietnamese, were liberalized in 1925; after that, while the *livret universitaire* was still required, the Governor General's permission was dispensed with. Five years later, when French officials began to review the errors they had made in formulating a policy for Vietnamese students, they came to consider this liberalization a significant mistake.[18]

The overwhelming majority of those who could make their own arrangements for French study were, inevitably, the sons of the rich of Vietnam, though later in the decade a surprising number of poorer students contrived ways to get to France. But every account agrees that the first Vietnamese to come after the war had money. Many were the sons of the landowners of Cochinchina, from rice-growing regions in the south of Vietnam. These landowners were a *nouveau riche* class whose wealth was the direct consequence of French land policies, and they were the most pro-French social group of Vietnam.[19] They lived in Western style homes, mostly in Saigon, wore Western clothes, drove automobiles. Described as a bourgeoisie by some scholars, the landowners lacked the managerial skills of the true bourgeois; more importantly, they held no political power. They chafed under their lack of it, and struggled for more: the Vietnamese Constitutionalist party was a vehicle created for that purpose. But they never struggled too hard, or for too much: one of their primary demands was for easier access to French citizenship. A Vietnamese contemporary has described them as the happiest class of men in colonial Vietnam. Often lacking higher education themselves, the landowners wanted higher French education for their children, which was hardly available in Vietnam. Though the colonial administration, like the *colons*, tended to depict the Constitutionalists as potentially dangerous nationalists, this demand for more French educational opportunities was one of the easier Constitutionalist political demands to accede to, and in the heady period of Vietnamese economic growth that followed the war, the financial sacrifice of sending their children to France for study was one that quite a number of Vietnamese families were in a position to make.[20]

Not only did the Vietnamese students tend to be rich, they were, for the most part, from the South. In the first years after the war no particular organ of the French government was responsible for either monitoring what the students studied, or even determining where they came from, so that precise information about their origins is difficult to come by. But the University of Paris, at least, classified Vietnamese students by region, and throughout the interwar period roughly two-thirds of the students registered there came from Cochinchina.[21]

The fact that the preponderance of Vietnamese students were southern and wealthy allows one to infer that few of them had been touched directly by the Sino-Confucian tradition. The land-owning classes in the South had collaborated with the French since the nineteenth century—and as a group were not linked to the old mandarin scholar gentry. Thus most of the Vietnamese students who came to France, unlike their compatriots from Annam and Tonkin, were two generations removed from the Confucian tradition.[22]

This initial wave of several hundred Vietnamese students who came in the first few years after the war avoided close surveillance by the French government because of their relative lack of political engagement. The vocabulary the French newspapers used to describe the Vietnamese students reflected France's own satisfaction with the prestige of her culture and the generosity of her colonial policies. The Vietnamese were portrayed in the press as gentle, well mannered, and hard-working—and certainly grateful to have the opportunity to drink at the well springs of French culture and science.[23] Even officials who were concerned that the student migration would create hotbeds of nationalist agitation found little to worry them.[24]

## Early Misgivings

During this initial calm, however, men more knowledgeable about Vietnam, or in closer contact with the students themselves, were suggesting that the government's lack of a coherent and well-organized policy towards the Vietnamese students was having regrettable consequences. Albert de Pouvourville, the author of dozens of literary and analytical works about Indochina, and a fierce and prominent partisan of French colonial rule, was one of the first to express his misgivings. The purpose, he asserted, of letting Vietnamese come to France went beyond giving them the professional training necessary to fulfill a more prominent role in Indochina's economy; it should be France's goal, as well, to create "a solid and lasting moral and intellectual bond" with them, so that they would feel as much at home in France as they did in Vietnam. But this would not happen if the French neglected them. "If our young men arrive in France with a determination to work," De Pouvourville observed, "they also come with a certain shyness . . . children of an old and courteous people, they are also fearful of their first contact with the civilization of the conqueror." France was letting them remain that way. He described the Vietnamese traveling about Paris in groups, behaving correctly, but "not mixing in French life, feeling intimate with no French sentiment. While their intelligence and their spirit approach the heights of our own, their soul remains foreign and shut off." He closed with a plea for Frenchmen interested in the colonies to make more of an effort to invite Vietnamese into their homes, to give them a sense of French family life, and he observed that it was shameful that Parisian society was willing to dote on the students from China so much more than on the Vietnamese.[25]

Another troubled description of Vietnamese student life in France came from a regional committee of the *Alliance Française*—the organisation dedicated to the global spread of French language and culture. One of its officials, the headmaster of a *lycée* in the southern city of Aix-en-Provence, wrote in early 1923 a detailed report on the one hundred or so Vietnamese students preparing their *baccalauréat* throughout the Midi region.[26] He pointed out that the students often started off well—they were diligent and well behaved. Some did well in school, though many were hampered by poor spoken French and experienced difficulties in the physical and natural sciences "for which their civilization has badly prepared them." But the real problem was that there was no organization to guide the students when they weren't in school. Those among the Vietnamese who were boarding students and subject to the continuing discipline of the *lycée* tended to do better academically with each passing year. But those who came only as day students lived under the supervision of guardians who were chosen capriciously—or by the students themselves. These young men worked less and less, until they "ceased appearing at the *lycée* at all."

The *Alliance* suggested that some mechanism be set up to control the student migration: to check on the health of students before they came—for the change in climate caused many of them to fall gravely ill—and to place them with guardians whose responsibility was guaranteed. It was also necessary, the *Alliance* contended, that the students be guided away from the liberal professions, law and medicine, and steered towards engineering and the applied sciences. Above all, the report concluded, there was a need for some French organization to exercise both a tutorial and disciplinary role for the young Vietnamese who lived outside of the *lycée*. Furthermore there was a need for an official body charged to communicate accurate information about French living conditions to the parents—who in many cases sent their sons to France with inappropriately large sums of money, which the young men used for gambling.[27]

The *Alliance Française* report was read and commented upon by officials at the Ministry of Colonies; when it reached the colonial government of Indochina, in Hanoi, however, it ran into a dead end. In December 1923 Governor General Merlin replied to the Ministry of Colonies that the recommendations would be excellent if it were France's intention to encourage the "dispersion of native youth from their natural centers of intellectual formation." But this was not French policy, and Merlin proudly pointed out that Vietnamese could attend both technical schools and *lycées* in Hanoi or Saigon; the government would be "contradicting itself" if it made excessive provisions for students to go to France for study. But if the colonial government would do nothing to influence the student migration to France, neither would it undertake to stop it. It would be impossible, Governor General Merlin asserted, to prevent Vietnam's rich families from sending their children to France; those who went could probably not be persuaded to forsake the pursuit of law and medical degrees for the study of subjects like agronomy.[28]

## The Tangled System

Merlin's reply was significant. It meant that the French would skirt the effective choices available to them. Even then it was clear that France should either try to monitor and shape the student migration or simply forbid it. But Merlin would do neither. He acknowledged that Vietnamese would seek education in France so long as there were not comparable facilities in Indochina, but he was disingenuous in claiming that Vietnamese students could easily study for the French *baccalauréat* in the colony. The year

Merlin wrote, only eighteen Vietnamese received the degree in Vietnam, and this figure did not grow significantly until the 1930s.[29]

Just as it was in metropolitan France, the opportunity to obtain the *baccalauréat* was a key issue of educational controversy. The degree was the sole and necessary key to the doors of the French universities, and thus to the liberal professions. It could be acquired only through study in the *lycées*, which charged tuition, thus shutting out from access to the liberal professions the majority of students whose families could not afford to pay. Only 2.5 percent of French students of *lycée* age attended them—and perhaps one-eighth of these received some sort of scholarship.[30] The rest attended primary and upper primary schools, which were free, and noted for inspiring in their students patriotic sentiments toward the Third Republic. These schools prepared students for vocational training as well, but as they did not prepare for the *baccalauréat* exam even their best graduates could not go on to the university. While this two-tiered system was under serious attack by French educational reformers after World War I, the idea that access to secondary level elite literary education should be limited was acceptable to most sectors of French society. Just as Frenchmen who wrote about native education in the colonies worried that too much of it would stir up ambitions that could not be sated, the men who founded the French primary school also worried that the creation of *déclassés*—working class people with excessive intellectual pretensions—would be dangerous to the health of the society.[31]

For a Vietnamese who aspired to a French university education, the doors were shut tighter still. The *franco-indigène* system initiated in 1917 by Governor-General Sarraut granted a local *baccalauréat*, which was useless for getting into a French university, and of little value in the colony. And while Sarraut had initiated the practice of allowing Vietnamese to attend the French *lycées*, the actual number who could do so remained extremely small. One limitation was expense: yearly tuition was equal to the full salary of a Vietnamese school teacher. Another was the number of places open: Vietnamese could initially apply only for the places that remained open after the French applicants had been considered. When more Vietnamese gained admission to the French *lycées*, in the mid 1920s, the *colons* complained bitterly to the government about Vietnamese crowding them out of "their" schools.[32]

Thus the usual course for a Vietnamese student who knew the French language and whose family could give him financial support was to stay in school in the colony to receive the local *baccalauréat*, then go to France and begin preparation for the *baccalauréat* all over again—so as to be able to enter the university. In the early 1920s many Vietnamese tried to circumvent the system once they reached France by taking the *baccalauréat* equivalency exam designed for foreign students; because it was French policy to encourage such students, this exam was not demanding. But when Vietnamese, after taking this less circuitous route, attended French law school and returned to Saigon and Hanoi to seek jobs in French law offices, the *colons* complained. Vietnamese who had not received the French *baccalauréat*, argued a spokesmen for the colonial bar, would be unable to "understand the motives behind our activities, or the spirit behind the formulation of our laws."[33] This complaint, entirely typical of the *colons* who had for years done everything in their power to limit Vietnamese access to education, was soon heeded by the colonial government. Officials in Hanoi and Saigon regularly reminded the Ministry of Public Instruction that Vietnamese, because they were "protected subjects" and not "foreigners," should not be permitted to take the *baccalauréat* equivalency exam.[34]

Thus in the first years after World War I, France's policy towards the Vietnamese students can be characterized by its inability to choose between tight restriction of access to education in France and a genuine effort to make the Vietnamese more fully loyal to France by encouraging, and molding, the migration. No serious barrier stopped the Vietnamese from coming to France; no organization guided them in their choice of studies; no governmental body provided a credible guiding hand to either aid or discipline. Opposed in principle to allowing students to come to France, and not eager to alienate those classes of Vietnamese who could afford to send their children there, the colonial government took refuge behind the belief that the *franco-indigène* system under construction in the colony could satisfy the hunger of the Vietnamese for French learning and diplomas.

## Ho Chi Minh and the First Communists

We have alluded to the relative political calm that had reigned in Indochina since 1908, which surely contributed to a certain French complacency on the education issue. At the time French policy choices were made it was not yet clear that a Western-educated counter-elite would replace the generation of traditional patriots who had unsuccessfully opposed French rule for years. There was in Paris a small number of anti-colonialist Vietnamese who had lived in France during and after the war; among them were the aging nationalist intellectual Phan Chu Trinh, the talented radical lawyer Phan Van Truong, and the revolutionary Ho Chi Minh, then known under his earlier pseudonym of Nguyen Ai Quoc. But there was little reason for the French to think that these men and their ideas would escape from the confines of sectarianism and political marginality.

To many Americans who grew up during the 1960s the biographical highlights of Ho Chi Minh's early life are more familiar than those of America's own founding fathers; they are related in similar fashion in the many biographies that Ho's life has inspired.[35] He left his Northern province of Nghe An in 1911 at about age 20 and took a job as a cabin boy on a French steamer that made stops in Africa and the Mediterranean. He then worked at a variety of odd jobs in London before coming to Paris in 1917. In Paris he earned a sparse living as a retoucher of photographs, worked diligently to learn the French language, and forged ties with other Vietnamese opponents of French rule. He began a tireless campaign of writing and agitating against French colonial rule, and soon became known to several members of the French Socialist party. As a delegate to the famous Socialist party conference at Tours in 1920, where French socialism split into a pro-Leninist Communist party, and a reformist Socialist wing, Ho voted with the Communists—because, as he later related, it was they who "sided with the colonial peoples."[36]

But it is important to remember that Ho was not a central figure among the Vietnamese living in France at the time, and did not become a major force in Vietnamese politics until leaving Paris for Moscow in 1923, after which the Comintern gave him significant backing. In France, Ho was already known for the personal asceticism and complete devotion to the Vietnamese national cause which were to become part of his legend. Nontheless, the anticolonial pro-Communist newspaper he edited and wrote for, *Le Paria*, lost subscribers regularly after its founding in 1922; the Communist front organization which directed it, the *Union Intercoloniale*—an organization designed to bring together black Africans, West Indians, North Africans, and Vietnamese in a common struggle against French colonialism under Communist leadership—never managed to achieve a membership of more than one hundred.[37]

The Vietnamese students who came to France after the war were, in general, indifferent to Ho Chi Minh's message; once in Moscow, Ho lashed back at them to condemn their lack of patriotism and their general air of insouciance. His testimony, included in his well-known polemic *French Colonization on Trial*, corroborated the accounts of the students appearing in the French press: they had little political consciousness, and were indifferent to Marxism-Leninism. Ho complained that they spent their time in billiard halls and night clubs, and were, unlike the Chinese students in France, indifferent to the fate of their nation under French rule. He entreated them to come to the Soviet Union's "University of the Toilers of the East," where they could, he claimed, elect their own soviets and participate in Soviet political life; he warned that if the youth of Vietnam did not awaken from their laziness, the Vietnamese nation would die.[38]

Ho's lament over the Vietnamese students in France was echoed by many who did not share his revolutionary hopes. He was right to point out their lack of interest in Communist politics: the Ministry of Colonies, in 1923 found little to fear about the politics of the student emigration. But several men whose hopes for Vietnam were diametrically oppposed to Ho's agreed with his depiction of the students' frivolity and shallow moral character. By 1925 there existed a considerable body of testimony from several sources about the collective psyche of these young men who had traveled across the globe to be educated in France, and it added up to a very troubling portrait.

## Reformist Laments

In 1924, the prestigious *Académie des Sciences Coloniales* heard presentations from Sylvain Lévi, a noted scholar of Indian civilization, and Diep Van Ky, a Vietnamese student with ties to the Constitutionalist party. Both discussed education in Indochina, and felt deep misgivings about the direction in which things were going. Diep Van Ky expressed frustrations about a system that was a "masterpiece of complications" for a Vietnamese who wanted a higher French degree—the core problem being the worthlessness of the Indochinese *baccalauréat* which had no value outside of the colony. He lamented the literature that advocated limiting the Vietnamese to technical and practical education; nothing, he suggested, could be more hideous than Western civilization stripped of its intellectual and artistic components. He observed that the academic performance of the Vietnamese who had come to France up to this point had been poor, and argued that scholarships for gifted students could change that. The real problem was the French made no provision for those who came: no guardians, no supervision, and perhaps most importantly, no chance to sit down with a French family. Diep Van Ky was eager for close ties between France and Vietnam and, at the end of his talk, he invoked the possibility of creating a transcultural elite that would work simultaneously for the interests of France and Indochina. No Frenchmen could hope for a more eloquent expression of pro-French sentiment from a Vietnamese. But Diep Van Ky's insistence that "the education of the native populace is the only justification of the colonial effort and the most legitimate of Vietnamese demands" was sincere and his complaint that the French were failing was well grounded.[39]

Professor Sylvain Lévi painted a still bleaker picture. An expert on India, and widely traveled in all of Asia, Lévi made the argument that France and Britain faced colonial rebellions that were at root psychological. He jarred his audience by stating what few men in the French colonial establishment ever heard in one another's company: that a "prodigious amount of hatred of Europe and Western civilization" had build up in the Orient which most Europeans were not aware of. According to Lévi, this hatred was not generated so much by the fact of Europe's dominance as because of its unfulfilled promise: "Throughout [Asia] the reproach is the same: 'Europe came, disturbed our normal development, dazzled us with the technical advances of its civilization; we ourselves abandoned our own traditions . . . and we are left nothing at all.'" Lévi had no specific solutions to the dilemma. He suggested that France try to let the Vietnamese choose which elements of French civilization they wanted to adapt for themselves, and take care not to impose upon them what France wanted them to take.[40]

### The Passion of Paul Monet

There may have been no Frenchman who cared more passionately about French efforts to educate the Vietnamese, or was more acutely conscious of the failings of their policies, than Paul Monet. A wounded war veteran and a man of some personal means, Monet went to Indochina after the war as a representative of the *mission laïque*. He became an irrepressible publicist against both the injustices of French colonial rule and the arrogance of the Vietnamese elite—who obstinately refused to heed his advice about what they should try to learn from the West.[41] At the University of Hanoi, Monet established a *foyer*, a dormitory which he outfitted with a library of French literature and history. He lectured the Vietnamese student residents on the importance of acquiring Western knowledge for its own sake and not for the administrative jobs that a diploma would provide. He tried to establish a similar institution in France, on a larger scale—a sort of boarding school for Vietnamese students who would attend the *lycée* in Toulon and spend their free time on healthy outdoor pursuits and closely monitored educational field trips. Monet bought a property for his venture, but to his great disappointment failed to receive the financial or political support he had expected from either the colonial government or wealthy Vietnamese.[42]

Behind Monet's efforts was his conviction that the educational and cultural impact of France upon the generation of Vietnamese that was coming of age in the 1920s was catastrophic. His description of the Vietnamese students in France, who wandered through the French school system almost without supervision, was harsher even than Ho Chi Minh's: "They receive too much money from their parents, and spend it on gambling and women—and then return to Indochina depleted, tubercular and syphilitic and anti-French, having completely broken with their familial traditions."[43]

What France was doing, Monet thought, was giving the Vietnamese half an education—enough to strip away at the respect which Vietnam's younger generation felt for its elders and thus striking at what remained of the colony's Confucian moral code. Yet the full benefits of French culture were denied them: France made it difficult for them to attend good French schools, and many jobs in the colony were reserved for French citizens. He exhorted the youth of Vietnam to study more, to open their minds to Western learning, to recognize that only a whole class of *philosophes* and their students made the French Revolution possible. He told them to ignore French clothes, and French manners, and chastised the students at his own *foyer* for their obsessive interest in examinations, rather than learning.[44]

Monet exhorted the colonial government to increase its energy in both directions: to "give more generously and govern more firmly." He urged it to increase dramatically the number of scholarships available for Vietnamese to study in France, and to open a far greater number of administrative jobs to Vietnamese employees. At the same time, he wanted the government to take control of the lives of Vietnamese students who went to France, to dictate where they lived, what they studied, and how they spent their leisure.[45]

Monet believed it was possible to form a Vietnamese elite that was conversant with French culture, loyal to France, and yet not severed from its own social roots. He was prescient enough to recognize that the formation of such an elite required a far greater effort than the colonial government was making, and much of his writing was permeated with despair over France's lost opportunities. In none of his endeavours did Monet receive sufficient money or political support, despite his dogged lobbying efforts. His books read as a litany of complaint against rich Vietnamese, *colons*, and French officials who undermined his plans after initially agreeing that he was correct. Hostile to communism, Monet nevertheless did not shy away from attributing the colonial bureaucracy's reluctance to open more administrative jobs to Vietnamese to naked economic self-interest. He ended his career in the 1930s, sharing platforms in France with speakers from the French Communist party and others whose condemnation of the French presence in Indochina was far less equivocal and nuanced than his own.

## The Politics of Stalemate

By the mid 1920s such troubled portrayals of the Vietnamese generation gestating in the French *lycées* and universities were heard with increasing frequency. By 1925, they reached high levels within the government. In

September of that year, the Ministry of Colonies held a conference attended by the minister, several high officials, and the designated Governor General of Indochina, Alexandre Varenne, to discuss the politics of Vietnam's "youth" problem.[46] By then French officials recognized that they faced generational discontent along a broad front. The discussion centered on the question of how the colonial government might provide more jobs for Vietnamese graduates. Even with this limitation, the debate was notable for the inability of its participants to pursue questions to their conclusion. Again and again, speakers stressed the need to keep the youth of Vietnam in the colony, away from the "pernicious" influences of metropolitan France. But a certain reluctance to consider decisive measures, typical of the interwar Third Republic, was evident at this meeting. This lack of enthusiasm for dealing with the issue remained characteristic of governmental measures so long as the French were facing the educational problem. It is noteworthy that despite the concern which all French officials voiced about the students, the possibility of actually prohibiting them from coming to France was not even raised.

## Notes

1. See Chapter 1 for an analysis of the arguments of Jules Harmand and Louis Vignon, and French response to them. This kind of accent was also prevalent among politicians. The deputy Marcel Habert proclaimed, in 1920, "we have just shown you how we must turn an affectionate eye on the natives in order to ensure ourselves their aid . . . having secured the material life of these natives, we must give them education. Which education? . . . Let us not waste our time by giving them primary education, let us not give these children, whom we need as workers, courses in history or literature, let us give them technical education. . ." quoted in Rudolph von Albertini, *Decolonization: The Administration and Future of the Colonies, 1919-1960.* trans. Francisca Garvie (Garden City: Doubleday & Co., 1971), 586.

2. Estimates of the number of Indochinese students in France during the early 1920s were compiled for the Ministry of Colonies by the Controle Général des Troupes Indochinoises—the office which monitored the demobilization and repatriation of the Indochinese soldiers sent to France during the war. This office estimated, in 1922 that there were 500 Vietnamese students in France. Slotfom III, 33. Another Ministry of Colonies document estimates that there were 300 students, out of a total Vietnamese population in France of 3000. Slotfom I, 4. An estimate given by the journalist Louis Roubaud from *Le Quotidien*, July 9, 1924 is 400 students.

3. In 1919 the Ministry of Colonies' new Inspector General of Public Instruction argued this point against others in the Ministry of Colonies who urged extreme caution in allowing Vietnamese greater access to French schools. But typically for the time, even the argument for Western education was hedged: France's aim was "less to create an intellectual elite than to bring elementary education to the masses." See Archives Nationales, Section d'Outre Mer: Nouveau Fonds, Indochine (hereafter ANSOM: NFI) Carton 259-2223(1).

4. Herriot's remark and other similar opinions are cited in the unpublished dissertation of Ralph Schor, *"L'Opinion Française et les Etrangers en France, 1919-1939"* (University of Nice, 1980), 602-607.

5. This grand and common sentiment is elegantly expressed in Czeslaw Milosz, "Starting From My Europe," *Partisan Review* 2, 1983, an excerpt from his memoir *The Witness of Poetry*. Statistics on the student enrollment at the University of Paris can be found in Archives of the Rector of the University of Paris, (hereafter ARUP) Carton 227.

6. Annie Kriegel's "Aux Origines Françaises du Communisme Chinois" in her *Communismes au Miroir Français* (Paris: Gallimard, 1974) is an evocative source for information on Chinese in France from 1900-1920. See also Conrad Brandt, "The French Returned Elite in the Chinese Communist Party" in E.F. Szezepanik, *Symposium on Economic and Social Problems of the Far East* (Hong Kong, 1961).

7. Ibid.

8. Among them Chou En Lai and Teng H'siao Ping.

9. Kriegel persuasively argues this point. A Soviet historian, Garuchiants, has stressed the importance of French Communist contacts, without citing specific sources. See Kriegel, "Aux Origines Françaises du Communisme Chinois."

10. The article by René Waltz on the Chinese students in Lyon, in *France-Indochine* December 23, 1922 was not atypical: "Already they attach themselves to France. One of the things that strikes them most when they compare us to other peoples that they know, is, they tell us, the gentleness of our customs; that is what conquers them. Between them and us there is an affinity of the heart, which, underneath all the differences of race, nature, and habit, constitutes the profound link . . ."

11. A damning description of France's education policy in Africa is given in Jean Suret-Canale, *Afrique Noire: Occidentale et Centrale: l' Ère Coloniale* (Paris, Éditions Sociales, 1977), 460-490.

12. In Slotfom VI-9 there is a cursory census of colonials in the Paris region in 1924, which mentions only 5 African students. Another, and perhaps more thorough estimate, from the same source estimates that in all of France there were 25 students from Africa and 50 from Madagascar in 1926. According to University of Paris records, no students from French West Africa attended the university until 1929. See ARUP 227.

13. Until colonial students engaged in the kinds of political activities that caught the attention of the French government, it is generally difficult to find a central and authoritative estimate of their numbers. Even when the students were subject to a serious census, French accounts of how many there were differed substantially. Guy Pervillé, in his unpublished doctoral thesis "Les Etudiants Musulmans Algériens, 1908-1962" (Écoles des Hautes Études En Sciences Sociales, 1980), ch. 2 estimates that there were "about thirty'" Algerian students in Paris in 1928. Most Algerians who could attend university, did so at the University of Algeria, an institution up to the standard of a French provincial university. For the Moroccans, see John Halstead. *Rebirth of a Nation: The Origins and Rise of Moroccan Nationalism, 1912-1944*. (Cambridge: Harvard University Press, 1967), 137. He estimates that thirty Moroccans received a French university education in France before 1932.

14. René Grousset, *Le Réveil de l'Asie* (Paris: Plon, 1924).

15. Ibid., iii; 113.

16. Ibid., 239-248.
17. It has not been possible to determine the exact number of Vietnamese students who received government scholarships for study in France on a yearly basis. Coyle in "Indochinese Administration and Education," (Ph.D. diss., Tufts University, 1963), 204-205 finds there was funding for 15 scholarships for study in France for the year 1938-1939. A government document in AOM-Indochine, 51534 states that six scholarships per year were funded by Hanoi between 1927 and 1931. These figures are close to the number of scholarships for French study that were funded early in the century, before World War I: see the speech by M.A. Salles describing the careers of the 9 Vietnamese boys who received scholarships from the government in 1908, reprinted in *L'Asie Française*, December, 1924.
18. The requirements both before and after the law of December 1, 1924 are discussed in ANSOM: NFI, 259-2226, "Rapport de Mission de M. Thalamas sur l'Emigration Scolaire Indochinois," (1930). Official rationalization for eliminating the need for the "policelike" permission of the Governor-General, in 1925 is found in AOM-Indochine, 51524.
19. Perhaps no policy of French colonial rule in Vietnam had more pernicious consequences than its land policy. Before the French arrived, all land, a commodity always in short supply, belonged in theory to the emperor, while the peasants who farmed it exercised de facto ownership rights. With the French conquest, both peasants and the mandarin agents of the emperor fled the French presence in the South, leaving the conquerors in the possession of large plots of land, which they expanded through dramatic improvements in the irrigation system. Then French officials auctioned the land off; the only Vietnamese class with a realistic chance of buying it were those who had learned the French language and had some knowledge of the bureaucratic red tape involved. Prices were cheap, however, and the Vietnamese collaborators did well. When peasants returned to their land, they found themselves transformed into tenant farmers, so that by the late nineteenth century, the French had created two classes previously unknown to Vietnam—landless peasants and absentee landlords. Buttinger, *Vietnam*, 160-167, contains an excellent discussion of the land question.
20. The political and social style and goals of the southern landowners and the Constitutionalist Party are discussed in Ralph Smith, "Bui Quang Chieu and the Constitutionalist Party of Cochinchina." *Modern Asia Studies*-III, 2, 1969, Milton Osborne, "The Faithful Few: The Politics of Collaboration in Cochinchina in the 1920's" in Walter Vella, ed., *Aspects of Vietnamese History*, (Honolulu, University of Hawaii Asian Studies, 1973), and Pierre Brocheux, "Les Grands Dien Chu de la Cochinchine Occidentale Pendant la Période Coloniale," in Jean Chesneaux, Georges Boudarel and Daniel Hemery, *Tradition et Revolution au Vietnam* (Paris, Editions Anthropos, 1971).
21. See ARUP 227 for a yearly record of the numbers of students from Tonkin, Annam, and Cochinchina registered. The percentages throughout the interwar period roughly match those of 1916, when 57 of the 95 students came from Cochinchina. See note 24, chapter 1. Because the generic French term for all Vietnamese was "Annamites" it is likely, however, that the number of Vietnamese from the central province of Annam was overstated, and in fact the number of students from the South was greater than roughly two thirds. Most non-numerical indications suggest that as many as 90% of the students came

from the South, particularly after 1924. See the Thalamas report, ANSOM: NFI, 259-2226.

22. Thus neither in the early 1920's nor later did the Vietnamese students in France fit into the category of what Alexander Woodside has labeled "the mandarin proletarians"—descendants of the old scholar gentry who assumed leadership positions in the Vietnamese Communist movement. See Alexander Woodside, *Community and Revolution in Modern Vietnam* (Boston: Houghton Mifflin, 1976), 234-239. In a related vein, Joseph Levenson, speaking of the modern political legacy of the Confucian tradition in China, has argued that Marxism was seen as an attractive doctrine by those in the Chinese intelligentsia who felt that Confucian culture had contributed to Chinese decay because it satisfied the need to reject Confucianism without embracing that part of the West perceived as responsible for China's humiliation. While a similar phenomenon may have been at work among those Vietnamese raised in regions where memory of the Confucian tradition was strongest, in Annam and Tonkin, Confucianism was no longer even something to rebel against in Cochinchina, except in so far as it was incorporated into the new syncretic religions such as Cao Daism. See Joseph Levenson, *Confucian China and its Modern Fate* (Berkeley: University of California Press, 1958), 134-146.

23. Typically enthusiastic depictions of the first wave of post-war Vietnamese students can be found in *L'Opinion*, July 20, 1922, *Le Quotidien* July 9, 1924, and *La Dépêche Coloniale* Aug. 2, 1922.

24. For example, a letter from the Ministry of Colonies to the Minister of Public Instruction on February 1922, asking for the latter's cooperation in obtaining information about the students, betrays litttle anxiety about their political commitments and activities. See Slotfom, III, 33.

25. *La Dépêche Coloniale*, July 7, 1923. De Pouvourville was not the only observer to regret this phenomenon. *L'Opinion*, July 20, 1922 described the Vietnamese students as a "hermetically sealed group" which was cordially welcomed around Paris, "though it was often the sort of interested kindness that welcomes, generally, all those who can pay and pay well."

26. AOM-Indochine, file 51536.

27. Ibid.

28. Ibid.

29. Coyle, "Indochinese Administration," 180-181.

30. See the discussion by John Talbott, *Educational Reform in Post War France* (Princeton: Princeton University Press, 1969), 3-33.

31. Talbott, *Educational Reform*, 27 and Antoine Prost, *Histoire de l'enseignement en France, 1800-1967* (Paris: Armand Colin, 1968), 327.

32. Gail Kelly "Conflict in the Classroom: A Case Study from Vietnam," Unpublished Manuscript. (privately communicated)

33. Letter from the President of the Committee of Discipline of Lawyers and Defenders for the Saigon Court of Appeals, AOM-Indochine, 51523.

34. Ibid.

35. Among the best of the many books on Ho Chi Minh are David Halberstam's *Ho* (New York: Random House, 1971), and Jean Lacouture, *Ho Chi Minh: a Political Biography*, trans. Peter Wiles (New York: Random House, 1968).

36. The citation is from Ho Chi Minh's article "The Path Which Led Me to Leninism," *L'Echo du Vietnam*, July 1960 quoted by Lacouture, 30.

37. Reports from the French Colonial Ministry analyzing the politics of the anti-

French activists in Vietnamese exile community during Ho Chi Minh's French period can be found in Slotfom I, 4. Their conclusion, in April of 1923 was that Ho was too radical to achieve a wide following among Vietnamese. A sympathetic discussion of *Le Paria* and the Union Intercoloniale, which nonetheless acknowledges the group's sectarian marginality (unlike Ho's biographers) can be found in Claude Liauzu, *Aux Origines des Tiers Mondismes: Colonisés et Anti-Colonialistes en France, 1919-1939* (Paris: Editions L'Harmattan, 1982), 99-136.

38. Nguyen Ai Quoc, *Le Procès de la Colonisation Française* (Hanoi: Editions des Langues Etrangeres, 1962), 136-150.

39. Diep Van Ky, "L'Enseignement des Indigenes en Indochine" *Académie des Sciences Coloniales* Tome 4, 1924-1925.

40. Sylvain Lévi, "L'Enseignement en Indochine" *Académie des Sciences Coloniales* Tome 4, 1924-1925.

41. Apart from an occasional newspaper reference, I have found no other source of information on Monet than two of his books, *Français et Annamites* (Paris, 1925) and *Entre Deux Feux* (Paris, 1928), I have only conjectural evidence for supposing Monet's personal wealth.

42. For Monet's bitter disappointment at his failure to receive support for his *Institut Franco-Annamite de Toulon* see Monet, *Entre Deux Feux*, 90-134.

43. Ibid., 90-91.

44. Ibid., 364.

45. Ibid., 89, and *Français et Annamites*, 92-96.

46. ANSOM:NFI, 231-1900.

# 3

# The Heyday of the Vietnamese Student Migration, 1925-1930

During the late 1920s the Vietnamese student community in France emerged as a thorny problem for French colonial officials. The political exploits of several hundred young Vietnamese in France became a frequent topic of French complaint in Indochina, within the Colonial Ministry, and eventually in the Chamber of Deputies and the popular press. By 1930, the knots of Vietnamese students in Paris and other university centers—whose frivolous politics and lifestyle had been disparaged by Ho Chi Minh a mere half a dozen years before—were leading a revolution in the political attitudes of Vietnamese youth. The student community in France had become sufficiently radicalized that it was able, throughout the ensuing decade, to feed Vietnam's nascent Communist movement with dozens of valuable cadres and potential leaders.

The first rumblings of this transformation showed themselves not in France but in Indochina itself. Historians have observed these new signs of political turbulence emerged at the same time as a number of new social developments within the colony. One salient factor stands out however: during the 1920s the older generation of Vietnamese nationalist leaders was fading away, and their place gradually taken by young men who have been exposed to Western education and ideas from adolescence onward.[1]

## The Turbulent Twenties

There had been, from 1908 until the mid 1920s, a remarkable period of political peace in French Indochina. During this time, while Europe was shaken to its foundations by war and revolution, nationalist opposition to French rule was limited to the plots, conspiracies, and violent outbursts of men who had neither advanced education nor mass followings, and the French authorities managed to isolate and suppress them without difficulty.

Governor General Albert Sarraut pacified Vietnam's small but restless educated class with eloquent promises of liberal political innovations in the future. Such men as Phan Boi Chau and Phan Chu Trinh, the most able educated opponents of French rule, were aging and in exile—unable to exert much influence inside the colony.

In the years immediately following the war, Vietnamese efforts to change the terms of French rule were led by Bui Quang Chieu's Constitutionalist party. Chieu was of an older generation. Born in 1873, he came from a mandarin family, had attended French schools in Saigon and Algiers, and held a number of posts in the colonial administration. His followers were usually men of some means, who owned land, were employed in the colonial bureaucracy, or both, and they assumed that the French would remain in Indochina for the rest of their lives. However irritating the Constitutionalist newspapers and demands for political representation were to the French *colons*, who dominated both the finances and the politics of the colony, they were backed by no threat of force. Vietnam's aspiring bourgeois party eschewed violence in practice and principle. Its members made no effort to take their case to Vietnam's peasantry or its urban poor. The challenge they posed to French rule was limited.[2]

By 1925, however, it was apparent to both French and Vietnamese observers that this interlude of relative political calm was coming to an end. The social structure of the colony, particularly in Saigon and other parts of Cochinchina, where the French influence on Vietnamese society had penetrated most deeply, was undergoing significant changes. In the years after the war, the rise in popular literacy in both French and *quoc ngu* made possible an explosion of publishing activity in the South. The new press was written by the small advance guard of a new Vietnamese intellectual class—men who had received some French education in the colony, or in France itself, but who were ignorant of the Confucian classics and Chinese characters. The audience for the new newspapers was a growing class of white collar workers, some of whom could be moved to participate in strikes or urban demonstrations. One result of this new mixture was that Vietnam's new anticolonial leaders grew up learning a political lesson that the generation of scholar-mandarin rebels who had preceded them had never mastered: that the most expeditious route to acquiring political power in colonial Vietnam was through mobilization of the lower classes.[3]

One of the pathbreakers of the new generation of anticolonialist leaders was Nguyen An Ninh, the politically active publisher of the French-language Saigonese newspaper *La Clôche Felée* which proclaimed on its masthead that it was a journal "for the propaganda of French ideas." Nguyen An Ninh was the son of a Confucian scholar who had been active in the "exodus to the East movement" a generation earlier; he attended Indochina's best French schools before traveling to Paris in 1918 to study law. In France he translated Rousseau's *The Social Contract* into Vietnamese and was in contact with both Ho Chi Minh and Phan Chu Trinh. This energetic young publicist was one of the first of a generation of young men whom the conservative essayist Pham Quynh aptly described as "rebels in the French style, for French reasons." Nguyen An Ninh was able to publish in such progressive French intellectual publications as *Europe* where he proclaimed that the Vietnamese could not be stopped from imbibing the political lessons of Montesquieu and Voltaire, and called upon "Republican" France to take control of Indochina away from the *colons* who ruled in its name. At this stage, his political demands focused on such matters as freedom of the press, of public expression, and of movement. In one essay written for a French audience he described himself as one of the multitude of Asian youth who had discovered that the "secret" of Europe's "material power" lay in its "critical spirit" and democratic ideals.[4] French reluctance to allow the spread of these ideals to Indochina is aptly summarized in an exchange between Nguyen An Ninh and the French Resident General in Saigon, Maurice Cognacq. When pressed by the young Vietnamese for greater press freedom, Cognacq replied "If you want intellectuals, go to Moscow; we don't need any of them here." It was advice that Nguyen An Ninh followed after a fashion. By the mid-1920s, after being arrested several times, he turned more radical; in a speech in Saigon in 1926 he proclaimed that the French had "nothing more to do in Indochina" and soon after gravitated into the political orbit of Vietnamese communism.[5]

In Paris, French officials were uncertain of what posture to strike in the face of this new turbulent climate. When the moderate left-wing Cartel des Gauches government came to power in 1924, they sent the respected reformer and Socialist party member Alexandre Varenne to Indochina to serve as the colony's Governor General.[6] Before his departure, Varenne discussed the colony's problems with the Colonial Ministry's highest officials. At one meeting, the group concluded that discontent among Vietnam's youthful intellectuals was the greatest long-term threat to stability in the colony. Albert Duchêne, the ministry's director of political affairs and a prolific author on matters concerning the French empire, argued that France had time to reverse the trend; he thought that the biggest reason for unrest among the educated youth was the lack of job opportunities commesurate with their skills and diplomas. The solution—one always close at hand when French officials considered liberalizing measures—was to open up more job opportunities for Vietnamese in the colonial administration. The top jobs, as always, were reserved for French citizens. This category included some naturalized Vietnamese, but, as Duchêne pointed out, the number of Vietnamese requesting naturalization was small. The meeting concluded that the administration should search for new categories of administrative jobs to be opened to noncitizens.[7]

There were elements of both wisdom and good politics in this analysis; lack of job opportunity was already part of the litany of Vietnamese student complaint.[8] But even modest reforms such as giving Vietnamese law graduates access to the Indochinese bar, clashed directly with political and economic interest groups in the *colon* community. Furthermore the diagnosis that simple career frustration was at the root of the new unrest was, at the very time the officials spoke, being overtaken by new symptoms. By 1925 the chief instigators of the new student turbulence were voicing distinctly nationalistic demands, of the sort that could not be satisfied by tinkering with the job qualifications for mid-level posts in the administration or expanding the law school at the University of Hanoi.

When Varenne arrived in the colony in late 1925, he was quickly confronted with evidence that the new discontent was widespread and difficult to contain. The first of these outbursts spilled forth in the aftermath of the arrest by French agents in Shanghai of the aging revolutionary Phan Boi Chau. The elder statesman of the Vietnamese resistance movement was returned to Hanoi and put on trial for treason. After a well-attended trial, he was sentenced to death.[9] Long before the trial began, however, word of Phan Boi Chau's arrest had spread, and the proceedings went on against a background of sit-down strikes and petitions for clemency, and large student demonstrations in the streets. The pressure made an impact on the French authorities, and one of Varenne's first actions after arriving at his post was to commute the aging rebel's sentence to house arrest in the imperial capital of Hue. Phan Boi Chau would spend fifteen years of his old age in Hue, but it was not many months before the youth rebellion in Indochina was lit by another spark.

This time the catalyst was the death of Phan Chu Trinh, the scholar and nationalist intellectual who had returned to Saigon in 1925, after fifteen years of exile in France. Phan Chu Trinh's political legacy was complex and ambiguous enough that many political factions within Vietnam would try to appropriate it. Fifteen years abroad had not changed him essentially. He emphasized that the only real route to Vietnamese independence lay in the country's modernization, which required a willingness to borrow from the West. His rejection of violence made him basically reformist, and had he lived, the synthesis of the Chinese classics and European enlightenment authors which he urged on the youth of Vietnam might soon have made him an anachronism. But once dead he could be remembered for his personal integrity and refusal to be co-opted by the colonial regime, and his funeral procession in March of 1926 turned into the biggest political demonstration in Saigon's history. Vietnamese political leaders from the Constitutionalists to more radical factions formed a funeral committee, which organized a week of observances, while in the schools Phan Chu Trinh's funeral was an occasion for students to bait school authorities by wearing black armbands, and to paint the grafitti "A.B.L.F." (A bas les Français) on walls and blackboards. Disciplinary actions followed, and in the spring of 1926 a student school boycott spread around Cochinchina. During that period more than a thousand Vietnamese students were expelled from schools in Cochinchina for disciplinary reasons. In Saigon in particular there was a flurry of small political grouplets and the voluminous printing of tracts and manifestos. Both reformist Vietnamese like the Constitutionalist leader Bui Quang Chieu and radical nationalists like Phan Boi Chau criticized the student strikes, arguing that the youth of Vietnam would serve the country better by becoming educated. But by the summer of 1926, the radical politicization of Vietnamese youth had acquired its own powerful momentum.[10]

## The New Wave of Students

In the midst of this agitated and politicized climate the rate of Vietnamese student migration to France began to climb. The unrest in the colony transformed the voyage to France into something more than the means to a higher French diploma and remunerative employment back in Indochina. For some of the students who had been expelled from school in the 1926 student strikes, going to France was a way of continuing their schooling, as education officials in France were unwilling and unable to cooperate with their counterparts in Indochina in disciplining and punishing students.[11] But beyond the practical appeal, the voyage of the young became infused with a new aura. For a generation of Vietnamese youth, particularly those from the Saigon area, study in France came to be seen as sort of a patriotic gesture. Not only did France represent science and modernity (as it had a generation ago both to some Vietnamese collaborators and to the founders of the Dong Kinh Free School movement) but some of the best known leaders of the new nationalism, such as the late Phan Chu Trinh and the young Nguyen An Ninh had recently returned from France themselves; embarking on the long steamer trip across the ocean thus came to be seen as a sort of daring sacrifice that one would make for one's country. Ta Thu Thau, a Vietnamese student leader who would travel to France himself one year later and there emerge as the leader of Vietnamese Trotskyism, expressed the new spirit in an address at dockside to a group of students setting sail for Marseilles in 1927:

We students must pick up and conquer the education that we are refused in our country ... Do you know my dear friends that at each ship departure, some young Annamites who have neither relatives nor friends aboard abandon their work in order to be present at the pier? They inform themselves of the number of those leaving and their joy rises with the number of emigrants ... These compatriots who thus accompanied us at the departure represent Annam for us, and their hopes are those of the fatherland.[12]

It is worth repeating that no conscious policy of the French government encouraged this increase in student emigration. In private French officials lamented the surge. Scholarships for study in France—one key indicator of where France wanted its colonial students to study—remained tiny in number: about one dozen a year, including study grants from both the government and large French companies that sent future employees for technical training in France.[13]

In part the surge was the unanticipated consequence of an easing in visa procedures that the French had initiated in December 1924. Since that date written authorization to leave the colony from the office of the Governor General—a requirement that served as a sort of political background check for students applying for student visas—was no longer demanded. According to French officials the requirements that remained, such as the *livret scolaire,* the scholastic record, were easily circumvented by young Vietnamese. Students from wealthy families set out for France with tourist visas, while poorer ones hired themselves out as cabin boys on the ships. So it was that this combination of new circumstances—the spread of French language instruction, particularly in Saigon, to a growing Vietnamese middle and lower middle class, somewhat relaxed bureaucratic regulations, and an unforeseen outburst of youthful rebellion inside the colony—produced what one official woefully described as an "invasion" of emigrating Vietnamese students.[14]

The "invasion" was not large, except in relative terms. French authorities never managed to compile internally consistent and comprehensive statistics of the number of the students who arrived, a noteworthy fact considering France's reputation for well-organized and meticulous bureaucracy. But according to rough estimates the number of Vietnamese students nearly tripled between 1925 and 1930. Most ministries agreed there were about 600 Vietnamese students in France in 1925, a figure that rose to 1700 in 1929. A sense of the surge can be gleaned from the more precise enrollment figures near the top of the educational pyramid—the University of Paris. There the number of Vietnamese pursuing degrees rose, before its peak in 1931, as follows:

1925: 45
1926: 70

1927: 98
1928: 122
1929: 166
1930: 179
1931: 203[15]

Nor did French authorities collect rigorous documentation of the social and regional origins of the students. As we have mentioned, at least two-thirds of the students came from Cochinchina, the southernmost third of Vietnam, and the region of Indochina in which the French cultural and educational presence was most deeply entrenched.[16]

## Social Origins of the Migration

The most informed official analysis of the social origins of the migrating students was the Thalamas report, compiled in 1930 by Indochina's director of public instruction. According to the report the student movement was fed by three streams. The first involved a class of Vietnamese who had been coming to France to study since before the war. These were the sons and (very infrequently) the daughters of Vietnamese notables who were employed by the French administration in the colony; their parents had mandarin backgrounds, and were that part of the former Vietnamese ruling class which had come to terms with French rule. According to the report, there were never more than several dozen students from this sort of background in France. Most were capable students, and took jobs in the government administration when they returned. These students, who were just as likely to come from Annam and Tonkin as Cochinchina, were not at all a problem for French authorities. Their numbers had risen in a regular and steady rhythm since the end of the war, which French officials thought of as "natural."[17]

The accelerated immigration after 1924 was fueled by two new elements, both from Cochinchina. One consisted of students who had been expelled from the schools in the South for disciplinary or scholastic reasons, especially in the aftermath of the student strikes of 1926. Participants in the strikes had included students attending the French *lycées* in Saigon, whose families were usually wealthy, as well as students from more modest backgrounds, who were enrolled in *franco-indigène* schools. The turbulence was centered around Saigon. Among the students caught up in the ferment was a hard knot of bright and ambitious boys from Vietnam's lower middle class—the sons of lower-grade teachers or small merchants. It was not uncommon for such boys to receive financial assistance for the voyage to France from wealthy Vietnamese, perhaps in return for the promise to marry an otherwise difficult-to-place daughter.[18] Other boys from the lower middle classes took jobs as cabin boys on ships or simply stowed away, and survived in France by taking odd jobs and engaging in various scams and hustles in the Vietnamese student community. Several of these young upstarts would become student leaders in France, and would be instrumental in changing the political climate for a generation of Vietnamese intellectuals.

The number of student migrants from the lower middle classes was small however—and represented only a fraction of the larger group—those who came to France by shortcutting the established procedures. The Thalamas report quoted the Vietnamese Constitutionalist paper *La Tribune Indochinoise,* a French language paper that expounded moderate nationalist views, as boasting that it had arranged 147 clandestine departures in one year. This can be read as an indicator that the Vietnamese business and professional classes favored the student migration, and were willing to circumvent French regulations to help their children get to France.

The third stream of the migration was made up of the offspring of the rich of Cochinchina. The Thalamas report depicted this component as originally the numerical equal of the rebellious contingent during the middle 1920s. Towards the end of the decade it continued to grow, so that, by 1930, it was the largest single component of the Vietnamese student migration. As we have noted, the richest class in Cochinchina was the landowners in the Mekong Delta, most of whom were not themselves well-educated. Somewhat amusingly, the Thalamas report likened their children to *nouveau riche* Americans,—that is rich, vulgar, uneducated, and status-conscious. They were, for the most part, weak students with a lot of money to spend; the report noted several who received monthly allowances well in excess of the sum the French government allotted for a full year's scholarship.[19]

In France, these streams tended to blend in with one another, and the political divisions that later emerged do not seem to have been based upon class background in the colony. What emerged in the blend, the report concluded, was "a mass dominated by the lazy and discontented."

Thus a rough sociological portrait of the Vietnamese students' background would show it was mostly, but not exclusively, Southern, mostly, but not exclusively, wealthy, and almost entirely comprised of young men. What distinguished it from earlier groups of Vietnamese students who had studied in France was that it was, to a great extent, self-selected—made up of Vietnamese who chose to come to France on their own, without the prodding, or even the permission, of the colonial government. Another factor was that it contained within it a small number of ambitious boys from Vietnam's lower classes, several of whom would later demonstrate a prodigious talent for political organization.

How many were Catholic? It is interesting that no one in the French government asked this question, for Vietnamese Catholics, who made up ten to fifteen percent of the population of Vietnam, had always been more favorably disposed to the French than the rest of the Vietnamese population. Oddly enough, there are signs that it was not a question that occurred to the French Catholic church until the migration was well underway. For example, when the publication *La Documentation Catholique* took a reading of Vietnamese students in 1932, a year or so after the numerical peak of the migration, it found that less than two dozen of the 333 Vietnamese enrolled in *lycées* were attending Catholic institutions.[20] There was a small residential *foyer* for Catholic Asian students set up by the archbishop of Paris in 1929; in the first three years of its operation, 51 Vietnamese students had lived there—a very tiny percentage of the Vietnamese students in Paris.[21] A somewhat greater number participated in the activities of the nonboarding *foyer* in Paris, also under the archbishop's jurisdiction. By the 1930s, however, a Vietnamese Catholic student club apparently had less than two dozen members.[22] Commenting on this weakness, Father Paul Catrice, who wrote frequently for Catholic publications on matters concerning foreign Catholics in France, suggested that the Church pursue its apostolic role among the students more vigorously, perhaps by setting up the kind of larger boarding institution that had been unsuccessfully attempted by the Protestant Paul Monet. But this suggestion, never carried through, was made quite late in the history of the student migration.[23] We do not know how many of the Vietnamese students came from Catholic backgrounds, or privately attended Mass. But the available evidence indicates that few of them, somewhere between two and ten percent, came into contact in France with a Catholic *lycée, foyer* or student club.

### The Collapse of the Collaborators

Because much of the student migration took place in the wake of the 1925-1926 events in Cochinchina, many of the students arrived in France already committed to what the French authorities would habitually describe as "clear anti-French attitudes." Education in France did little to mitigate such sentiments; in most cases it inflamed them. Even for those students who did not join the various radical activist factions of the Vietnamese student milieu, the years spent in France had a corrosive effect on their willingness to accept the existing arrangements in colonial Indochina. The trend of Vietnamese student politics during the five or six years after the student "invasion" was towards the radicalization of Vietnamese sensibilities. Many of the students who arrived in France infused with no more than simple patriotism returned as active Communists. Those who opposed the Communists, or who remained attached to the colonial ideals of Franco-Annamite collaboration were intimidated into an apolitical silence and lost the influence they once wielded within the Vietnamese student organizations.

To explain the radicalization that took place in the 1920s, it is useful first of all to explore the political weakness of those students who might have stood against it. At the time of Ho Chi Minh's departure from Paris in 1924, there were at most a handful of Vietnamese students attracted to communism, and the ranks of the radical nationalist expatriate organizations were thin as well. This changed rapidly in the years ahead. Before the surge in Vietnamese students going to France, the strongest voice of protest in postwar Vietnam was that of Bui Quang Chieu's Constitutionalist party. Under the leadership of the Paris lawyer Duong Van Giao, they were the most visible Vietnamese political presence in France as well. The Constitutionalists were generally Saigon-based men of means. Many were businessmen or doctors and owned land outside the city. A good number were naturalized French citizens. They were forthright in asserting that their material wealth made them "disinterested" and thus worthy of playing a greater role in Vietnamese politics. In the years immediately following the war, they founded several newspapers, and had some successes in contesting with the *colons* elections for the Saigon colonial council. But it was a movement that produced no important political leaders or thinkers.[24]

For the plain fact was that there was a great weakness, or paradox in the Constitutionalist position, and this weakness was passed across the ocean and through the generations to their political (and literal) heirs among the Vietnamese students in Paris. The ultimate political aim of the Constitutionalists was self-determination for Vietnam, perhaps with the colony remaining under some ill-defined dominion status. But they sought to achieve this aim through collaboration with the French, and indeed the idea of collaboration weighed more heavily with them than the idea of independence. No men in France or Vietnam were more sincere believers in the phrase "Franco-Vietnamese collaboration." They were willing to challenge specific injustices of colonial rule; they were contentious about the difficulties Vietnamese faced in joining the Indochinese bar; they complained about the tiny numbers of Vietnamese whom the French permitted to become naturalized Frenchmen. But they did not want to achieve Vietnamese self-determination against the French, and were basically comfortable within the colonial context—which, after all, was where they had achieved their own success. In the colony they seemed uncertain whether they should try to prove their good will and responsibility so that France would accede to their demands, or actually to challenge French authority. The idea of collaboration, which had made a certain amount of sense in the nineteenth century, had acquired a passive, self-serving, and defensive ring to it after the Russo-Japanese War, the ongoing turmoil in China, and the Russian Revolution. French rule, which at the turn of the century could have been perceived as something that would sweep out the cobwebs, no longer wore the face of progress.

Moreover, the political strategy of collaboration rested on a dreadfully flawed notion—that the French could be persuaded to grant the Vietnamese what they wanted. Concessions to the idea of Vietnamese independence had been hinted at many times by Sarraut, without result. When the left-leaning Cartel des Gauches came to power in 1924, Bui Quang Chieu, the leader of the Constitutionalists, came to France for a speaking tour and lobbying effort. Chieu even paid for the opportunity to write opinion pieces for such pro-government publications as *Le Quotidien* and *Annales Coloniales*. His immediate demands were for termination of French censorship of journals in *quoc ngu,* granting to Vietnamese the right to free assembly, and greater Vietnamese access to responsible government jobs; his broader plan was making enlightened French opinion aware of the discontent brewing in Vietnam. While he was received politely, he returned to Saigon empty-handed in 1926. The following year the minister of colonies explained the government's distrust of the Constitutionalists:

> My department's opinion has never varied on this point and considers this allegedly moderate party every bit as sinister as the most clearly defined extremist party. Its goal is the same; it differs only in the timetable and perhaps the means.[25]

The French minister was correct in stating that the final implication of the Constitutionalist's activity was the independence of Vietnam. But it was short-sighted in the extreme not to recognize that differences as to the timetable and the means by which independence would be won were political distinctions of the first order. The French granted to Bui Quang Chieu and his party no concessions that might have demonstrated to Vietnamese, particularly of the younger generation, that constitutionalism was a force to be reckoned with. The moderate collaborationist nationalism had less and less influence with each passing year among the Vietnamese who were flowing into French schools in the middle of the 1920s.

Yet the failure of the collaborationist tendency among the Vietnamese students to sustain itself after the student flow intensified has sources that go beyond the purely political. The French never helped the collaborationists to win any victories, but moderate nationalism suffered from its own internally generated handicaps as well. The older generation of Constitutionalists were always in a morally ambiguous position when demanding reforms from the French; their social position, after all, was intertwined with the colonial system. But the heirs and children of the Constitutionalists suffered from all of the uncertainties of their parents, and from some newly minted ones as well.

## The Politics of Alienation

One fruitful way to explore the eclipse of collaborationism is within the context of the personal estrangement and alienation suffered by the Vietnamese, both in France and after their return. Of course these experiences were relevant to all colonial students who were in Paris and London between the wars. Even men as successful as the future Prime Minister of India, Jawaharal Nehru, were caught up in such feelings, Nehru's self characterization—"I am a stranger and an alien in the West. I cannot be of it. But in my own country also, I sometimes have an exile's feeling"—is often cited as typical.[26] The point here, often expressed more painfully by men less at home in the world than Nehru, is that the experience of Paris and London cut the student off from the emotions of his own people. In the case of North Africans, for instance, this feeling was exacerbated because many had lost touch with the Arabic language: "The French language is my exile," said the Algerian writer Malek Haddad, speaking (in French) before an Afro-Asian writers conference.[27] But even when estrangement merely meant that the student educated in the *métropole* no longer felt comfortable speaking with his parents, and out of tune with the rhythms of life in colonial society, the educational migration was a deeply unsettling experience.[28]

Such feelings, then, are a typical and perhaps inescapable part of the colonial student's world. But in the Vietnamese context they acquired a particular *political* resonance, which makes it necessary to understand the way such feelings of uprootedness were experienced and used by contending factions within the Vietnamese student migration.

Nearly all Vietnamese who came to France between the wars shared certain experiences in common. Probably all the students, for instance, lived in a mental universe quite different from that of their parents. They were the children of people who, more likely than not, had elaborate village kinship ties even if they had moved to the city, who believed in ghosts, and whose own marriages had been arranged. Such assumptions and beliefs were no longer held by their children; they had been undermined by the *franco-indigène* school system and the more general process of modernization in the colony even before the students got to France.[29]

The next step in the students' mental evolution involved beginning to think of themselves in a different light in relationship to Frenchmen. In the colony, Frenchmen seemed remote, powerful, and distasteful. With the exception of the small number of privileged children attending French *lycées,* Vietnamese students in the colony probably had little contact with French boys their own age, and, with the possible exception of a teacher, little positive personal experience with any French people. Even in the *lycées,* relationships between French and Vietnamese students could be hostile, particularly during the politically charged years of 1925 and 1926.[30] Relationships with French adults were likely to be unsatisfactory. To a young Vietnamese in the colony, an adult Frenchmen was quite possibly perceived as a corpulent and perspiring figure who was perpetually demanding something, and who had created a social system under which his demands had to be attended to, and who was himself full of contempt for the Vietnamese.[31]

But this picture might begin to change as soon as the Vietnamese got on the boat. The Vietnamese novelist Nhat Lien, himself a student during this period, has provided a whimsical depiction:

> . . . the further the ship got from Vietnam and the closer it got to France, to the same degree the more decently the people aboard treated me. In the China Sea they did not care to look at me. By the Gulf of Siam they were looking at me with scornful apprehension, the way they would look at a mosquito carrying malaria germs to Europe. When they entered the Indian Ocean, their eyes began to become infected with expressions of gentleness and compassion . . . and when we crossed the Mediterranean, suddenly they viewed me as being civilized like themselves and began to entertain ideas of respecting me. At that time I was very elated. But I still worried about the time when I was going to return home.[32]

Once the Vietnamese arrived in France, the nature of their personal and emotional experience, particularly in regard to French people, took different turns. Varying emotional reactions to being in France took on a political meaning. If these students' emotional response to being in France did not always precede their political choices, they nevertheless seem to have been an important element in their choices.

## The Perils of Loving France

For some Vietnamese, being around the French proved to be quite congenial. As Ly Binh Hue, a law student and the editor of the moderate *Journal des Étudiants Annamites* put it in an "open letter" to a compatriot who had not yet decided whether to come to France, what was striking about French life was that one was treated with dignity, respect, and the complete absence of racial prejudice—so much that "even at the Opera, no one dared stare at you, even if you had an orchestra seat." He stressed that one found in France a completely different species of Frenchman than was in the colony. Teachers in the *lycées* "like us as well as they like their French students, that is to say they confuse us with them, and forget that we are Annamites."[33] Beyond that there was Paris, and a wealth of opportunities. Friendships with French students, both male and female, could flourish while Paris itself opened up a dazzling array of intellectual and artistic opportunities. One young writer who came to France on a government scholarship and eventually went on to earn his doctorate in French literature described the city as permeated with "an air of liberty, gaiety, and tolerance"—and France as the only country that would acknowledge his intelligence.[34]

We don't know how many Vietnamese felt like this. To fall in love with France, it would be necessary first of all to speak French well, and probably to be at least a capable student.[35] If this was a minority experience, it was not that rare. It is, for example, the Paris portrayed by the Vietnamese protaganist of the novel *Nam et Sylvie* which concerns a love affair between a Vietnamese student and a French girl.[36] In this novel there is no mention of French racism or cultural condescension, and the complications between the Vietnamese student and his lover have nothing to do with the relationship between "the colonizer and the colonized." In some of the letters sent home by Vietnamese students one can see photographs that convey this atmosphere. In pictures of dances held on special occasions at the Indochina House in Paris, or at the Vietnamese student associations at Bordeaux, there are portraits of happy students—Vietnamese young men, young French women, a few French males—all exuding an air of gaiety and normalcy.[37]

This sweetness of life in France was not necessarily something decadent but could be exciting, because it involved intellectual effort and growth. Such was the argument of Nguyen Manh Tuong's *Sourires et Larmes d'une Jeunesse*.[38] In that collection of short stories, the young Vietnamese writer (who received his doctorate in French literature in 1936) dwelled on the possibilities of Paris, which he described as "the center of all that human genius can create in the realm of art, elegance, intelligence." In this Paris, a Vietnamese could live a somewhat French life if he had mastered the nuances of the language, if he was fortunate in his French friends. He could feel that Paris was not only the artistic and intellectual capital of the world, but, as French colonial rhetoric suggested, his own capital city. Even when Nguyen Manh Tuong's stories take a bitter turn, where France is involved, the tone rises to the level of high drama. A Vietnamese student commits a crime of passion, because a bourgeois French father tries to break up his daughter's engagement with him. A student dies from tuberculosis while his friends gather round. Another student stays in Paris, walking the streets in poverty, because his parents, trying to force him to return, stop sending him an allowance. He prefers the freedom of Paris to the alleged security of the Vietnamese hearth, as do all of Nguyen Manh Tuong's characters. These are stories about loving France, and in an off-key way, about loving the French.

And yet this is a tragic book, which fully expresses the emotional difficulties of the Vietnamese who got closest to the French. Once they are forced by circumstance or filial obligation to return home, true sadness begins. There they feel stifled, unable to express themselves, haunted by guilt over their perception that the family hearth has a "sinister" feel to it. Once Nguyen Manh Tuong's characters return to Vietnam, they begin to die within, their spirit weakened by the feeling that they cannot be understood by their countrymen, their parents, their future wives. *Sourires et Larmes* is a collective profile of a certain type of Vietnamese student, who, by embracing France, lost contact with his own people.

This loss of roots was also a concern of Pham Quynh, the most gifted of Vietnamese conservative intellectuals. Born in 1892, Pham Quynh graduated from the French school for interpreters in the colony, learned Chinese on his own, and in 1917 became the editor of the literary journal *Nam Phong*. As an essayist, editor, and for a short time an officer in Emperor Bao Dai's cabinet during the 1930s, Pham Quynh may have been the Vietnamese intellectual who worried most about the dangerous political consequences that would flow from a Vietnamese generation growing up without a solid sense of its own cultural and national moorings.

Pham Quynh would be executed by the Viet Minh in 1945 and receives severe treatment in most recent histories of Vietnam for a number of reasons.[39] His journal *Nam Phong* received subsidies from the colonial government, and he served the French in several official capacities. Most importantly Pham Quynh argued in a variety of ways that Vietnam could prosper under French rule. There is no doubt that Pham Quynh was guilty of collaboration; he seemed to take France's rule of Vietnam as an unalterable fact of life, and advocated that the Vietnamese learn as much as possible from the French in order to find their way in the modern world.[40] In some of his writing he crossed the line into procolonialist propaganda; his suggestion, for example, that Vietnam was on the way to becoming a "laboratory where the reconciliation between East and West was preparing itself" had little basis in reality.[41] Too often for the good of his own posthumous reputation, Pham Quynh approvingly cited French authors associated with reaction against both modernity and the Third Republic. But much of his commentary on Vietnamese youth in the 1920s rings true.

According to Pham Quynh, Vietnamese youth was growing up without cultural bearings; it was equally ignorant of Vietnam's own Confucian intellectual heritage and the intellectual rigor of the French *philosophes*.[42] His remedy was, in part, more education; he recommended that young Vietnamese immerse themselves in both the Confucian and the French classics. He also urged the French to define their educational mission more broadly: the people of Vietnam needed not just technical education but literary education as well. But Pham Quynh saw French education as a double-edged proposition for the Vietnamese. In one essay he discussed the state of mind of a young French-educated Vietnamese, a hard working member of Vietnam's rising elite. The young man complained that foreign education had "completely separated us from our country and our people," and admitted "shamefully" that he no longer felt any "instinctive solidarity" with the broad masses of his people. Like the protagonists of Nguyen Manh Tuong's stories, Pham Quynh's young confidant avoided all conversation with his parents, claiming that when he spoke his mind he offended them. He ruefully concluded, "The only gain we got from our foreign education was a critical spirit which we trained on everything around us."[43]

Pham Quynh's own interpretation of this generational malaise was equally severe. As one way out of the feeling of unrootedness, he and other writers associated with *Nam Phong* emphasized the study of language. They often cited the writings of Charles Maurras to stress the mystical importance of language in defining a people's national identity. For the people of Vietnam, Pham Quynh advocated the creation of a national Vietnamese literature in the new written language of *quoc ngu*. The young Vietnamese growing up in the 1920s dismayed him because he felt they knew neither Vietnamese nor French; they spoke and even thought in a hybrid mixture that was neither Vietnamese nor French. As a result, Pham Quynh contended their thought processes lacked discipline and any concrete sense of what words really meant; the Vietnamese young were thus uncritically receptive to any faddish ideological system.[44] It was a diagnosis that rang more true than the proposed remedy. Pham Quynh and other writers around *Nam Phong* never stopped trying to modernize Confucianism, or to utilize other traditions to forge an intellectually respectable conservatism; in colonial Indochina such efforts amounted to little more than marks made upon the sea.[45]

The type of self-division and sense of cultural homelessness described by Nguyen Manh Tuong and Pham Quynh tended to be exclusively the problem of the collaborators. The writing in the moderate student newspapers, like the *Journal des Étudiants Annamites,* is shot through with phrases that implied self-doubt, self-questioning, and self-division—emotions that were certainly sure to paralyze a young man aspiring to political activity or leadership. Those among the Vietnamese who learned, in France, to feel comfortable with the French, to esteem French society, found that they not only wanted French esteem in return, but that they no longer knew exactly what they wanted for the Vietnamese people. Their sense of group allegiance, and of national identity, was fragile, and complicated. It is not surprising that they would prove no match in energy or will for those other Vietnamese students who realized early on that they wanted nothing from their stay in France but the tools to drive the French out of Indochina.

The students prone to this sort of self-division could not maintain their leadership positions in the burgeoning Vietnamese student movement in France for very long. The last time Vietnamese of moderate political tendencies held much sway in student opinion was at the Vietnamese student conference held in Aix-en-Provence in September 1927. The conference, bringing together one hundred fifty Vietnamese students, was organized by several students with ties to the Constitutionalist party. The conference was held in the municipal hall, and the mayor of Aix opened the proceedings with a graceful speech, after which the students formed a procession to lay flowers in the local cemetery for French and Vietnamese who died in the Great War. These rituals—the choice of a government building, the visit to an emotional symbol of shared French-Vietnamese sacrifice—displayed the intended nature of the gathering. Few Frenchmen regarding the photographs of these well-scrubbed young men posing in ill fitting oversized suits might imagine that young Vietnamese would soon become the vanguard of the world movement against French colonialism.[46]

But these symbols of French-Vietnamese good will obscured the fact that this first conference of Vietnamese students in France was most unusual: it was the last occasion for a very long time in which a number of young educated Vietnamese could gather and pass resolutions that did not condemn French rule over Indochina and France itself. Even the spirit of political calm that prevailed during the five-day gathering was possible only because the conference organizers explicitly forbade any floor discussion of political resolutions.[47] The conference's fourteen resolutions, which were unanimously adopted, were "corporate" in character; they were designed to touch educational issues only. It is unlikely that a radical condemnation of French colonialism would have achieved much support. When one student made a well-received speech urging young Vietnamese to cease their pursuit of law degrees—and concentrate instead on engineering, he suggested as suitable role models Henry Ford and André Citroën, whom he claimed had more impact on their societies than any jurist. No one reproached him for his choice of heroes.[48]

But the "educational" resolutions displayed a considerable degree of uneasiness. The young Vietnamese accused the colonial authorities of a "total absence" of any doctrine for education in Indochina, and demanded more schools in Indochina, more scholarships for study in France, as well as such measures as the building of special residences for Vietnamese students to make student life in France more convenient. There were as well some tell-tale signs of national-cultural confusion: one resolution called for the colonial government to help develop the "public spirit" of the Vietnamese by reproducing and translating (from Chinese) documents from the Vietnamese past, and to make more of an effort to teach Chinese. French teachers, it would seem, were to be entrusted with the difficult dual mission of bringing young Vietnamese into the modern world by educating them in France, and simultaneously restoring their historic sense of themselves by reconciling the students with their Chinese-influenced past.

But for its Vietnamese organizers and the French officials who observed it, the conference succeeded because it avoided political controversy. Conference organizers were satisfied to note that their activities received approving coverage in the local French press; if the reporter from *La Voix Provençale* and the mayor of Aix considered that the future leaders of Vietnam had been present that week, perhaps that was confirmation enough that things would go well for these young men who aspired to be the ruling elite of Vietnam.[49]

Although these student demands were quite moderate, they did not receive the serious consideration of French officialdom. Amadée Thalamas, the colony's director of education, wrote an ungenerous critique of the conference that summary rejected not only the students' resolutions but the very idea that Vietnamese students in France might legitimately formulate their own demands on the French government.[50] In any case, by the fall of 1927 the tide had begun to turn: the Vietnamese in France were becoming, in ever greater numbers, committed radical nationalists, available for recruitment into the Communist movement.

### The Spirit of Separateness

This growth of radical nationalism among the students has a dimension very much rooted in the emotions stirred up by being in France. Here, the student did not become estranged from his own people, or at least admitted nothing of the kind. Rather, he learned to use his newly acquired proximity to Frenchmen as a way of defining himself against the French. What seemed to take place was another side of alienation, in which the French milieu repelled, rather than enticed the Vietnamese. It was a sentiment much more likely to lead to energetic political commitment.

Perhaps too, the phenomenon described by Tocqueville, in his depiction of the relationships between noble and bourgeois prior to the French revolution is relevant. Tocqueville's point was that as the two classes became closer in manner, function, knowledge, and behavior, and as the privileges belonging to the nobility diminished, any remaining differences in status and privilege became less tolerable.[51] Can one say that Vietnamese nationalism was felt more intensely by the Vietnamese students once they found themselves, in France, studying at the same schools as French boys, and in some cases doing the same work? Could they, after being treated as well as Frenchmen, not come to feel in their bones that they were just as qualified to run their country as the French?

In general, this proximity produced a social situation that was more equal (in comparison with Vietnam) but still separate. Most Vietnamese students did not have a social life that revolved around dances with French girls, cultural appreciation of Paris, and intellectual achievement. To be receptive to French intellectual life—to be able to perform well in a French *lycée* or university, to be stimulated by French professors, or literature, a Vietnamese student needed either a solid academic background in the colony or unusual intellectual gifts; this excluded the majority. Either inclination, or lack of language skills, or pre-existing nationalist convictions kept most Vietnamese students apart from the French. Astute French observers had noted this in the immediate postwar years, before the Vietnamese posed any political problem,[52] and it was a social symptom that did not disappear when the Vietnamese migration increased.

There were many indications of this separateness. The prefect who reported on the Vietnamese in Toulouse described them as a "closed circle" who hardly ever were involved with French people; Vietnamese who didn't have anti-French attitudes fit in with difficulty.[53] A professor at Montpellier wrote, in 1929, that the Vietnamese had "no real contact with French life" and suggested, unsuccessfully, that the government sponsor a mixed French-Vietnamese *foyer* of Vietnamese students.[54] A letter home from a Vietnamese to a friend in Saigon dwelt on the Vietnamese problem with dating and girls; according to him, it was possible to date, but the girls most accessible to Vietnamese in France were secretaries and shop girls—beneath the perceived station of the Vietnamese student. Thus involvement and marriage was something to be feared and avoided lest a student have to return with a French wife to Saigon and spend the rest of his life "nourishing an enemy of his race."[55] A French Catholic student paper lamented, as late as 1936, that student-to-student contact between French Catholics and colonial students was negligible.[56]

Academic failures also may have nourished a Vietnamese sense of apartness. There were of course talented Vietnamese students who did well in French schools at every level. But there is much evidence that many Vietnamese students were lost academically, having arrived in French *lycées* without suitable preparation, and gained entrance into the university without appropriate skills. Even those equipped to do well might have encountered some subtle condescension from their teachers, who were not slow to conclude that the Vietnamese were "unable to grasp our style of thinking."[57] Another reason for academic difficulties may have been the fact that the relationship between academic performance and career possibility was muddied by the colonial situation. That a Frenchman who worked in the colonial administration was paid nearly twice the salary of a Vietnamese doing the same job was of course an irritant; so too was the reality that Vietnamese still were barred from the highest positions in the administration and judiciary of their country. Careers in politics and the press, though possible, existed only under the confining rules of ultimate French sovereignty.[58]

Furthermore there may have been at work a more general Oriental cultural aversion to the West. The East's rejection of Western individualism is a difficult subject to generalize about, for quite clearly the personal freedom that is part of life in France is attractive to many Asians, including Vietnamese. But it is true that the Western sense of the individual's value is not taken for granted in Asian societies, as many scholars have noted.[59] Vietnamese in particular came from large and generally cohesive families, and could easily be put off by the customs of "individualist" France. Once cultural feelings became politicized, as began to happen in the late 1920s, it could be a short step from estrangement to denunciation. One student writer touched on this when he contrasted the warm Vietnamese hearth, where everyone ate "from a single food tray," with what he disdainfully labeled the "each person one room, each person one plate" French family system. The Vietnamese student leader Ta Thu Thau, fresh from a violent confrontation in a Left Bank cafe with members of the right wing *Jeunesses Patriotes,* commented that at least his opponents had managed to transcend the "accentuated individualism" that was destroying Europe.[60]

Under different circumstances, a nationalist student movement rejecting the West might have sought new political moorings by looking backward, and searching for ideological anchors in the historic recesses of its own political tradition. But among the Vietnamese students in France, one finds no evidence of efforts to mine their own past for an ideology to deal with the present. Vietnamese conservatives, like Pham Quynh in Hanoi, tried to weave traditional Vietnamese heroes and concepts into an ideology to deal with the problematic present. In Vietnam, Communists, with much greater success, would learn to infuse their movement with the spirit of the redemption of the Vietnamese past.[61] But, perhaps because they were removed from that tradition both by the distance, and—particularly in the case of Southerners, simple lack of knowledge—the Vietnamese students in France attempted nothing like this, and were not stirred by anything resembling fundamentalism. To those Vietnamese in France who sought an ideological system expressive of their rejection of France, French colonialism, and French culture, Marxism proved to be completely satisfactory. For not only did it categorically condemn that part of the West which had humiliated their country, but it brought with it the possibility of organizational assistance, and powerful allies—elements which should never be underestimated when gauging the appeal of an ideology.[62]

By the late 1920s it had become apparent that the brightest and most energetic Vietnamese students in France had come to define themselves in political terms, and were won over to a radical nationalism, usually permeated with simple Marxist analysis; for many this kind of nationalism was a stepping off point along the way to a life-long embrace of the Communist movement. It is quite possible to summarize this phenomenon in the language of sociology. The French historian Daniel Hémery has described the Vietnamese student movement as a nascent intellectual class that was prohibited from fulfilling the functions of governance and ideological dissemination that similar groups in European society were able to carry out: the only way these young Vietnamese could fulfill their function as intellectuals was to transform themselves into a revolutionary intelligentsia.[63] This is persuasive; still it doesn't catch all of the elements of envy, frustration, and estrangement that were vented into the Vietnamese student movement, and of which that movement made effective political use. Becoming a student militant meant rejecting the French, and implied nearly open warfare against those Vietnamese who showed themselves able to get along with the French. Militant nationalism, then, solved a great many of the emotional dilemmas experienced by young Vietnamese half a world away from their homes, and much more than a generation away from the world of their parents.

Militant nationalism involved, prior to acceptance of any doctrine, a series of rejections. First of all it required an outright rejection of the right of France to "lead" Vietnam into the modern world; it became commonplace in the myriad, evanescent journals of the radical Vietnamese students to reiterate the line that first appeared in the writings of Nguyen An Ninh: France, which had given liberty to its own citizens had in Indochina "imposed slavery on a free people who possessed a rich civilization at the time when the French were still living in caves."[64]

Another convention that was rejected was the compulsion to perform academically, particularly if the goal was professional success in colonial Vietnam. This rejection took the form of minor revolts—as when students in Toulouse turned in blank papers for an examination question (for the *baccalauréat*) which asked them to describe how their feelings towards "La France protectrice" had evolved during their stay.[65] It took the form of student agitation against preparing for jobs in the "prison of the bureaucracy," as well as the formation of study groups that tried to win student promises not to work for the colonial government when they returned to Indochina. It also took the form of a carefully defined kind of elitism—by which the French-educated students talked about their "sacred duty" to spread their knowledge and their ideas among their less-educated countrymen, while at the same time vowing to put themselves under the guidance of Vietnam's "workers and peasants" who were to "correct their faults." This brand of intellectual elitism and radical analysis coexisted comfortably: a telling example is the student paper which argued that the Chinese, Egyptian, and Indian nationalist parties had consistently collaborated with their colonial oppressors—and that Vietnam's "national bourgeoisie" would also always commit treason against the popular masses; two pages later it pleaded for support from Vietnam's "future elite corps- the fifteen hundred Annamite intellectuals in France" to support their paper.[66]

Militant nationalists also rejected lives of middle class comfort by making choices that involved real sacrifice. The two Vietnamese students who played the most crucial roles in leading their peers to the Communist Left, Ta Thu Thau and Nguyen Van Tao, both pursued politics at the expense of personal or material comfort. Ta Thu Thau, who would become the driving force of Vietnamese Trotskyism, was born into a poor family of six children, and had supported his studies at a *lycée* in Saigon through menial odd jobs. Still he rejected the colonial government's offer of naturalization and a full scholarship for his studies in France; when he arrived he lived in poor quarters, and supported himself by tutoring. His sometimes ally and eventual foe, the future Communist minister Nguyen Van Tao, never finished his degree, and for some time subsisted as school security guard.[67] Among the radicals there grew something of cult of hardness and self-sacrifice. Years before he emerged as the most prominent Vietnamese Communist in France, Nguyen Van Tao wrote home to a friend in Saigon "It is written already that I must work for the resurrection of my country, that I must offer my life, my energies, my happiness to Vietnam. I have a duty to accomplish, and no need to make calculations about joy or sadness. I must suffer because I am a man. I hope you will do the same."[68]

This striving for a kind of revolutionary purity blended with other aspects of the stance of defiant nationalism. Because the student felt himself on an equal ground with the French, he could contrast the situation in France with the reality in Indochina. "Here there is equality, and I fear nobody," one young Vietnamese wrote home. "But if a Frenchman from Indochina shows contempt for us as if he were still in Annam, we would insult him immediately. That is the great pleasure for all our countrymen in France."[69] And yet in France too one could cultivate one's separateness, and make that into a political act. By the late 1920s the style of being a Vietnamese rebel in France involved rejection of French society, French mores, and even social interaction with the French. More than the repetition of Marxist slogans, these attitudes reveal the emotional sensibility that grew up within the Vietnamese students in France.

By 1930, radical Vietnamese students had made the rejection of social interaction with the French into a political imperative. When students who resided at the government-sponsored Indochina House of *Cité Universitaire* held a dance and invited French girls, the other Vietnamese ripped down the posters and used the event to demonstrate their political and moral superiority. "None of us have ripped up your posters, my dears" exclaimed one political flyer posted in the student restaurant at the *Cité Universitaire.*

> French students have learned from these posters what kind of people they are going to dance with on Sunday. They will see how, in an "oriental decor" you plan to celebrate the condemnation of your countrymen and how you acclaim the terror and dictatorship in Indochina. Don't worry about your posters, they haven't disappeared. They are too beautiful. We will make thousands of copies of them and plaster them over all the walls in Indochina. Your parents and your friends will see how you live in this huge palace on the Rue Emile Faguet, and what shame you are bringing on yourselves.[70]

The expression of such sentiments became more and more frequent. By the late 1920s and all through the following decade, Vietnamese who mixed socially with the French were subject to harsh attack from their fellow students.[71] The trappings of social equality that a Vietnamese could find in France—which had seemed interesting to students early in the 1920s—were not satisfying once a climate of political rebellion had grown in the student community. Soon any kind of social contact could be subject to political analysis, and become an occasion for the venting of political hatreds. One young Vietnamese wrote home (in a letter opened and internally circulated by officials in the Ministry of Colonies) of a particular realm where politics and more private feelings intersected:

> No one denies that Paris is the most beautiful city in the world . . . as for the "women" there, there are countless numbers, many of them so beautiful that the sight of them turns you around. But we have no feelings toward them, we like them only to satisfy our sexual appetites. There are some with skin as white as ivory, who, completely naked, solicit us for a price of ten francs, half the going rate. Seeing them like this, we pity them, especially when they are performing deprayed and slavish acts. If these pretty women were in Viet-

nam, they would push us away exclaiming "dirty Annamites"—perhaps they would be the wives of high French officials. When we contemplate that, we suppress our pity, and oblige them to do even more depraved things.[72]

This combination of political and more visceral attitudes left the Vietnamese student community permeated with a spirit of latent violence that fully foreshadowed the civil war which would break out a generation later. By 1930 it was no longer possible for a Vietnamese student in France to write an article or attend a social function that supported "Franco-Vietnamese collaboration" without risking physical reprisal. There were instances in which flying squads of students traveled from city to city to give "collaborators" make-shift show trials, or simply beat them up. More courageously, radical Vietnamese in Paris went out of their way to disrupt meetings of the right-wing French youth group the *Jeunesses Patriotes.* In a widely reported incident in a Paris cafe in 1929 several Vietnamese brought knives and broken bottles with them to fortify their efforts to stop the young Frenchmen from hearing another Vietnamese student speak on "Franco-Annamite collaboration." Those young people who had to be hospitalized after this lively battle did not come from the ranks of the Vietnamese radicals.[73]

In the myriad small struggles for control over Vietnamese student associations and student journals this kind of militant spirit proved unstoppable. "Just about everywhere, the disruptive Indochinese elements are gaining ground" was the assessment given by the Ministry of Colonies' principal undercover agent towards the end of 1926, and within three years his pessimistic assessment proved justified.[74]

Changes in power at the organizational level tell the tale. First the *Association Mutuelle des Indochinois,* an organization founded in 1923 which had received considerable financial support from the Ministry of Colonies was taken over by an alliance of Constitutionalists and more radical young Vietnamese in late 1926. The following year its subsidy from the Ministry of Colonies was withdrawn and its premises vacated. In 1927 the *Parti Annamite de l'Indépendance* was revived under the leadership of Ta Thu Thau, and soon established itself as the most significant Vietnamese political grouping in France. The PAI gained support both from students and from skilled Vietnamese workers, particularly from those in the lacqueur trade. The French government banned the PAI in 1929, but by that time it had completely replaced the Constitutionalist party, which French officials, by year's end deemed "no longer functioning."[75]

Similar changes took place in the groups run explicitly by students. In 1929 the medical student Tran Van Doc was forced out of the leadership of the largest student organization in Paris, the *Association Générale des*

*Étudiants Indochinois,* for speaking of France's "genius" at a ceremony for the ground breaking at the Indochina House of the *Cité Universitaire.* The left-wing nationalist students who gained control of the group tried to use it as a springboard to establish one large Indochinese student organization which could exert centralized control over all the Vietnamese student clubs in France.[76] Radical gains in the AGEI were mirrored by similar developments in Marseilles, Toulouse, and Aix, the other French cities where Vietnamese students numbered in the hundreds.[77]

One clear conclusion could be drawn from these shifts, and the attitudes that generated them: France was failing utterly in its efforts to train a generation of educated Vietnamese who would be willing and able to forge durable links between France and Indochina in future decades. One cannot assert that a majority of the Vietnamese who came to France became anti-French activists; there were no comprehensive polls taken of Vietnamese attitudes. But a Paris prefect of police report on Vietnamese student attitudes in 1929 claimed that most Vietnamese were hostile to the French presence in Indochina.[78] And the predominance of radical attitudes among those Vietnamese who were politically active and effective—those who were willing to start or write for a student newspaper, participate regularly in a student organization, or demonstrate—was striking. The fact that there may have been merely two-or three-or four hundred such students out of the few thousand who attended school in France was never a source of reassurance for the French; no colonial official came forth to proclaim the attitudes among the Vietnamese students were really not so bad because there may have been a "silent majority" of the Vietnamese who didn't actively oppose French rule.

The ferment among Vietnamese youth had been, of course, predicted many times—and not only by those whose solution was to prevent Vietnamese from receiving any higher education at all. The experience of France did not begin the road to rebellion for many of the students; Vietnamese radical nationalism was rooted in the many anomalies of the colonial situation in Vietnam, and in the Vietnam's own past. But the years in France did more to inflame the nationalist passions of Vietnam's youth than to calm them.

The youth rebellion represented both threat and opportunity to the diverse elements in the French political community. To the French colonial establishment it signaled a major obstacle in the way of France's plans to keep hold of Indochina. To the adherents of the world Communist movement in France, and its leaders in Moscow, the militancy of the young Vietnamese represented an important opportunity—the chance to turn the passions of revolutionary nationalism in a disciplined Leninist direction. Between those two groups stood many others, among them French liberals and Socialists and representatives of the Catholic Church, who surveyed the student scene and saw that the stage was being set for a political catastrophe. But these groups had neither ideas to resolve the dilemmas nor the power to impose their solutions.

Those representatives of the French state who were the main French actors in the struggle for the minds of the young Vietnamese generation saw France's failures all too clearly. But the difficulties faced by the colonial power as it tried to enforce its rule over an unwilling foreign people—while proclaiming its own adherence to liberal ideas, and while its policy choices were restricted by liberal institutions—were considerable. They would prove impossible to surmount.

## Notes

1. This generational change in the leadership of Vietnamese anticolonialism is stressed in David Marr, *Vietnamese Anticolonialism* (Berkeley: University of California Press, 1971), 248-277.
2. Thomas Hodgkin in *Vietnam: The Revolutionary Path* (London: Macmillan, 1981), 216-226, describes the immediate postwar years as "the only period in Vietnamese history when the collaborating elite was able to exercise a certain initiative." See also David Marr, *Vietnamese Tradition on Trial* (Berkeley: University of California Press, 1981), 15-53 for an analysis of the balance of social forces in Vietnamese society in the mid-1920s.
3. The emergence of a publishing industry in Vietnam and of a new class of urban intellectuals with a new political style is discussed in Marr, *Vietnamese Tradition on Trial*, 44-53, and in Daniel Hémery, "Ta Thu Thau: l'Itineraire Politique d'un Révolutionaire Vietnamien," in *Histoire de l'Asie du Sud-Est: Révoltes, Réformes, Révolutions*, ed. Pierre Brocheux, (Lille: Presses Universitaires de Lille, 1982), 194-204.
4. Nguyen An Ninh, "La France et l'Indochine," *Europe*, 15 July 1925.
5. See Hémery, "Ta Thu Thau," 197-207 and Hodgkin, *Vietnam*, 219-220. Pham Quynh's remark is cited in William Frederick, "Alexandre Varenne and Politics in Indochina," in *Aspects of Vietnamese History*, ed. Walter Vella (Honolulu, University of Hawaii Asian Studies, 1973). The remark from the Resident General Maurice Cognacq is quoted in Daniel Hémery, *Révolutionnaires Vietnamiens et Pouvoir Colonial en Indochine: Communistes, Trotskystes, Nationalistes à Saigon de 1932 à 1937* (Paris: Maspero, 1975), 67.
6. For an assessment of Varenne's role, see Frederick, "Alexandre Varenne" and Walter Langlois, *André Malraux: The Indochina Adventure* (New York: Praeger, 1966), 163-181.
7. ANSOM: NFI, 231-1900.
8. See chapter 4 for a discussion of the job shortage for educated Vietnamese.
9. Several Vietnamese and Western scholars have maintained that Phan Boi Chau was invited to a rendezvous by Ho Chi Minh in Canton, who then tipped off the French police, thus simultaneously procuring reward money and a martyr for the cause of Vietnamese independence, while eliminating a rival leader of the anticolonial movement. See Buttinger, *Vietnam: A Dragon Embattled* (New

York: Praeger, 1967), 80. This version has always been denied in Vietnamese Communist writings.

10. For accounts of the 1926 disturbances, see Hémery, "Ta Thu Thau," 197-207 and Gail P. Kelly, "Conflict in the Classroom: A Case Study from Vietnam, 1918-1938," unpublished manuscript, privately communicated.

11. See chapter 4 for a discusion of the lack of cooperation between various branches of the French government.

12. See Daniel Hémery, "Du Patriotisme au Marxisme: l'Immigration Vietnamienne en France de 1926 a 1930," *Le Mouvement Social* January 1975. Ta Thu Thau's dockside speech, quoted from *La Tribune Indigéne,* 23 December 1927, is also cited here.

13. AOM-Indochine, 51534 indicates that the Governor-General's office in Hanoi gave only six scholarships a year from 1927 to 1931. Other sources of quasi-governmental scholarship money were available, from organizations such as the government sponsored *Association pour la Formation Intellectuelle et Morale des Annamites*; also the *Distilleries de l'Indochine* and the *Charbonnages de Tonkin* paid for the professional education of future employees; still the percentage of Vietnamese students in France who were scholarship recipients was tiny. For official French dismay over the surge, see the report by Thalamas, the colony's director of public instruction, ANSOM: NFI, 259-2226.

14. Thalamas report, ANSOM: NFI 259, 2226.

15. See Slotfom VI, 9 for the Ministry of Colonies 1925 estimate. The larger figure, from a Ministry of the Interior estimate is from Archives Nationales, (hereafter AN) F-7, 13412. University of Paris enrollments are found in ARUP 227.

16. The police commissioner of Toulouse reported that seventy-two percent of the Indochinese students there came from Cochinchina in 1928. This figure roughly corresponds to the number of Cochinchinese who were enrolled at the University of Paris, though the regional statistics from there are often uneven and contradictory. One difficulty is that Annam, the central province of Vietnam was the seat of the imperial capital; thus "Annamites" was a generic name for all Vietnamese, including residents of Saigon. See ARUP 227.

17. Thalamas report, ANSOM: NFI, 259-2226.

18. Marr, *Vietnamese Tradition,* 43-44 mentions the scholarship in exchange for marriage phenomenon.

19. See the Thalamas report, ANSOM: NFI, 259-2226. Teacher comments like the one from the *proviseur* of the *Lycée Lakanal* were typical: he wrote that the Vietnamese were poor students not "because of their ethnic origin, but because they were recruited by wealth and social origin rather than intellectual aptitude." See AN: AJ-16, 2708.

20. *Dossiers de la Documentation Catholique,* 19 March 1932.

21. "Les Étudiants Orientaux en Europe," *Documents de la Vie Intellectuelle,* 20 October 1931.

22. Slotfom III, 32.

23. "Les Étudiants Orientaux en Europe," *Documents de la Vie Intellectuelle,* 20 October 1931. This article is unsigned, but brings together several signed pieces written by Catrice for this publication and for *La Documentation Catholique.* The question of the Catholic Church's response to the student movement is explored in chapter 4, below.

24. The most incisive treatment of the collaborators is Milton Osborne, "The Faithful Few: the Politics of Collaboration in Cochinchina in the 1920's" in

*Aspects of Vietnamese History.* See also Hémery, "L'Immigration Vietnamienne," and R.B. Smith, "Bui Quang Chieu and the Constitutionalist Party in French Indochina, 1917-30," *Modern Asian Studies* 3, 2 (1969).

25  Letter from Minister of Colonies Leon Perrier to Varenne of 28 September 1927, quoted in Hémery, "L'Immigration Vietnamienne." Ministry of Colonies reports of Bui Quang Chieu's visit are contained in Slotfom III, 3.

26.  Nehru's full paragraph is as follows: "I have become a queer mixture of the East and West, out of place everywhere, at home nowhere. Perhaps my thoughts and approach to life are more akin to what is called Western than Eastern, but India clings to me as she does to all her children, in innumerable ways; and behind me lie, somewhere in the subconscious, racial memories of a hundred generations of Brahmins. I cannot get rid of either that past inheritance or my recent acquisitions. They are part of me, and though they help me in both the East and West, they also create in me a feeling of spiritual loneliness not only in public activities, but in life itself. I am a stranger and an alien in the West. I cannot be of it. But in my own country, also, sometimes I have an exile's feeling." Jawaharlal Nehru, *An Autobiography* (London, 1936), 597-598, cited in Edward Shils, *The Intellectual between Tradition and Modernity: the Indian Situation* (The Hague: Mouton, 1961), 61.

27.  Haddad, quoted in David Gordon, *North Africa's French Legacy: 1954-1962* (Cambridge: Harvard University Press, 1964), 36. See Gordon, 35-46 for a broader discussion of alienation among French-educated North Africans.

28.  The subject is a vast one, and beyond the confines of this study. Some of the most useful discussions of cultural alienation of non-Vietnamese colonial students are in Gordon, *North Africa's French Legacy* and Shils, *The Intellectual between Tradition and Modernity.* Also useful are Albert Memmi, *The Colonizer and the Colonized* translated by Howard Greenfield, (Boston: Beacon Press, 1967) and Malek Bennabi, *Vocation d'Islam* (Paris, 1954.) Frantz Fanon's *The Wretched of the Earth* translated by Constance Farrington (New York: Grove Press, 1963) is the most influential argument for the need of Third World elites to rid themselves of their remaining deference to European culture. *Négritude* discussed in chapter 7, below, is one example of how gifted French-educated blacks dealt with their own sense of deracination. For a broader discussion of the experience in France of students from other colonies see chapter 7.

29.  See David Marr, *Vietnamese Tradition on Trial,* 8-13.

30.  Gail Kelly, "Conflict in the Classroom: A Case Study From Vietnam, 1918-1938" unpublished paper, privately communicated.

31.  Leon Werth in *Cochinchine* (Paris: F. Rieder, 1926) provides a vivid depiction of *colon* attitudes and habits. One sample of his ear for dialogue is his rendition of one of the first pieces of *colon* advice he received upon arrival in Saigon: "The annamite has a sense of justice. Don't ever punish him without reason. But if the punishment is fair, he accepts it. It inspires no rebellion in him. Moreover, he would be contemptuous of you if you didn't punish him" (p. 19). For his elaboration on how the *colons* made him ashamed to be European, see pp. 35-56.

32.  Quoted in Alexander Woodside, *Community and Revolution in Modern Vietnam* (Boston: Houghton Mifflin, 1976), 4.

33.  *Journal des Étudiants Annamites,* 15 May 1927. This journal was one of several published by groups of Vietnamese students in France. Other, similar papers

were *L'Annam Scolaire* in Aix-en-Provence, and *L'Annam de Demain*. Such forums of opinion, tolerated in France but not allowed in Indochina, typically ran a half dozen issues or so before closing. While they constantly exhorted their readers for subscriptions, they presumably received some funds from Vietnamese political groups in the colony.

34. See Nguyen Manh Tuong, *Sourires et Larmes d'une Jeunesse* (Hanoi: Editions de la Revue Indochinoise, 1937), 70-79 and 104-107 and passim.

35. Vietnamese academic performance is discussed in chapter 4, below.

36. Nam Kim, *Nam et Sylvie* (Paris: Plon, 1957).

37. Slotfom, III, 25.

38. Nguyen Manh Tuong, *Sourires et Larmes*.

39. See the discussion of Pham Quynh in Marr, *Vietnamese Tradition,* 110-115 and 152-157. A more sympathetic assessment can be found in Bernard Le Calloc'h, "Le Role de Pham Quynh dans la Promotion de *quoc ngu* et de la Littérature Vietnamienne Moderne," *Revue Française d'Histoire d' Outre Mer* tome LX-XII (1985).

40. Pham Quynh, *Essais Franco-Annamites* (Hue: Bui Huy Tin, 1937), 223.

41. Ibid., 334.

42. Ibid., 205-214.

43. Ibid., 302-304.

44. Ibid., 223.

45. Woodside, *Community and Revolution,* 102-108.

46. Photographs of those who attended the conference can be found in Slotfom III, 16.

47. Resolutions and a discussion of the conference can be found in the *Journal des Étudiants Annamites,* October, November 1927.

48. Ibid.

49. Newspaper clippings on the conference are in Slotfom III, 16.

50. See AOM-Indochine, 51527 for Thalamas' detailed and biting rejection of the conference demands, which was of a piece with the colonial government's stonewalling of Constitutionalist demands in the colony.

51. Alexis de Tocqueville, *The Old Regime and the French Revolution,* trans. by Stuart Gilbert, (Garden City: Doubleday, 1955), 77-96.

52. See above, chapter 2.

53. AN: F7-13410.

54. Slotfom III, 25.

55. Slotfom III, 28.

56. *L'Étudiant Catholique* 3rd trimester, 1936.

57. This was the phrase of the proviseur of the *Lycée Lakanal* as part of a report on "foreign" students in French *lycées*. Other headmasters and teachers reported quite the opposite: that Vietnamese students did well, except that sometimes they were a year or two older—a fact easily explained by the confused educational system linking the colony and France. AN, AJ- 16 2708. When they passed out of the *lycée* to the university, Vietnamese students failed in large numbers; by 1932 one half had failed their exams for the *license* in Law; see Slotfom III, file 36. See chapter 4 for a fuller discussion of French academic policies and attitudes towards the students.

58. For an example of the common complaint about salary and job discrimination, see the letter to the editor from "a group of Annamite students" in *Le Petit Méridional* 10 February 1929.

59. For a concise introduction to this theme, see Lucian Pye, *Asian Power and Politics* (Cambridge: Harvard University Press, 1985), 26-27.
60. For Ta Thu Thau's comment on the *Jeunesses Patriotes* see *La Résurrection* January 1929. The reflection on eating habits is from *Than Chung*, Saigon, 8 January 1929, "The Situation of People who Study Abroad," quoted in Woodside, *Community and Revolution*, 96.
61. See Woodside, *Community and Revolution*, 234-245, and Frances FitzGerald, *Fire in the Lake: the Vietnamese and the Americans in Vietnam* (Boston: Little Brown, 1972), 212-227.
62. For a discussion of the relationship between Vietnamese students in France and Communists and other forms of Marxism, see chapter 5, below.
63. Hémery, "Ta Thu Thau."
64. *L'Annam de Demain*, 15 October 1928.
65. Slotfom, III, 32.
66. *L'Annam de Demain* 15 October 1928.
67. Hémery, *Révolutionnaires Vietnamiens*, 70-71.
68. Slotfom XII, 2. Letter by Nguyen Van Tao. This file contains several dozen letters that were opened by the French authorities in Indochina, translated, and circulated among officials at the Colonial Ministry—for the purpose, according to the cover letter, of demonstrating the wrongheadedness of the belief that "instructing conquered people in our language would be sufficient to attach them to us forever."
69. Ibid.
70. The flyer is in AN, F7, 13410. For a more favorable perspective of the dances held at Indochina House, see Nam Kim, *Nam et Sylvie*.
71. See also the student publication *Anh Sang*, 1 March 1935 for a similar sort of attack: "They danced when eight of our brothers were condemned to death, and they danced some more when their children disappeared. It's the elite, you know, the elite. Last year, when the guillotine blade was suspended over the heads of our comrades, you know what they did: they danced. Rhumbas followed tangos, alternated with fox-trots . . . they were so sad, so sad, what was going on in Vietnam was hurting them so much that they would die of heartache if they couldn't dance."
72. The letter is found in Slotfom XII, 2.
73. Slotfom III, 25 recounts one instance where a dozen Vietnamese students took the train from Aix to Marseilles to "try" and beat up a student who wrote a pro-French article for *Journal de Marseilles*. A variety of accounts of the so called Café Turquetti incident, where members of the Vietnamese nationalist group the *Parti Annamite de l'Indépendance* brawled with the *Jeunesses Patriotes* can be found in Slotfom, III, 23. See chapter 4 below.
74. See Slotfom III, 25 for the report of "Agent Désiré."
75. See Slotfom III, 32 for a succinct summary prepared by the Paris prefect of police of the organizational history of the various Vietnamese groups and parties in the Paris region.
76. The year-long campaign for control of the AGEI and against the "valet" Tran Van Doc is chronicled in Slotfom III, 14.
77. For reports on these changes in Toulouse, see the Ministry of Interior's analysis in AN, F7 13410. Accounts of Vietnamese student politics in Bourdeau can be found in Slotfom III, 25.
78. Slotfom III, 42.

# 4

# Vietnamese Students in France and the Dilemmas of French Policy

The history of the French governmental response to the surge of the Vietnamese students is essentially one of French failure. Though French officials tried both blandishments and discipline, they were never able to gain political initiative with their students. The reasons for France's failure are varied. In part it can be attributed to lack of creativity on the part of French colonial bureaucrats; in part to the very limited resources the government was willing to allocate to the problem. Of greater significance is the larger ideological context in which French colonial decisions were taken. Both France's internal liberalism and the French sense of what her empire meant restricted the measures French governments could actually take to try to deal with Vietnamese student radicalism. These limitations make France's difficulties broadly symptomatic of the dilemmas encountered by all governments which were at once liberal, democratic, and imperialist.

## The "Humanitarian" Colonial Consensus

The rise of radical nationalism among the Vietnamese students in France during the late 1920s came at a time when France's own sense of itself as an imperial power was undergoing subtle but significant evolution. The satisfaction felt about the *force noire* and "the France of one hundred million" had not lasted long past the end of the war. Albert Sarraut's ambitious program for turning the empire into a single dynamic economic entity had floundered in the face of lack of funding and economic complementarity. By 1925 the French faced a messy little insurgency in their Moroccan protectorate and the renewed rumblings of anticolonial sentiment at home—exemplified by the French Communist party's call for French soldiers to desert and fraternize with the Moroccan rebels.

These difficulties did not begin to tear at the political consensus that supported the French empire—a consensus that stretched across the French spectrum from the leadership of the Socialists to the spokesman for the right-wing nationalist leagues. But they did provoke a growth in French awareness of problems in the colonies. The rise of France's imperial consciousness—the fruits of sustained efforts of the various procolonial lobbying groups, had been accompanied by a parallel rise of organizations and sentiments antipathetic to French colonialism. And if outright anti-imperialism remained, for the most part, the property of the extreme Left, there was considerable growth of a French guilty conscience about empire, which showed itself in the moderate Left, the Catholic Church, and in a variety of publications.[1]

André Gide's *Voyage au Congo* published in 1927 and serialized in the Socialist paper *Le Populaire* was one instigator of the new conscience. Gide's work included a vigorous condemnation of the exploitation of Congolese laborers by a French forestry company—though he balanced his depiction with recognition of the positive effects of the French presence in Africa. Leon Werth's *Cochinchine*, published the previous year, was another example of incisive French self-criticism.[2] By 1930 the Catholic Church began to assert a greater interest in colonial matters. Catholic manifestos rejected what was described as the "selfish and brutal colonialism of the nineteenth century," and opposed as well a colonialism based on the strategic or economic interests of France. The sole justification of French colonialism, claimed Joseph Folliet, an influential Catholic voice on colonial matters, was "service to humanity." In 1930 the Catholic seminar *Semaines Sociales* held a session on the colonial problem, which concluded that the main focus of colonialism should be the "well being of the native." The penetration of such themes into the French conception of her empire brought into prominence what the historian Charles-Robert Ageron described as "the humanitarian conception of colonialism."[3]

The growth of the "humanitarian conception" did not challenge French rule as such, and did not greatly affect the attitudes towards the empire held by France's colonial professionals—the intellectuals, functionaries, and politicians whose careers were most intertwined with the empire. Since before the war, these men had supported "association" as the guiding concept of French colonial strategy, and the word dominated discussion of the political shape of the empire between the wars. Association had been developed by French colonial thinkers as an alternative to assimilation: it meant that French rulers should "respect," so far as possible, the indigenous institutions and local elites in her colonies, and develop the art of ruling through them. Though "association" was initially conceived as a modern and reformist alternative to the unthinking policy of making natives French and destroying their local culture in the process, it was a conception that easily lent itself to conservative arguments against giving France's colonial subjects the rights of French citizens or exposing them to Western education. Political reforms put forth by the exponents of association went no further than expanding the rights of colonial subjects to elect representatives to advisory panels for the local French administrator. In no case was association conceived of as a way station along the road to independence.[4]

Throughout the 1920s, those colonial writers and ideologists close to political power in France were united in their belief that the independence movements in the colonies would never amount to anything. This was as true for Left-leaning governments, like the Cartel des Gauches, as for the Right. Léon Archimbaud, a Radical Socialist deputy who was the reporter on the colonial budget in the Assembly, published *La Plus Grande France* in 1928, and his views might be taken as representative of a vast number of deputies of the moderate Left. About the growth of internal nationalist movements in the colonies, Archimbaud wrote "Apart from a few brainless young people whose opinion is of no value, the Annamites have never demanded that France should evacuate Indochina." His views on colonial matters borrowed much from Albert Sarraut's *La Mise en Valeur des Colonies* which had been published five years earlier, and apparently nothing that had happened since 1923 had changed the Radical Party's concept of the forces challenging the French empire.[5]

The idea of a humanitarian colonialism and the inadmissibility of colonial independence served as the two pillars around which discussion of French colonial policy revolved between 1920 and 1936, and even the election of the Popular Front did not greatly change matters. Arguments such as Archimbaud's demonstrated that the Radical Socialists did not have a vastly different conception of the empire than did the *Chambre Bleu Horizon*. The two conceptions defined the outer boundaries of the colonial consensus, and limited French options. Education was, after all, one of the few tangible benefits France could really offer the young Vietnamese, and by most colonial conceptions, education was an inextricable part of France's humanitarian and civilising mission. On the other hand, all French officials who were familiar with the students recognized that exposure to France was making many students more hostile to French rule. This made for a dilemma of the first order. The political development of the Vietnamese students illuminated the contradiction between the ideals justifying empire and the discipline necessary to sustain the empire. Because the Vietnamese were the first colonial students to come to France in any number, they posed the problem in a fresh form. But the problem was a classic one for governments that were internally liberal and outwardly imperialist.[6]

French governmental responses to the dilemmas posed by the students can be fairly described as indecisive, contradictory half-measures. One could argue that the response reflected the lack of creativity within the colonial ministry. This could be attributed more to the ministry's permanent bureaucrats than to the minister of colonies himself. Nine politicians headed the Ministry of Colonies in the six years after Sarraut left the post in 1924. This turnover probably served to shield the top officials from political meddling, and conceivably from fresh ideas. There was continuity in the top post: Albert Duchêne, the director of political affairs for the ministry during this period, was the man more responsible than anyone else for forging France's response to the Vietnamese students. Duchêne had reached late middle age, and his intellectual interests ran more to the financial structure of empire and early French colonial history than to the new social forces that were making themselves felt in France's colonial domain.[7] Younger men, like the Africanist Robert Delavignette, who would give the Ministry of Colonies a new look in the 1930s, were, during the previous decade, serving in their first overseas posts, often in Africa. The Ministry of Colonies had never been known as a fount of fresh and innovative thinking in comparison with other French ministries, and its posture towards the Vietnamese students throughout the 1920s bore the stamp of mediocrity.[8]

But the dilemmas posed by the students challenged the very heart of the French notion of itself as a modernizing, humanitarian colonial power, and forging a policy to deal with them would have strained the capacities of even the most innovative government officials. Official French efforts to grapple with the problem ranged from programs to help Vietnamese students adjust to academic life, to the disciplining of the most intransigent student rebels by returning them to Indochina. All of these measures were carried out before a rhetorical background of glowing public optimism, which was revealing both of French imperial ideology and of the restraints that governed French choices.

The public ceremonies at the ground-breaking for France's Indochina House in 1928 and its completion two years later put this optimistic French discourse on full display. The new building, part of the newly opened *Cité Universitaire* in Paris, was designed as a lodging and social center for about one hundred Vietnamese students; its thinly veiled ulterior purpose was to put Vietnamese students in a place where Frenchmen could both watch them and shelter them from disruptive political influences. Those who spoke at the Indochina House ceremonies were informed and not unrealistic men, who fully recognized that the influx of Vietnamese students into France was producing political turbulence. They were businessmen who had lived and worked and enriched themselves in Indochina, or colonial officials well briefed in the police reports about the political agitation sweeping through the younger generation of educated Vietnamese. Like most men in public life, they were not conscious hypocrites; the words they spoke reflect what the procolonial Frenchmen wished to be true about the French education of Vietnamese.

At the first Indochina House ceremony, Minister of Colonies Léon Perrier placed the need for the new building in the context of what France had done to bring the spirit of modernity to young minds of Vietnam. He stressed that France was bringing to the Vietnamese the chance to escape from stultifying tradition, and the intellectual tools to give man power over nature. These were common themes in French colonial thinking. "As soon as he enters the French schoolroom," Perrier exclaimed, "the young school boy has the impression of entering another world, which is bathed in a seductive glow. One speaks to him of France as a divine guardian; one liberates his soul from ancestral terrors, one communicates to him a confidence in the future and a sense of progress to replace the tedious effort at memory which had paralysed the intellectual activity of his race." To the young Vietnamese attending French schools, France was replacing "the cloud of mysticism" in which "his fathers floundered like frightened birds" with a "world of logic." France was showing the youth of Vietnam the ways in which "sentiments of dignity and a sense of the power of man could arise."[9]

When the building was completed two years later, the ceremony was larger; in attendance were the president of the Republic, several ministers, and a large roster of educational and colonial officials. The speeches contained the characteristic combination of self-congratulatory patriotism with an added emphasis on the "familial" nature of the relationship between official France and the colonial students. A.R. Fontaine, the businessman and director of the Indochinese liquor company *Distilleries de l'Indochine*, who had been in charge of raising money for the new edifice, opened the ceremony by noting the role Indochina House could play in shielding the young Vietnamese from "the unforeseen temptations and perils" of the French capital. The French owed it to the parents of the students to maintain their "respect for tradition" as well as to "open their spirits toward the clarity of our modern and scientific civilization."

Another speaker was the new minister of colonies, François Piétri, who asserted that the central doctrine of the French Republic was to "raise all peoples to an equality of mind." The experience of study in France, Pietri continued, would demonstrate to the youth of Vietnam that France contained much more than productive factories and that "despite the magnificence of France's technical accomplishments" the Vietnamese would be more deeply touched by "the ideal of reason which has illuminated the world for centuries." Students, who had first learned "respect for tradition" in Vietnam would learn from France the need for "organised work, and positive effort." When they returned, they would communicate "to their own parents, friends, and later their children what is the nature of the greatness of the people which watches out for you, what is the worth of this family—the French collectivity, which today regards you as its most treasured children."[10]

In private communications and in occasional published writing, French officials showed themselves far more skeptical about the relationship between the *métropole* and its "most treasured children." They did not wish to deny higher education to the Vietnamese, though elements of both the French and Vietnamese Left accused them of this. Nothing would have made the French happier than for the young Vietnamese to return home with the kind of cultural imprint that bound their allegiance to France— and to the French idea of "Franco-Vietnamese collaboration" forever. But officials in the Ministry of Colonies recognized early in the postwar period that their ideological harvest of students educated in France would be slim. As a consequence, the strategy that actually guided French policy was that of minimizing the flow of students to Paris. Once the students arrived, the government sought ways to channel and control them. That the French government never managed to shut down the flow of students who came to France by their own resources is indication both of an inconsistency in policy and a reflection of how the humanitarian ideological themes that the French used to justify their empire made stern or repressive measures towards Vietnamese students impossible to carry out. Far away from Paris, in the Moroccan Rif, or in Indochina itself, the French could protect their colonial possessions with all the brutality necessary, but in view of what the French thought of themselves, a restrictive policy towards the educational aspirations of Vietnamese in France proper was beyond the government's capacity.

For despite the rhetoric French officials used at ceremonies like the opening of the Indochina house, they did not, in fact, want Vietnamese students to come to France. Ever since the doctrine of colonial "assimilation" had come under criticism a generation before, there had been a consensus that French education should be given out in measured doses. Since the end of World War I and particularly since the beginning of the surge of Vietnamese students to France in the mid 1920s, internal documents showed the French colonial ministry to be of a radically different turn of mind than the words spoken at ceremonial occasions would indicate.

What French officials really thought can be traced through a number of internal documents that circulated through various branches of the Ministry of Colonies in the 1925-1930 period. One of the first of these was the Fabry report, prepared in early 1927 by the deputy and former minister of colonies Jean Fabry. Fabry was a political figure and a right-winger, but his views on the question of students display generally the same conceptions, and weaknesses, as those of the ministry's civil servants. While Fabry's report nominally concerned all French subjects from the colonies who were resident in France, nearly half of it was devoted to the problem of Vietnamese students. Fabry acknowledged that "one might consider it interesting to see a young elite come to our schools, to know us better and to assimilate our mentality and morals. One could hope that they would feel the usefulness for their country to be supported by a great European nation, and that, upon returning, they would become useful auxiliaries for our administration, as well as for industry and commerce." But such a happy outcome would be impossible if the young elite was not "protected" against Communist influence, which was inspiring them to revolt against French rule. Such protection, Fabry noted was part of what France had "implicitly promised" when it took over the territories in the first place.[11]

Fabry blamed the student problem on Communists, which was simplistic, or at least premature. Like many conservatives of that period, Fabry used the word "Communist" to signify almost any leftist political tendency he opposed, and was unwilling to distinguish between Communist and non-Communist anticolonial nationalism. Certainly he made no analysis of the extent of Communist organizational and ideological links with the Vietnamese student groups in France.[12]

To combat "Communist" influence, Fabry suggested rather mild measures. He accepted as axiomatic that it was impossible to keep students from coming to France: "France" he wrote, "could not keep students from coming to France with their own money" because it "could not take measures that would be considered by her subjects as harassment." The remedy therefore was a tightening of administrative controls on student emigration: a document from the school system in the colony certifying that the students were prepared to attend the schools in France should be required, as would a promise from their parents to send them sufficient funds throughout their stay. Fabry also suggested measures for improving government scrutiny of the students, placing a surveillance organization directly under the jurisdiction of the minister of colonies. He advocated tighter cooperation between the various police and surveillance offices and the university authorities, and suggested that vacation residences be constructed at the sea shore and in the mountains, so colonial students could be tracked by the government when school was out. All of these proposals received the approval in principle of the Ministry of Colonies, but in a pattern typical of the French bureaucracy's response to the student problem, the only recommendation that was implemented was the transfer of the small surveillance office from the Ministry of War to the Ministry of

Colonies. One looks in vain for reasons why recommendations received no follow-through. With the Fabry report, there is no evidence of policy disagreement; a more likely explanation has to do with shortage of money—which was evidence of the low priority given the student problem by the French state.

Education officials in Indochina also were formulating pessimistic analyses of the student problem. In June 1927, Henri Gourdon, an inspector general of public instruction in Indochina, circulated a report that sharply criticized the educational system in the colony. Gourdon had a scholarly background in oriental art and culture, and had been involved with reformulating the educational system in the colony in the decade before the war. Imbued with a traditionalist's sensitivity, Gourdon stressed that Vietnamese parents throughout the colony were complaining about the lack of filial piety among children who were attending French schools. The educational system, he claimed, was completely failing to deal with the "inevitable disequilibrium of morals" that accompanied economic and social change. He advocated measures to reorganize the University of Hanoi, which, he noted, was attracting very few students. And he raised the fascinating suggestion that France consider the resuscitation of Chinese characters, particularly in the northern regions of Vietnam, and infuse the curriculum of the primary schools in the colony with Confucian "morality instruction." As for the exodus of students to France, Gourdon wanted it limited to those who were engaged in programs of study that could not be pursued in Indochina. One suggestion was carried out—the construction of a residence for Vietnamese students at the *Cité Universitaire*—which would become Indochina House. But the other measures were not implemented, including the most ambitious one—that France take the lead in reintroducing Confucianism in the schools of Indochina as a measure to facilitate social peace.[13]

Gourdon was not the only official in Indochina who advocated playing the Confucian card. Henri Delétie, another Asia scholar associated with the colonial administration and with the *Académie des Sciences Coloniales* also argued that the youth rebellion could not be quenched by bringing French reason or modernity to the Vietnamese. Delétie, who in 1910 had published a book on the traditional Vietnamese education system, had become increasingly critical of the subject matter taught in the *franco-indigène* system; it was, he felt, too similar to what was taught in France. French literature, with its themes of "passion, fantasy, caprice and paradox" only confused Vietnamese. Delétie's ideas were similar to those of the conservative writer Louis Vignon. He urged the government to create textbooks that taught Confucian aphorisms and inspired filial piety, respect for authority, and an ethos of self-improvement, and his writing included vivid examples of Confucian precepts that might make Vietnamese youth more amenable to French rule. Delétie was one of the few French writers who drew the logical conclusion that Vietnamese should be forbidden to study in France, even, he emphasized, if they came at their own expense.[14]

Arguments such as Gourdon's and Delétie's seemed to represent the only alternatives put forth within the ministry to the educational policies actually in place in Indochina. One cannot say how seriously such arguments were taken. Vietnamese conservatives like Pham Quynh were also advocating a return to neo-Confucianism. It was a doomed idea, not least because Confucian doctrine was then under heavy attack at its source, in China. But for Frenchmen to advocate a Vietnamese return to Confucianism would seem to require a considerable degree of cynicism, considering that most Frenchmen viewed the system as quaint and reactionary. It is curious, therefore, that no other solutions for solving the Vietnamese student problem appeared in the main journals that treated colonial issues, or among the options under consideration at the Ministry of Colonies. Paul Monet, a gadfly critic of French policies who advocated energetic efforts to form a Frenchified Vietnamese elite, seemed to be the only important exception.[15]

In the absence of better alternatives, the French response to the student flow continued to be characterized by passivity and stalemate. This is evident in the lengthy report on Vietnamese students in France, produced in 1930 by the highest ranking French educational official in Indochina, the former University of Paris historian, Amédée Thalamas. Thalamas characterized the young Vietnamese in scathing terms. His report, prepared during the numerical peak of the Vietnamese student migration, contained not a trace of the paternal benevolence and good feeling found in French official rhetoric. Yet Thalamas acknowledged that no restrictive policy towards the students was politically feasible. Recapitulating many negative reports on the Vietnamese students' academic performance and affinity for radical politics, Thalamas laid the blame on the liberalization measures undertaken by the colonial government that had been designed to mollify discontent in Indochina. Accordingly, the key French error was the retraction, in 1924, of the regulation that required young Vietnamese to receive permission from the Governor General's office in order to leave the colony. This measure, which Thalamas characterized ass "undertaken for political reasons which I have never understood," was compounded when former Governor General Alexandre Varenne proclaimed in public that the University of Hanoi left much to be desired as an academic institution. Such words and actions, Thalamas complained, legitimated Vietnamese student travel to France. Thalamas was critical not only of the anticolonial political agitation among the Vietnamese, and their poor academic performance. In language much like that of the typical *colon* he also rued the psychological effect that the stay in France had on the students. He complained that the "unbridled vanity" of the Vietnamese drew them to France, plus the belief that once they returned they could "deal as equals with all of the individuals of the protective power."[16]

Yet for all his irritation Thalamas felt that not much could be done. It was impossible, he pointed out, to return to the pre-1924 regulations; in addition to the political problems it would create in Indochina, such a move would be "difficult to explain to metropolitan and parliamentary opinion" and would be "irreconcilable with the fundamental principle of liberty which is at the base of our entire educational structure . . . so that any return to the old arrangement of authorized departure would be condemned in the name of our own principles."

The Thalamas recommendations were therefore tame; indeed they were a mere continuation of the policies that French officials had begun in the mid-1920s when they first discussed trying to stem the accelerating student movement. He advocated that no scholarships be given to Vietnamese students to pursue in France any course of study that could be completed in Indochina; this recommendation had been promulgated by Governor General Varenne in 1927. For the rest, Thalamas recommended that France continue to "follow and survey the students as soon as they get off the boat" and that the government in Indochina make a special effort to warn parents of the risks and perils involved in letting their children go to France to study.

### The Limits of Surveillance

The French state, therefore, did not encourage a student exodus, but acted as if it was powerless to prevent it. Indeed the only student policy that the French carried out with any consistency was that of official surveillance, and even this was done by half measure. Some surveillance of Vietnamese in France was carried out by the Ministry of Interior, but the principal arm of the French government responsible for spying on Vietnamese in France was the *Service de Contrôle et d'Assistance aux Indigènes* (the CAI) which was organized in 1919 by the Ministry of Colonies. The CAI was the bureaucratic successor to an office at the War Ministry charged with the surveillance of the colonial troops who had been brought to France during World War I. It was financed by the government of Indochina, and always worked in close contact with the Indochinese branch of the *Sûreté*, the police organ of the government.[17]

But the organization was hardly the powerful secret police apparatus that its initiators may have wished it to be. The CAI's bureaucrats described their mission in grandiose world historical terms: as one memo-writer put it, France needed a "single front of surveillance and counter-revolutionary propaganda in order to oppose the revolutionary front." But the organization entrusted with counteracting the work of the Third International and all other instigators of anticolonial sentiments among the workers and students from Indochina and colonial Africa operated from an office in Paris that employed, in October 1925, a grand staff of four officials from the Ministry of Colonies, one retired police officer, one translator and two secretaries. The office in Marseilles, which opened and read the mail Vietnamese sent home, employed one official from the Ministry of Colonies and three Vietnamese readers.[18]

All that the CAI could do was hire informers and compile dossiers on individuals; it had no authority to arrest its charges, or discipline them in any way. Nor was it always easy to find Vietnamese who would report on their fellows to the French; after the wave of students began in the mid-1920s, the CAI recruited students who had run out of money or failed their exams, and feared returning to Vietnam without diplomas.[19] Nevertheless, in the Paris area in particular, CAI benefited from the reports of several men with good and steady contacts in the Vietnamese radical circles.[20]

The problem with a policy towards the students that was based primarily on surveillance, French officials soon realized, was that while they could compile considerable dossiers on the students, chronicle their radicalization and monitor their newspapers and small political parties, they could not actually do anything about these trends. The power of any political police must rest, finally, on its capacity to inspire fear, to dish out punishments and, if necessary, to imprison people. But French officials were all too well aware that those Vietnamese students who were busily organizing themselves into radical cells were breaking no French law.

The traditional means used by the French state to deal with foreigners who engaged in undesirable political activity was to expel them, and the Ministry of Interior and the Paris prefecture of police sent a steady stream of requests to the Ministry of Colonies for funds to do just that. The publishing of the radical journal *Vietnam Hon* was one transgression the Ministry of Interior considered deserving of explusion.[21] But officials at the Ministry of Colonies replied that treating the Vietnamese like foreigners created its own difficulties. Indeed, when Indochina's Governor General Varenne received several requests for funds for the repatriation of Vietnamese political activists in the summer of 1927, he balked. Varenne claimed that radical activists could do much less damage to French rule in France than they could in Vietnam, and that it was much easier to keep track of their movements in the *métropole*.[22]

Varenne's telegram produced a sharp controversy at the Ministry of

Colonies, and prompted a reply from Duchêne, the director of political affairs, that revealed much about France's official dilemmas. The problem, Duchêne argued, was that even if it was easy enough to keep an eye on radical Vietnamese in France, there was "absolutely no possibility to thwart their activities." Duchêne blamed "those who run the press" for blocking the actions of the Ministry of Colonies, saying that judicial sanctions sought for allegedly political reasons were impossible to obtain. In frustration Duchêne cited a long list of political incidents, some of them violent, in which French judges were unable or unwilling to prosecute Vietnamese students. To clinch his argument, Duchêne reminded Varenne of the latter's frequent complaints about the effects, in Indochina, of anti-French newspapers that had been written and published in France by Vietnamese students. He concluded, "to prevent a Vietnamese journal published in France from appearing in Saigon there is only one way, and that is to deprive the journal of its editors by chasing them out of France." He added that the Parisian police would take a dim view of reporting on the activities of Vietnamese radicals in France if they were "refused satisfaction" by officials in Indochina.[23]

Duchêne's reply was a vivid example of a dilemma that ran through all levels of French dealing with her colonial students: keeping the lid on movements that threatened French rule in Vietnam demanded measures that rubbed against the grain of a democratic regime which justified its imperial role with rhetoric from the revolutionary Republican tradition. After Varenne left the top post in Hanoi in 1928, he was replaced with men more willing to arrange for the repatriation of unruly students. But stern measures involved French authorities in legal acrobatics. The problem, of course, was that the Vietnamese were not "foreigners" (*étrangers*) but *protégés français*; therefore they were not subject to the legislation France used to expel foreigners.

After considerable effort, a plausible way around this embarrassing dilemma was found. As Ministry of Colonies officials publicly explained, Vietnamese students needed permission to study in France from the office of the Governor General (though this had come to involve no more than possession of the official *livret scolaire*). However, permission could be withdrawn if the students misbehaved in France, thus implying that the student could be repatriated. This line of reasoning, as one internal document from the Ministry of Colonies dryly noted, "did not rest upon a solid juridical foundation." When French officials used such logic to repatriate several dozen students in 1930, their action provoked ridicule from left wing deputies in the National Assembly and squalls of complaint from the League of Rights of Man and other groups.[24]

The other method adopted by successive French governments to tame the wave of student radicalism was to attempt to coddle them and immerse them in a network of French-sponsored hostels, clubs, and student assistance organizations. This policy had its roots in the early post war years when the Ministry of Colonies had sponsored a *foyer* in Paris and in other cities where Vietnamese *emigré* workers could receive lodging and a place for social events, and where French officials could keep an eye on them. One of the initial rationales behind such institutions as the *Foyer Indochinois* was to encourage the Vietnamese to create "open" groups that were more easy for the French police to watch, and not push them into creating "secret societies" whose activities were difficult to penetrate.[25] By the late 1920s, however, French officials recognized that such hostels and mutual aid associations were no panacea; one official, in trying to discourage the government of Indochina from sponsoring a new *Foyer Indochinois* in Montpellier, claimed that Vietnamese revolutionaries found the foyers to be simply a "protected haven" where they could carry out their propaganda "at their leisure."[26] Nevertheless, by the late 1920s, France had constructed other student centers, which took account of the lessons of previous failures. The *Foyer Vaquelin* in Paris, sponsored by a group of colonial publicists and industrialists organized by *Distilleries d'Indochine* director A.R. Fontaine, sought to avoid the politicization that had occurred at other hostels. The by-laws for Fontain's *foyer*, for example, were written so as to make the selection of Vietnamese officers more or less meaningless by giving the student board a purely consultative role, and holding separate elections for students in each branch of studies. Furthermore, the rules of the new dwelling strictly forbade "political activity." This example was followed by the much larger Indochina House, which opened the same year.[27]

The *Foyer Vaquelin* and the construction of the Indochina House at the *Cité Universitaire* were the result of French efforts to bring a sense of order and equilibrium into the lives of Vietnamese students and to brake their movement towards the Left. Governor General Varenne was the main figure in French officialdom to advocate methods to deal with the student problem that didn't smack of police repression. In his suggestions, one can find one of the few glimmers of an independent conception of colonial policy on the part of the moderate Left. In a letter sent to the minister of colonies in March of 1927, Varenne exclaimed that "it is necessary to take the Vietnamese in hand as soon as they get off the boat in Marseilles, and follow them during their entire stay in France."[28]

The vehicle by which the Government of Indochina and the Ministry of Colonies sought to accomplish this was the *Service d'Assistance Morale et Intellectuelle* or SAMI. SAMI, it was hoped, would "give moral assistance" and help to "shield them from the influence of extremist parties" as well as dispense advice on more mundane matters such as lodging and possible courses of study. SAMI was intended to show the students a softer edge of the French government and the men who organized it took care that it would be perceived as having no associations with the French police. It did of course; the SAMI files show that it was in regular contact with the Indochinese *Sûreté* and other branches at the Ministry of Colonies. But SAMI did act as the students' advocate in much of their dealings with the government, helping them when they found themselves short of funds or facing bureaucratic difficulties.[29]

But like nearly every other institution that France created to deal with the Vietnamese students, SAMI was limited in size and authority. An organization entrusted to "take the Vietnamese student in hand as soon as he gets off the boat" could count on an absurdly small staff of five people, of whom two were Frenchmen; its offices occupied two rooms. Four years after SAMI was founded, its chief Henri Lemaire noted wistfully that "to form contacts with individuals who are not in any way obliged even to converse with SAMI, in order to take preventive action against the development of pernicious ideas in their heads is a difficult and long-lasting task."[30] Indeed the task may have been impossible. SAMI had difficulty in accomplishing even the most mundane part of its work—keeping track of which Vietnamese students were in the country, what schools they were studying in, how they were doing. Understaffed as it was, SAMI had no recourse but to write the various schools and ask for information about Vietnamese enrollment and performance. But many school officials refused to cooperate with what they perceived as "police-work" by the Ministry of the Colonies. As a result, five years after SAMI's creation, its files contained extremely incomplete information about the whereabouts and academic activities of the Vietnamese students in France.[31]

## The Catholic Church

The Catholic Church was one nongovernmental institution that complemented the government's feeble efforts to enforce a modicum of academic and political discipline over the Vietnamese students. Catholic missionaries had been active in Vietnam for three centuries, and the French conquerers of Vietnam had skillfully used the banner of "freedom of religion" against Vietnamese mandarins who were oppressing Vietnamese Catholics. One consequence of this history was that Vietnam's one-to two million Catholics became one of the nation's social groups most amenable to "Franco-Vietnamese collaboration."[32] By the 1920s relations between the Church and the government were cooler, which disrupted possible cooperation. In Hanoi, the local archbishop orchestrated an unsuccessful campaign against the naming of University of Paris historian Amédée Thalamas as the colony's top educational official; his book about Joan of Arc was considered hostile to the Church.[33] One can make a case that the residue of France's Church-state conflict was damaging to the colonial interests of both parties.

All tendencies of the Catholic Church in France were in favor of the country's colonial mission, though by 1930 significant voices arose within French Catholicism. These elements called on the French state to do much more for education and economic development of the colonies and to eliminate many of the brutalities that accompanied colonial rule.[34] The Catholic Church in Indochina was a deeply conservative institution, and ever since the student strikes of 1925-1926 it had expressed alarm over the increasing moral turmoil in Vietnam. In 1929 the apostolic vicar of Hanoi wrote to Tonkin's resident superior; he noted that the loyalty of the Vietnamese population was weakening with each passing day, and placed the main blame on the French school system. The solution, he suggested, was a massive expansion of confessional schools.[35] Needless to say, the government did not delegate its educational prerogatives to the Church as the vicar suggested. In France the colonial ministry collected information on Catholic efforts with the students in a cursory fashion, and displayed little interest in whether the Vietnamese involved in such programs performed better academically or were more loyal to the French colonial government.[36]

The Catholic effort was, in fact, modest but not insubstantial. The focus of Catholic interest in the students was the *Foyer des Étudiants d'Extrême Orient* founded by Father P. Lebbé, which had residences in Bourg-la-Reine and a nonresidential *foyer* in Paris. The Bourg-la-Reine dormitory had space for twenty students; by one account fifty-seven Vietnamese had stayed there before 1929, though their numbers dwindled once the government opened up Indochina House. Residences that shielded the students from anti-French agitation seem to have competed with one another. The *foyer* sponsored a student newspaper called *L'Amitié Indochinoise* and tried to keep afloat a Vietnamese Catholic student club, the *Action Sociale Indochinoise*. The Paris hostel was used, according to one report, by fifty Vietnamese in 1927—a considerable number. Subsequently little was heard of it, even in the Catholic press; perhaps it was a casualty of the Vietnamese radicalization. The boarding residence took in Chinese and Japanese students as well, and by 1929 only five Vietnamese were living there. The Vietnamese Catholic student group seemed to have no more than a dozen members and mainstream French Catholic student organizations did not have much contact with the Vietnamese.[37] Ngo Dinh Nhu, the ill-fated brother-in-law and confidant of South Vietnamese president

(1954-1963) Ngo Dinh Diem was active in the *foyer* and club, and later made a somewhat artificial effort to transplant to Vietnam aspects of French "social Catholicism."[38] But generally the Catholic imprint on the student migration seems less than one might suppose. Outside the *foyer* some Vietnamese studied in French seminaries: a Church publication in 1932 mentioned three.[39] When French clergymen convened in Marseilles in 1930 to discuss the broader question of colonialism, the Father from *Missions Étrangères* who spoke about Vietnamese elites gave a vague account, and made no mention of the several thousand Vietnamese students in France.[40] When, after 1930, French Catholics began to think about making greater efforts to organize the Vietnamese students in their midst—or at least wrote more about them—the Vietnamese student migration had already begun to decline.

If the French Catholic mainstream was slow in concerning itself with the Vietnamese in France, at least one group on the far right was alert to their importance. The *Jeunesses Patriotes*, a rightist faction headed by deputy Pierre Taittinger had, by 1929, enough contacts among young Vietnamese to invite twenty-five of them to a JP meeting on Franco-Vietnamese collaboration, held at the Café Turquetti on the Boulevard Saint Germain. When Do-Dinh Thach, a pro-French Vietnamese, spoke of future Vietnamese prosperity within the context of the French empire, radical Vietnamese students who had infiltrated the meeting hurled glasses at the speaker, and a nasty brawl resulted. One young French phalangeard was severely stabbed in the chest, and twenty-one Vietnamese were arrested.[41]

## Academic Questions

In our discussion of French policies towards the students, we have until now given very little emphasis to purely educational issues. The reason for this is simple enough: because the French government perceived the students as a source of political instability, an overwhelming preponderance of official concern about the students concentrated on their political activities, rather than on what they were learning. Thus in the one realm in which the French government could have collected information about the Vietnamese that was neither impressionistic nor based on opened mail or the reports of informers, it did not do so. In response to questions about what the Vietnamese students studied, how well they did, and the relationship between their study in France and their professional prospects in colonial Indochina, the available sources provide information that is considerably less detailed than that available about student politics.

Vietnamese in French schools had to overcome the common French prejudice that they never really could master Western intellectual disciplines. Louis Vignon and other colonial conservative writers had helped convince a generation of French officials that the psychological gap between Vietnamese and Frenchmen was impossible to bridge, that Vietnamese and other colonials would never think like Frenchmen, and that France could only spoil its relationship with Vietnam by trying to mold the minds of its subjects to French standards. There always was anecdotal evidence upon which such assertions could be based; one can even find it in the noted Indochina scholar Paul Mus's depiction of a hapless Vietnamese teacher from the prewar years. This teacher wondered, Mus reported, why his French employers made him teach Western science, when it was so obviously nonsense.[42]

The Vietnamese students in France in the 1920s were much more attuned to the modern than the poor man in Mus's example, but the evidence available says that most of them did not do well in school.[43] The majority of Vietnamese came to France to work on their *baccalauréats*, and the available statistics consistently show fewer Vietnamese attending French universities than were enrolled in the *lycées*. The Thalamas report, for instance, was sharply critical of the academic performance of Vietnamese students in France as a group, and complained that the Vietnamese sought out schools in applied science or letters where they could enroll without a diploma.[44]

Often poorly prepared in the French language, a great many of Vietnamese doubtlessly had difficulty. But in addition to academic hurdles, they faced a steep wall of French cultural condescension. There were certain assumptions that French colonial educators commonly held about their various charges. In the Vietnamese case, the most frequently expressed assumption was that they memorized well, but couldn't really reason or assimilate French concepts.[45]

In the early 1930s, the minister of public instruction periodically required the headmasters of *lycées* in the Paris region to report on how the "foreigners," including Vietnamese, were doing. The raw data of the reports give a mixed assessment subject to a variety of interpretations. Several French educators were enthusiastic about the work of "somehow touching these young people and winning their affections forever" and some were convinced that seeing another side of France and living with French people on a level of equality would make Vietnamese more attached to the French *mère patrie*. Such advantages, it was thought, might be worth considerable effort on the part of teachers.[46] But more often the *lycée* principals emphasized problems. Several complained of poor language preparation by the Vietnamese, and one wrote that in contrast to European foreigners, most Vietnamese seemed "incapable of grasping our method of thought and expression." While some *lycée* heads reported that

Vietnamese students did just as well as anyone else, such comments were rare. The general French attitude was closer to the spirit of the laconic remark of one teacher, who, noting that his Vietnamese students found it impossible to analyze and deduce, concluded that "the difference between Indochina and us is Descartes."[47]

Our knowledge, then, of what Vietnamese learned academically in France is imprecise. If such information interested the French, the government nevertheless did not organize the bureaucratic effort to explore the question; the ill-fated SAMI had difficulties in even getting its inquiries answered by the various university rectors. One 1930 study of Vietnamese academic performance estimated that one-third of the Vietnamese students enrolled in French *lycées* dropped out each year because of bad grades or illnesses induced by the cold climate, presumably to return home with no diploma of any sort in hand.[47] In the Paris region, in 1929, two-thirds of the Vietnamese students attended *lycées*, rather than universities, while a handful attended the elite Grandes Écoles. Nor was gaining admission to one of the faculties of the university (which required the *baccalauréat*) any guarantee of success. One of the sporadic SAMI reports, dated 1933, reported that over half of the Vietnamese students taking the law exam failed it.[49]

## The Bitter Harvest

The overall result was that out of the thousands of Vietnamese passing through French schools, France was harvesting very few who were both well-educated and politically loyal. One sign of the small number of talented collaborators was a memorandum, dating from the mid-1930s, from the office of the Governor General in Hanoi, listing Vietnamese who should, because of their educational achievements, be given special consideration for administration jobs. A grand total of four, all of whom had received doctorates, made the list.[50]

It has been argued here that successive French governments made little effort to mold the *mentalité* of the Vietnamese students because they never really had committed themselves to bringing Vietnamese students to France in the first place; French governments preferred, but did not have the will to enforce, a policy of keeping the students in Vietnam where they could study at the University of Hanoi. Nevertheless when one considers the sheer volume of human activity involved in the Vietnam student exodus—the thousands of students traveling thousands of miles, the dozens of informers hired, the thousands of police reports written and filed—one is forced to ask again why the French government tolerated such a disorganized and chaotic result. Of course the colonial government found more than the four students who were particularly qualified to receive responsible jobs—but there nevertheless exists no list that chronicles the records and employability of a significant number, say, one-quarter, of the nation's French-educated Vietnamese.

To assay even a speculative answer of why this should have been so, one must go beyond the records available in French government archives and concentrate not on the supply of trained students which French education produced, but rather on the demand for them in the colonial economy and governmental system of Indochina. Why did not France insist on forcing the Vietnamese to become engineers, clerks, designers of roads, accountants, bankers and even entrepreneurs, rather than tolerate a situation in which several thousand students made a vague stab at earning degrees in law and medicine, usually without success?

An answer to the question is suggested by the debate over the industrialization of Indochina that took place between several French economists in the late 1930s. For if it is true that France's domestic liberalism and idealized sense of the meaning of its imperial mission made it incapable of preventing Vietnamese from striving towards higher French education, it is also true that the colonial economy in Indochina had no need for greater numbers of educated Vietnamese.

The reason for this, as was pointed out in the late 1930s by several critics of French economic policy in Indochina, was that there was no French policy for the industrial development of the colony, and indeed, there were powerful French economic interests in Vietnam that were opposed to industrialization.[51] French investment in the colony was overwhelmingly concentrated in such industries as mining and rubber, the output of which was exported to France. As economists had pointed out for generations, there were favorable conditions for manufacture in Indochina. The colony had both raw materials and energy in the form of coal deposits, giving it the potential to manufacture steel, rubber, paper, glass, and textiles. But French customs regulations and the domination of the Vietnamese capital markets by the Bank of Indochina prevented French, Vietnamese or anyone else from importing foreign-made capital goods, and restricted any foreign investment. Those French firms that did invest in the colony's economy concentrated their efforts overwhelmingly in the extractive industries, which promised short-term profits to their investors. French companies that sold manufactured goods to Vietnam perceived no advantage in starting up enterprises in the colony, which would have directly competed with their operations in France.[52] The result of this closed system was that the biggest French businesses in Indochina were, in addition to the rubber and mining firms, not manufacturers, but the alcohol and salt monopolies, whose profits were regularly depicted as scandalous in the

French assembly. Authors writing from such diverse political perspectives as the pro-Communist historian Jean Chesneaux, and Charles Robequain, a writer well disposed to French colonialism, concur that the French customs regulations and the Bank of Indochina's singular domination of the colony's capital market served to severely inhibit Vietnam's economic growth.[53]

The question of whether France should encourage industrialization in Indochina was of course fraught with political consequences. There were Frenchmen, particularly among the *colons*, who feared the social consequences of greater economic development; they did not want to contend with a first generation Vietnamese proletariat. As one French critic of the government's policy put it, the *colons* "seemed to believe that factory workers were more dangerous than the starving in the countryside."[54] But if the French policy of nonindustrialization did manage to ensure that the Vietnamese proletariat remained small, it also prevented the development of a powerful and economically active Vietnamese middle class.

There were jobs for educated Vietnamese as government officials, as school teachers, or in modest positions in the existing French firms, but there were few professional positions in economically productive activities. French officials often expressed the fear that Vietnamese students would become *déclassés* because they would be unable to find work commensurate with their ambition. They also complained loudly and often that young Vietnamese sought only administrative jobs. Depending on the writer, this trait was either attributed to the "mandarin tradition" or to some innate or racial quality.[55] Before the French conquest, the ruling mandarins had indeed discouraged Vietnamese from entering the commercial professions, and young Vietnamese with high aspirations automatically looked towards a government career. Remarkably, for all the disruption of traditional patterns of life that French rule had meant in Indochina, nothing the French did with their control of the Vietnamese economy had much effect on this ancient tendency of career choice for young Vietnamese.

But advocates of opening up Vietnam's economy to foreign products and capital, such as the liberal economist Paul Bernard, argued that the French policy of nonindustrialization in Vietnam was truly fraught with pernicious political consequences. At the conclusion of his concise indictment of French economic policy in the colony, published in 1937, Bernard underlined the "contradiction" between France's policy of educating young Vietnamese and its economic policy of "restricting the country within the narrow boundries of peasant agriculture and artisan production." Only the industrialization of the economy, Bernard noted, "could offer the new class the jobs which could prepare it for the destiny it aspires to." Economic progress, Bernard maintained, could make the much proclaimed Franco-Vietnamese collaboration a reality. Economic growth would accelerate the number of contacts between elites from both societies, and inspire "the kinds of intellectual, moral, technical and financial exchanges between French and Vietnamese that would resolve the major problem of integrating Vietnamese elites in the French milieu."[56]

If the absence of economic growth amounted to a missed opportunity for "collaboration" between French and Vietnamese elites, it also enhanced Vietnamese bitterness towards the French. Bernard was correct in stressing that all young educated Vietnamese were aware that considerable economic progress was being made in Japan and even the Philippines, and blamed France for the lack of progress in their own country. This point, in fact, was the one element that all educated Vietnamese in the 1930s largely agreed upon: Vietnam needed industrialization, and the French were in some way responsible for the fact that very little industrial development was taking place.[57]

Frenchmen lamented that young Vietnamese, when they sought professional employment, invariably looked for positions in the government, but in fact there was very little else for them to do. Vietnam's middle class developed no economic power of its own, which ultimately diminished its social and political importance. French policies had the effect of preventing the middle class from occupying the position that the nascent bourgeoisie had achieved in countries which had undergone capitalist development. Such policies may have avoided the creation of a Vietnamese proletariat, but they did not create social stability. As Paul Reynaud, the French minister of colonies, remarked, after returning from an inspection of Indochina in 1939, "Behind a thin curtain of intellectuals, in the area where in Europe there is a middle class, you have here a vacuum. Aside from the landowners, whom our policy of increased rice acreage has created, and aside from a few people owning enterprises connected with our public works and a few rare men engaged in commerce, there is no middle class—nothing which constitutes the political structure of the countries of Western Europe."[58]

The absence of a dynamic industrializing sector in the Vietnamese economy would turn out to have great consequences for decades to come. French officials concerned with the education of Vietnam's youth, however, treated it more as a short-term problem, and did so with a marked lack of political vision. It has already been stressed that only a small percentage of the Vietnamese students who passed through France actually received higher diplomas. Official France assumed that the Indochinese government would be their employer of first resort. By the mid-1930s, however, French officials began to worry that the number of qualified Vietnamese job seekers, small as it was, was nevertheless beginning to outstrip the number of available posts. A decade earlier, the reformist Governor General Alexandre Varenne had significantly expanded the number of government jobs that Vietnamese would be permitted to hold, but by 1936 French officials had begun to argue that the "possibilities of absorption" of the local administration had reached its limit.[59]

By 1935, the effects of the global economic depression in conjunction with a number of French administrative measures had produced a considerable decline in the number of Vietnamese coming to France.[60] Nevertheless, by this time one can find examples of something practically nonexistent during the 1920s: the public acknowledgment by French officials and supporters of the French empire that there were too many colonial students in France. In a speech delivered in 1935 before the French Colonial Institute, the organization's director, J.L. Gheerbrandt, made this point. Gheerbrandt's subject was the sweeping theme of colonial youth. After several minutes of obligatory praise for France's "concept" of raising its colonial subjects to "the highest levels of intellectual achievement" Gheerbrandt pointed out that a considerable amount of "intellectual unemployment," long feared by French conservatives, was becoming a reality in the colonies. Restricting Vietnamese students to schools in Vietnam was necessary, Gheerbrandt asserted. Then he went further. "It seems to us that the day has come to . . . put the brakes on our educative efforts, and to direct a good part of the gifted colonial youth to professional or artisanal school," he said. Nothing else would stop a catastrophic rise in the number of the intellectual unemployed.[61]

This speech, which would be attacked by critics of French colonial policy,[62] amounted to nothing less than a frank admission that France had failed, not only with its Vietnamese students, but with its young *protégés* from Africa, from the Mahgreb, and even from the French Antilles. If France could not govern its far-flung empire by increasing access to French education, it could not govern it at all. For the French idea of empire could never rest upon simple force. Not only would such an idea have been resisted by a great majority of Frenchmen, but it would effectively deprive France of the possibility of attracting native collaborators, men convinced that association with France would bring their societies development and modernity, and themselves some desirable aspect of "Frenchness." Not all colonial officials were so pessimistic, or so frank, as Gheerbrandt. But his speech did serve to illuminate one of the fatal flaws underlying the French relationship with Vietnamese students and other young people in the French colonies. Simply put, France did not have the means or the political will to develop the societies that made up its empire. In underdeveloped societies, the untapped energies of educated men will always present problems of the first magnitude.

French colonialism, then, was well on the way to failure in finding channels for the ambitions and energies of the most academically advanced contingent of students from her empire, the Vietnamese. A not inconsiderable number of those Vietnamese who felt deprived of chances for satisfactory careers in government, or commerce, or in other areas that might have increased the political stability of colonial Indochina could find, in the 1930s, a number of other outlets for their energy and ambitions. Of these, one option was the career of professional revolutionary; once one had made this choice, it did not take long to find out that the brightest banner to rally under was that held up by the Third International and the Indochinese Communist party.

## Notes

1. For the rise of French imperial consciousness between the wars, see Charles-Robert Ageron, *France Coloniale ou Parti Colonial?* (Paris: Presses Universitaires de France, 1978), 250-259.
2. André Gide, *Travels in the Congo*, trans. Dorothy Bussy, (New York: Alfred Knopf, 1929). Leon Werth, *Cochinchine* (Paris: F. Rieder, 1926). Other widely read books which showed a renewed critical interest in the colonies were Louis Roubaud, *Vietnam: La Tragédie Indochinoise* (Paris: Valois, 1931). In the thirties, many more books critical of imperialism would be published.
3. For the renewed Catholic interest in colonialism, see the discussion in Rudolph von Albertini, *Decolonization*, trans. Francisca Garvie, (Garden City: Doubleday, 1971), 307-309, and *Semaines Sociales de France*, XXII session Marseille, 1930. Joseph Folliet's *Le Droit de Colonisation* and other Catholic writings are discussed in Ageron, *France Coloniale*, 36-41.
4. The best discussion of the association versus assimilation debate is in Albertini, *Decolonization*, 278-309. For the prewar debate, see Raymond Betts, *Assimilation and Association in French Colonial Theory, 1890-1914*, (New York: Columbia University Press, 1961.)
5. Quoted in Albertini, *Decolonization*, 304.
6. British experience with Indian students was not well known in France—but to the extent it was it was always used as an argument against allowing colonial students to come to Paris under any circumstances. See the discussion of Jules Harmand, above, chapter 1. On the contradiction between internal liberalism and colonialism, Raymond Aron has written that given their national sense of what they were and what they wished to be, neither Britain nor France had the capacity for violence necessary to maintain their empires under twentieth century conditions. See his *Espoir et Peur du Siècle. Essais Non Partisans* (Paris: Calmann-Lévy, 1957), 205.
7. Duchêne was born in 1866. His *La Politique Coloniale de France* (Paris: Payot, 1928) was a history of his ministry since Richelieu, and in its 320 pages it

contains not one mention of the dilemmas of ruling peoples who don't wish to be colonial subjects in the twentieth century.

8. The grouping of very senior officials around the Ministry of Colonies led one official to refer to the building on the Rue Oudinot—a stone's throw from Invalides, the wounded war veterans home, as the "Invalides" of the French empire. Hubert Deschamps, a younger official who had served in Africa, and would later be Léon Blum's *chef de cabinet* described the top bureaucrats at the ministry as possessed by "a kind of fossilization and a nearly total lack of vision" and lacking any "historical sense." See William Cohen, *Rulers of Empire* (Stanford: Hoover Institution Press, 1971), 134-135.

9. *La Presse Coloniale*, 21 July, 1928.

10. *Annales Coloniales*, 23 March, 1930.

11. Slotfom I,4 contains the Fabry report.

12. For a fuller discussion of communism and the Vietnamese students, see chapter 5, below.

13. The Gourdon report is filed in ANSOM: NFI, 259-2226.

14. Henri Delétie, "Le Problème Universitaire Indochinois," *Académie des Sciences Coloniales*, 1926-1927, Tome 8, and Deletie, "De l'Adaptation de Nos Programmes d'Enseignement au Milieu Annamite," *Académie des Sciences Coloniales*, 1929-1930, Tome 14.

15. For discussion of Paul Monet, see above, chapter 2. Vietnamese proposals for neo-Confucianism in Vietnam are discussed in David Marr, *Vietnamese Tradition on Trial* (Berkeley: University of California Press, 1981), 106-115.

16. Thalamas report, in ANSOM: NFI, 259-2226.

17. Slotfom I,4 and Slotfom III,1 contain information on the creation of the CAI.

18. See the Budin report in Slotfom I,4.

19. Slotfom I,7 contains a transcription of one session in which a reformer was recruited. A disconsolate young Vietnamese who had failed his exams and run out of funds agreed to enroll himself in a university outside of Paris and involve himself in and report on the most radical Vietnamese student organizations in return for CAI financial assistance that would allow him to remain in France.

20. The Slotfom archive contains a multitude of reports by an agent "Désiré" who fed French officials excellent information on Vietnamese radical activities in Paris from the mid 1920s to the mid 1930s.

21. Slotfom III,2.

22. Ibid.

23. Ibid.

24. For the colonial minister's public defense of repatriation as suitable discipline for the students, see *Journal Officiel*, 15 June 1930. Slotfom III, 2 and Slotfom I, 4 contain an extensive correspondence between the colonial ministry and the interior ministry and the Paris prefecture of police concerning what sanctions on the students could actually be carried out.

25. Slotfom I,4.

26. Slotfom III,25.

27. The prospectus for the *Foyer Vaquelin* which was circulated through officials at the colonial ministry, noted that "it was impossible to completely eliminate the system of elections" held by student residents of the *foyer*. See Slotfom III, 16. For a laudatory description of student life in the *foyer* see *Le Midi Colonial*, 6 February 1930.

28. AOM-Indochine, 51537.

29. AOM-Indochine, 51536.

30. Ibid.

31. Thalamas report, ANSOM, NFI. Carton 259, Dossier 2226, and Slotfom III,28.

32. Marr, *Vietnamese Tradition on Trial*, 82-86 and Alexander Woodside, *Community and Revolution in Modern Vietnam* (Boston: Houghton Mifflin, 1976), 11-12.

33. Gail Kelly, "Franco-Vietnamese Schools, 1918-1939" (Ph.D. Thesis, University of Wisconsin, 1975), 45.

34. See François Kempf "Les Catholiques Français" in Marcel Merle, *Les Eglises Chrétiennes et la Décolonisation* (Paris, A. Colin , 1967). See also the discussion by Rudolph von Albertini in *Decolonization*, 307-309.

35. ANSOM: NFI: Carton 326, dossier 2637.

36. AN: F-7, 13410 contains a query from the Ministry of Colonies to the Ministry of Interior asking if they had any information about the *Foyer des Étudiants d'Extrême Orient*. The CAI compiled one brief report on Catholic activities in 1927, and then apparently showed no more interest until the 1930s. See Slotfom III, 32.

37. See "Les Etudiants Orientaux en Europe," *Documents de la vie intellectuelle* October 20, 1931 and Paul Catrice, "Les Etudiants Orientaux en France," *La Documentation Catholique* no. 576, August 15, 1931. See also Slotfom III, 32 for a report on the Paris *foyer* in 1927.

38. Slotfom III, 32. For Nhu's efforts to use social Catholicism in Vietnam, see Joseph Buttinger, *Vietnam: A Dragon Embattled* (New York: Praeger, 1967), 785-786.

39. *La Documentation Catholique*, 19 March 1932.

40. Cours de R.P. Cadiere, "Elites Annamites" in *Semaines Sociales* Marseilles, XXII session, 1930.

41. Slotfom III, 23. See also Robert Soucy, *French Fascism: the First Wave, 1924-1933* (New Haven: Yale University Press, 1986), 206-207. I have been unable to uncover much about this curious alliance between the JP and the Vietnamese—though it gives grounds for speculation that conservative Vietnamese were both more courted and more attracted to the anti-parliamentary right than they were to mainstream French conservatism (or liberalism). Pham Quynh's affinity with Charles Maurras can be viewed in this light. This Vietnamese attraction to the extremes of the French spectrum was more pronounced on the Left—where Stalinism impressed the Vietnamese much more than democratic socialism. See chapter 5, below. A telling remark about the episode from the Trotskyite leader Ta Thu Thau, one of the radical students who infiltrated the meeting and attacked the speaker, should be recalled: "We admire the disciplined spirit of the Jeunesses Patriotes, who wish to continue the fine traditions of Sparta in the midst of this century where the Europeans are disorganized by accentuated individualism. But we will fight against those who oppose our march towards freedom." *La Résurrection* January, 1929.

42. Mus recalls a question asked of his father, a colonial school official, by a Vietnamese teacher some years before World War I: "You know I am a disciplined and punctual schoolmaster. Moreover, I have taken sides with you. I approve of the evolution you are trying to bring about in my country, and I'm doing all that I can to help you. Therefore you should treat me as a friend and have as much confidence in me as you have in your own people. Why don't you ever

give me the real reasons behind what you make me teach? For example, I've been teaching my students for fifteen years that the earth turns around the sun. I have always done it the best that I could. But even a child has only to look to the East every morning to see that the contrary is true as surely as two and two make four. You may be sure that I shall faithfully continue to teach that part of the curriculum. But what I would really like to know is why you make us say that. What result are you expecting? I can't understand what place it has in your way of doing things. Don't you have enough confidence in me to tell me your secret?" Cited in John T. McAlister and Paul Mus, *The Vietnamese and Their Revolution* (New York: Harper and Row, 1970), 104.

43. As acknowledged by Diep Van Ky, "L'Enseignement en Indochine," *Académie des Sciences Coloniales* Tome 4, 1924-1925.

44. ANSOM, NFI: 259-2226.

45. Delétie, "Le Problème Universitaire Indochinois" *Académie des Sciences Coloniales* Tome 8, 1926-1927.

46. See Maurice Lacroix, "Notre Enquête sur la Présence des Élèves Étrangers dans les Lycées et Collèges Français," *Revue Universitaire*, November 1931. For the full report see AN: AJ-16, 2708.

47. AN: AJ-16-2708. The question of whether Vietnamese could really learn or merely memorize remained a salient one for French educators throughout the interwar period. In 1936 a professor from the medical school at the University of Paris traveled to Indochina to report on the medical school at the University of Hanoi. He concluded: "It is true that the Annamite works very hard and tends especially to use his memory. Nevertheless it is certain that the best students know how to reason, and can establish relationships between diverse orders of information. I carefully arranged my examinations in a manner to discern the existence of this faculty, which many Europeans raise questions about, by posing questions not treated in the texts, which can only be answered by reflection and reasoning. The answers were generally good and sometimes excellent." ANSOM, Fonds Guernot, 22 ba, Report by Professor Champy.

48. AN, AJ-16, 2708.

49. For these academic results see Slotfom III, 28 and Slotfom III, 118.

50. ANSOM, NFI:1193.

51. The most important criticism of French economic policies in Indochina is found in Paul Bernard, *Nouveaux Aspects du Problème Économique Indochinois* (Paris: Fernand Sorlot, 1937) and Grégoire Khérian, "La querelle de l'industrialisation," *Revue Indochinoise Juridique et Économique* IV, 1938. The subject is well summarized in Buttinger, *A Dragon Embattled*, 181-199 and Isoart, *Phénomène National Vietnamien*, 172-190.

52. Buttinger, *A Dragon Embattled*, 180-192.

53. Jean Chesneaux, *Contribution à l'Histoire de la Nation Vietnamienne* (Paris: Editions Sociales, 1955), 161, and Charles Robequain, *The Economic Development of French Indochina* (London: Oxford University Press, 1944), 341-363.

54. Grégoire Khérian, as quoted in Isoart, *Phénomène National Vietnamien*, 189.

55. An official French expression of this view is the Gourdon report, ANSOM, NFI: 259-2226. See the discussion in Buttinger, *A Dragon Embattled*, 196-199.

56. Bernard, *Problème Économique Indochinois*, 173-174.

57. Khérian claimed that industrialization was "one of the rare problems on which the Vietnamese press expresses an astonishing unanimity." Isoart, *Phénomène National Vietnamien*, 190.

58. Quoted in Buttinger, *A Dragon Embattled*, 196-197.
59. For French claims that the bureaucracy had no further places open for Vietnamese graduates, see the Moretti report, ANSOM, NFI: 286-2942.
60. See chapter 6.
61. *La Dépêche Coloniale*, 27-29 October 1935.
62. See the anonymous article in *Espirit*, December, 1935.

# 5

# The French Left and
# the Vietnamese Students

While the French government engaged in its hapless effort to monitor and shape the flow of Vietnamese students into France, by the late 1920s the leftist opposition parties within France had themselves begun to pay attention to the students. For observers from the French Right, this was evidence that the Vietnamese students were politically restless because of the anti-French machinations of the French Left. In an article written under the headline "Left wing politicians, again, are working against France" the right-wing Parisian paper *L'Ami du Peuple* made the point in typical fashion. Vietnamese students, the paper warned, were not "harmoniously dividing their life between science and leisure" but had become the victims of a relentless propaganda barrage on the part of the Left. Among those responsible for the barrage, the author claimed, were the French Socialists, the League of Rights of Man, former Governor General Alexandre Varenne, and the French Communist party. The spectrum of Vietnamese under the spell of this diverse grouping was even broader: it involved everyone from from the Constitutionalist Bui Quang Chieu to Vietnamese working for the *Secours Rouge International,* a front organization of the Communist International. The piece closed by proclaiming that the roots of Vietnamese nationalism were to be found on the Left Bank, and it was there that the government should strike against it.[1]

This was the way much of the French Right spoke of the student question. It assumed that Vietnamese nationalist feeling was essentially the creation of French influences; it assigned comparable blame to all French critics of colonialism, from the League of Rights of Man to the Communist party; it made no meaningful distinctions between moderate reformists like the Vietnamese Constitutionalists and Vietnamese already integrated into the Communist movement.[2]

This kind of interpretation, however, was not without counterpart on the

Left. While French bureaucrats were lamenting the growing radicalization of the students, serious foes of French colonialism gloated. Daniel Guérin, a young left-wing Socialist who would become one of the most eloquent and persistent critics of the French empire was equally certain that Vietnamese radicalism was the consequence of French ideas. In 1930 Guérin wrote:

> What is paradoxical about the intellectual evolution . . . of the Orientals is that no one besides the Europeans taught them the ideas which they are now using against their masters. Never has the Western bourgeoisie brought about its own negation and fashioned its own grave-diggers in a more striking manner. Where did these young Annamites learn about the rights of man, if not in Republican France? And the rights of peoples to self-determination? This Wilsonian hypocrisy is at the base of the Treaty of Versailles. The revolutionary liberation of peoples? The workers of Europe sympathize tremendously. Moreover, it is not that these young men demanded to come to France in search of culture and enlightenment, but it is at France's own request, through the efforts of Albert Sarraut, that they have arrived.[3]

Guérin was of course greatly oversimplifying a complex question. As we have shown, French officials, including Sarraut, were never blind to the political dangers that might arise from allowing Vietnamese students to come to France. Perhaps it was a characteristic French conceit that enabled a leftist like Guérin to share with publicists of the Right the view that Vietnamese radicalism was principally the creation of French influences.

Guérin did not address the one question that may be most interesting to contemporary historians. For if it can be accepted that Vietnamese were learning in France how to be rebels, the question naturally arises as to what sort of rebels the Vietnamese were learning to be. Which elements of the varied French revolutionary traditions had the greatest influence on them? *L'Ami du Peuple* lumped together a coalition of "anti-French" propagandists that included the political heirs of every element of the Dreyfusard coalition. Guérin, in simultaneously invoking the "rights of man," the rights of peoples to "self-determination" and the rights of workers to "revolutionary liberation" passed over these political distinctions in like manner.

Since 1920, when the French Socialist party split at Tours over the issues raised by the Russian Revolution, such unity among the tendencies of the French Left implied by both Guérin and the French Right had been nonexistent: French Socialists and Communists were, most of the time, bitter foes. A contemporary historian is more interested in questions that colonialism's right-wing defenders and left-wing critics did not ask. Why was it that some elements of the French "revolutionary tradition" struck a responsive chord in the minds of young Vietnamese while others did not? Why were Vietnamese more likely to leave France with an appreciation for what Guérin called "revolutionary liberation" than with any particularly liberal sense of the "rights of man?" Why did several of the most politically talented Vietnamese of the 1925 student generation return from France as dedicated Communists, while no democratic socialist of consequence can be found among the Vietnamese who returned? Why, after all, did dozens of Vietnamese students return from their first deep encounter with France and the West not as admirers of Jean Jaurès and Léon Blum, but as activist followers of Lenin, Stalin, or in some instances, Trotsky? How did it happen that a figure like Jacques Doriot, for several years a Communist prominent in the party's anticolonial activities could act as serious manipulator among the various Vietnamese student groupings and factions, while a man such as Marius Moutet, the Socialists' principal spokesman on colonial affairs, could not speak before anticolonial gatherings in Paris without being vigorously heckled? And finally, what factors were at work that made the Vietnamese more receptive to Communist organization and doctrine than other colonial students?

Answers to these questions will be sought by examining the policies of French Communists towards colonial questions and towards the Vietnamese students, and the way in which the Vietnamese responded to Communist efforts. We shall also assess the policies of French Socialists towards the students. The comparative question of how colonial students from elsewhere in the French empire responded to the French Left will be treated in chapter 7.[4]

The French Communists greatly surpassed the Socialists in getting their message across to the Vietnamese students and in gaining allies among them. This superiority was due both to the content of the Communist message and the energy with which it was communicated. The French Communist party (the PCF) was the only major political institution in interwar France that advocated independence for Vietnam, as it did for the other French colonies. Initially this advocacy was carried out with a great deal of reticence, but the Moscow-based Communist International played a decisive role in pushing the PCF towards a vigorous anticolonial stance.

The Socialist party, by contrast, spoke of the colonial question with a deep appreciation of its complexities and ambiguities. Eloquent critics of the abuses of French rule, Socialists never made it clear to themselves or to others whether they wanted to reform French colonialism or abolish it. Such ambiguity would have been a severe handicap had the Socialists made a serious effort to win over the young Vietnamese. But the SFIO made few efforts in this regard, at least in comparison with the PCF. The result was that the PCF was not only the sole French party committed to Vietnamese independence but the only party devoting significant efforts to agitation and propaganda among the students.

## Roots of Communist Colonial Policy

When a majority of delegates from the old Socialist party voted, at Tours in 1920, to accept the conditions of the Communist Third International and become a Communist party, colonial questions remained well in the background. The majority at Tours did vote, however, for the Third International-inspired motion which proclaimed, "The Party is in full agreement with the Communist International in denouncing colonial imperialism, and taking the side of the peoples subjugated by European capitalism in their fight against oppression in all its forms." This formulation triumphed over two less forceful resolutions put forth by Jean Longuet and Léon Blum which expressed reservations both about the use of force by anticolonial peoples and the unprogressive nature of many of the anticolonial movements.[5]

The Communist International itself had, at the time of the Tours conference, only recently decided to place a particular emphasis on colonial struggles. The Comintern's first manifesto on colonial questions, drafted by Trotsky in March of 1919, analyzed colonial issues from a "Eurocentric" perspective that was not greatly different from that of the Socialist parties of prewar Europe. Colonial liberation depended upon Socialist revolution in Europe, an eventuality which, in the revolutionary months that followed World War I, seemed not at all farfetched. "The workers and peasants . . . of Annam, of Algeria, and of Bengal" the Comintern manifesto concluded, "will not be able to enjoy an independent existence until the day that the workers of England and France . . . take state power into their own hands."[6]

By the summer of 1920 revolution in Europe looked distinctly less likely. Revolutionary attempts in Berlin and Munich had failed, and the Hungarian Soviet Republic had collapsed. An Indian delegate at the second Comintern conference, M.N. Roy, put forth a proposal advocating that the world Communist movement should spare no effort to fuel revolution in the East—and indeed maintained that the fate of communism as a world movement depended on advances in the colonial areas.

Roy's arguments apparently had some influence on Lenin, who incorporated them into the Comintern "Theses" adopted at the second conference. Lenin's interest in the question of European colonialism could be dated to the Socialist International debates on the subject before World War I. In 1916 he had published the famous pamphlet, *Imperialism, the Highest Stage of Capitalism*, which developed the idea that colonial exploitation lay at the root of the corruption in the Western proletariat, because it enabled the Western bourgeoisie to encourage reformist and moderate tendencies in the working class, which sapped its revolutionary spirit. At the second Comintern congress, Lenin emphasized the importance of the anticolonial struggle to the future of communism, arguing that the peoples of the colonial nations were potential allies in the Soviet Union's struggle against the capitalist world. The main tactical point put forward in Lenin's "Theses" was that Communists should cooperate and enter into temporary alliance with anticolonial movements whether or not Communists held leadership positions within them.[7]

Though the PCF was influenced by Lenin's arguments, and committed itself to an anticolonial policy as one of the conditions for adhesion to the Comintern, such attitudes did not come naturally to the Party in its first years. Many of the PCF members who actually cared about colonial issues were residents of French Algeria, and when it came to the question of supporting movements to expel the French imperialists, *colon* Communists found their attitudes more closely resembled those of other Frenchmen than they did those of the Third International.[8] Other members of the PCF's rank and file perceived the colonial workers in France as potential strikebreakers; one party document lamented that propaganda among colonial workers in France was inhibited by the fact that the colonials were "habituated to servitude."[9] The PCF set up a colonial studies committee of ten members in August of 1921, but its report was not considered significant enough to be discussed at the annual Party conference in December of that year. After he had left Paris for Moscow in 1923, Ho Chi Minh complained that most French Communists thought that a colony was "nothing more than a country full of sands below and sunshine above, a few coconut trees and a few men of color . . . and they are completely uninterested."[10]

This inadequate attention to the Comintern line did not go unnoticed in Moscow, and at the fifth congress of the International in June 1924, PCF delegates received a dressing down from both Trotsky, who lambasted the Algerian section of the French Party for its "slaveholding mentality" and from Ho Chi Minh. Since he had moved to Moscow in 1923, Ho had become the Asian delegate of the Communist Peasants' International. At the fifth Comintern conference, he complained of the tentativeness of the PCF's anticolonial actions, and proposed that the Party commit itself to 1) the publication, in *Humanité* of a regular column devoted to colonial problems; 2) intensified recruitment efforts among the Vietnamese residing in France; 3) the dispatch of Vietnamese recruits to the Communist University in Moscow; 4) the organization of Vietnamese workers in France; and 5) the requirement that French Communist party members take an interest in colonial affairs.[11]

It took the shock of "Bolshevization" to bring the PCF around to a more vigorous anticolonial stance. This complicated purging process, which began in 1924, completely changed the face of the French Communist party. When it had run its course, two years later, the PCF was more youthful and more proletarian. Opposition groups of both the Left and Right were expelled. The Party emerged with its rump of former prewar Socialist parliamentarians reduced in size and influence; the Bolshevized PCF became a party of people both more alienated from French life and more willing to pursue energetically the disintegration of the French empire.[12]

The newly Bolshevized PCF chose Jacques Doriot, the twenty-six-year-old leader of the *Jeunesses Communistes*, to head the Party's new colonial commission. A burly former metal worker and a powerful speaker with great mass appeal, Doriot was a rising star of the new PCF. Almost immediately he had the occasion to demonstrate that in colonial matters, the Party was willing to go further than it ever had in taking the side of anti-French colonial rebels. In July 1924 the Moroccan tribal chieftan Abd-el-Krim went to war against French forces in the Moroccan Rif. Doriot shocked the French Chamber of Deputies by appealing to French soldiers to fraternize with the Moroccan insurgents. The Rif campaign was cut short the next year by decisive French miliary action. But the PCF's political response to the Rif war represented a telling sign that the PCF was henceforth willing to make good on the commitment it entered into upon joining the Comintern.[13]

While the Rif rebellion turned out to be a poor opportunity for the PCF to strike blows against the structures of French colonialism, the Party was soon presented with another opportunity. The upheavals that took place in Vietnam in 1925 led to an increase in the number of Vietnamese students coming to France. Unlike some of the colonial workers who, in the PCF's parlance, often behaved as if they were "habituated to servitude," many of these young Vietnamese were militantly anticolonial before they ever stepped on the boat. As a group they would turn out to be more receptive to PCF organization and propaganda than the small community of Vietnamese workers in France. From their ranks would emerge more dedicated Communists than from any other group of French subjects residing in the *métropole* between the wars.[14]

The PCF held some considerable trumps in its efforts with the Vietnamese. As mentioned above, it had the major advantage of having the anticolonial field more or less to itself. The PCF also benefited from the tactically flexible line initially mandated by the Comintern. In the aftermath of the 1920 Comintern conference, Communists were instructed to support, on a temporary basis, anticolonial groups led by "radical nationalists" (a concept sufficiently elastic to include a tribal chief like Abd-El Krim) and not to pay attention to whether such groups contained even latent Communist tendencies. In 1925 and 1926, the awareness of Marxism among Vietnamese was minuscule. Ho Chi Minh had moved from Moscow to Canton and established a small Communist grouping among Vietnamese exiles there, and some dissident newspapers in Saigon had published some excerpts and explanations of Marx. But an appeal to the Vietnamese on Marxist grounds alone would have had gone nowhere.

### Vietnamese Encounter the Communists

The most significant nationalist group among the Vietnamese in France was the *Parti Annamite d'Indépendance* (the PAI) which was founded by Nguyen The Truyen, a former associate of Ho Chi Minh, in 1926. The PAI was nationalist: its hero was the aging rebel Phan Boi Chau, and its literature was filled not with Communist slogans and analysis but with invocations of the "stolen fatherland" of Vietnam. PCF support for the PAI gave the small party a tremendous push. Communist printers printed the PAI's brochures, Communists protested when the PAI's meetings were broken up by the French police, and Communist speakers invited PAI leaders to share their podiums.[15] Not surprisingly, this stance won the Communists friends among nationalist Vietnamese. As Nguyen The Truyen himself pointed out, in an article printed in a Vietnamese student newspaper:

> The Communists themselves recognize that the colonies must go through a nationalist stage. What does that mean if not that, according to the opinion of communism's own advocates, that communism is not applicable to the colonies prior to their national liberation. In such countries, the struggle between races takes priority over that between classes . . (Y)et in Indochina there remains one fact: there are Annamites who sympathize with the Communists. Why? Simply because the Communist party is the only one which supports our national demands.[16]

There is some evidence that demonstrates what an effective and sometimes stunning impact the PCF's quite mundane activities could have on individual Vietnamese. One young student, a nephew of Nguyen The Truyen, recounted how the Party had first won him over. In 1925 he watched his uncle address a Communist meeting in Paris, and saw his talk warmly applauded. It was, the young man recounted, the first time he had ever seen a Vietnamese address an audience of French people; the sight left him bursting with pride and the young man went home to plunge eagerly into Bukharin's pamphlet *The ABC's of Communism*.[17]

For Vietnamese who had never had the opportunity to see a mass party in action before, even the small PCF of the mid-1920s was an impressive piece of work. One young man wrote home after observing a 30,000-strong demonstration the party had organized to protest the execution of Sacco and Vanzetti; with astonishment he recounted that the party could print leaflets and organize strikes completely without fear of government reprisal. "The Communists are powerful" was his breathless conclusion. For a Vietnamese who never had the occasion to see any group challenge the French government without receiving a crushing riposte, such a perception was a powerful tonic.[18]

While the main thrust of PCF colonial activity consisted of support for the PAI and nationalist groups of other colonial nations, it was also involved in trying to help the Comintern build the basis for a true Vietnamese Communist party. Ho Chi Minh was working with Vietnamese exiles in Canton by this time; but it was the responsibility of the PCF to find promising radical students in France and send them to the University for the Toilers of the East, in Moscow, where they could be trained as Communist cadres. Beginning in 1925, the PCF began to look for candidates for the Moscow school; those chosen were provided by the PCF with false Chinese passports, a medical examination and a limited amount of pocket money. The number of students sent to Moscow was never large: in 1927 French police estimated that there were nine Vietnamese at the Moscow school; by 1930 their number had risen to forty.[19] Nevertheless, these figures indicate that more Vietnamese chose to travel clandestinely to Moscow, and live in harsh conditions, than reside at the Catholic *foyer* located on the outskirts of Paris.

## The Colonial Third Period

The turnabout in Communist tactics signaled at the sixth Comintern congress in the summer of 1928 made the PCF's work with the Vietnamese more complicated. Prior to 1928 it had been Communist strategy to support all anticolonial movements that were not reactionary, all the while preserving the possibility of organizing explicitly Communist factions within those movements. Communists made no great effort to hide their intent to overthrow the "bourgeois nationalists" when they were strong enough to do so. But Chiang Kai Chek's forces, previously allied with the Chinese Communists, launched a preemptive strike against them in 1927. As a result, the policy, which rested on the conviction that the bourgeois nationalists would never understand what the Communists were up to, was left in tatters.[20]

The Communist debacle in China was one of several events that may have contributed to the Communist movement's sharp left turn in 1928. The Comintern had experienced a comparable setback when the British Trades Union Council failed to protest the British government's severing of diplomatic relations with the Soviet Union in 1927. Together these were enough to make both Soviet leaders and other Communists question the viability of united front tactics. Nevertheless, it seems that the abrupt and violent quality of the Comintern's left turn had its sources in Soviet domestic politics. The Communists' proclamation that the bourgeois world had reached a revolutionary "Third Period" and their attack on social democratic parties as "social fascists," were part of Stalin's maneuvers to isolate Bukharin and the "Right" within the Soviet Communist Party.[21]

The strategic line signaled by the Comintern's sixth congress called for the world's Communist parties to adopt a stance of sectarian aggressiveness towards all non-Communist forces—particularly those movements that had been previously considered progressive. This new "class versus class" strategy required the PCF to execute an about-face in its dealings with the Vietnamese in France. Suddenly it began to differentiate itself from the PAI and campaign against it. The PCF printed flyers making the quite ludicrous allegation that the PAI's new young leader, the mathematics student Ta Thu Thau, was acting in collusion with the right wing *Jeunesses Patriotes*.[22] The criteria by which the PCF chose Vietnamese to be sent to Moscow was also revised: henceforth French Communists were instructed to pay less heed to students, and make an effort to recruit Communist cadres from the small community of Vietnamese workers in France.[23]

One of the first manifestations of the new Communist line involved an effort by the PCF to create the nucleus of an independent Vietnamese Communist party. In April 1928, Henri Lozeray, a member of the PCF colonial commission, gathered together twelve Vietnamese who had formally joined the PCF in an aircraft hangar in St. Denis. Lozeray stressed the need to organize a group of Vietnamese militants who were trained in political agitation to work among all the classes of Vietnamese in France— students, sailors, and workers. Lozeray's intention was not only to create a special Vietnamese cell, under Party discipline; he also suggested the creation of a new newspaper, to be published in *quoc ngu*, that was critical of the PAI, followed the Communist line, and could be transported to Indochina. Such a paper could serve as a rallying point for a future Vietnamese Communist party. While some of the Vietnamese present reportedly took issue with Lozeray's criticism of the PAI, plans were drawn up for the creation of the newspaper *Lao Nong* (The Worker and Peasant). In a concrete manifestation of "Franco-Annamite collaboration" it was agreed that the paper's opening statement of purpose was to be written by French members of the PCF Colonial Commission, and translated by some of the Vietnamese present.[24]

The turnabout in Communist tactics, and the PCF's public and private campaign against the PAI did little to enhance the Party's prestige among

Vietnamese students, and by late 1928 French police were reporting that the new Communist line was meeting with a lack of comprehension among the Vietnamese.[25] But circumstances intervened that kept the PCF from paying too steep a political price for its new sectarian strategy: the PAI was eliminated.

Fortunately for the Communists, the French police obligingly disbanded the PAI themselves in March of 1929, just as the Communist attacks on the popular organization were becoming more shrill. This was not the first time (and would not be the last) that French authorities would eliminate the principal non-Communist organizations opposing their rule. Elimination of the PAI removed from the scene the main vehicle of political self-expression of radical Vietnamese students. When, a year later, the largest Vietnamese student organization, the AGEI, was disbanded as well, there remained virtually no Vietnamese anticolonial organizations left in France except those controlled by the Communist party.

### Ta Thu Thau and Nguyen Van Tao

The one radical tendency that did retain a sort of independence from Communist control was Vietnamese Trotskyism—a movement that owed its ephemeral existence largely to the unusual abilities of one young man, the mathematics student Ta Thu Thau. As noted above, Thau had been the leader of the PAI and the object of a bitter invective-filled campaign by the Vietnamese and French Communists. Though he had a noteworthy record as an anti-French activist, he was critical of the French Communists for what he termed "red imperialism" and wondered whether the PCF wished to maintain the Vietnamese in servitude "under another mask." But simple radical nationalism already seemed out of date to Vietnamese by the late 1920s. When the PAI was dissolved Ta Thu Thau himself initiated contacts with the French Trotskyist Left opposition, and began to publish in the Trotskyist journal *La Verité*. Ta Thu Thau and a few followers carved out a political position that was arguably to the left of Stalinism. They reproached the Communists for giving insufficient attention to Marxist education for the Vietnamese masses, and arrived at what one sympathetic historian has described as a "Luxembourgist" position, which rejected Vietnamese nationalism as such as outdated. But though Ta Thu Thau was more gifted as a political organizer than as a theoretician, Vietnamese Trotskyism always lacked organizational muscle; its leaders were prominent polemicists in the Parisian student milieu and played an important (and unique) role as allies of the Stalinists in Vietnam during the mid 1930s. But their independent prospects were dim, and their historical impact remains more a curiosity than anything more substantial.[26]

The PCF was also greatly helped by the arrival of the young student Nguyen Van Tao, who came to Paris from Aix in early 1928. Nguyen Van Tao was the son of small Cochinchina landowners and had smuggled himself to France in 1926 after being expelled from the *Lycée Chasseloup-Laubat* in Saigon for political activities. Intense, energetic, and tough, Tao first supported himself as a night-watchman at a *lycée*. He joined the PCF the next year, when he was nineteen. At the remarkably young age of twenty he accompanied the PCF delegation to Moscow for the sixth congress of the Communist International. Like many Vietnamese of his era he was possesed by intense political passions; his letters home that survive in the files of the French police repeatedly speak of his need to suffer and sacrifice for the resurrection of his country.[27]

Nguyen Van Tao stood out from his peers not only because of his energies and passions. He was willing to work closely with the French Communists and possessed a shrewd sense of how to operate within a Communist context—making him, in effect, a Communist model of the skilled collaborator. Tao's invitation to join the PCF delegation to Moscow in the summer of 1928 is a case in point. According to French police sources, he was included because he was willing to serve as Henri Lozeray's personal secretary when other radical Vietnamese had rejected the post, finding the PCF functionary personally offensive. In Moscow, Lozeray was called in before Bukharin, to answer allegations from several Vietnamese that the PCF treated the young colonials rudely and imperiously, and kept secrets from them. Bukharin smiled enigmatically when he heard these charges, but if he had any intention of reprimanding the French, he was cut short when Nguyen Van Tao leapt to Lozeray's defense, and pointed out that the Vietnamese making the criticisms came from bourgeois backgrounds.[28]

After his return from the Comintern conference, Nguyen Van Tao rapidly absorbed responsibilities within the PCF, and the PCF's visibility among Vietnamese students increased apace. Tao acquired a full time post on the PCF's colonial commission, and became the regular author of the *Humanité* column on the colonies. Under a variety of pseudonyms he wrote for *Les Cahiers du Bolchevisme* and *Pravda*.[29] He became a leading figure in the Communist student group, the *Union Fédérale des Étudiants*, which from 1929 onward campaigned regularly for Vietnamese and other colonial students to leave their "nationalist" groups and form new organizations under the umbrella of the UFE. He arranged meetings where French Communist professors spoke before audiences of Vietnamese students, and meetings where he spoke before French students. Though he had dropped out or been expelled from every French school he had attended since puberty, he criticized French instruction in Indochina and in other French colonies for its paucity. Whenever the French government moved to dissolve one of the larger Vietnamese student associations for nationalist activities, he made sure that the UFE was there to recruit those students.[30] In Tao's view the PCF never made an adequate effort to educate the French people about the colonial situation, and in 1930 he wrote a bitter critique holding the PCF responsible for the fact that the French people were ignorant of the turmoil then breaking out in the northern provinces of Vietnam. But he had the maturity to confine his criticism to a private letter to the PCF leadership.[31] As a public figure he worked incessantly to bring young Vietnamese into the Communist orbit. When several dozen Vietnamese participated in demonstrations in the spring of 1930, the French governnment seized the opportunity to arrest Tao, and he became the only Vietnamese student of the interwar period to spend several months in a Paris jail. During that time UFE journals and leaflets featured the slogan "liberate Tao" ahead of its calls of "Down with Fascism," *"École Unique Proletarianne"* and "Soviets to Paris."[32] When Nguyen Van Tao was finally expelled from France, in 1931, there were no major nationalist Vietnamese student groups left there except those organized under the direction of the French Communist party. By then some three hundred colonials of various nationalities were studying speechmaking and organizing skills at Communist training schools throughout France.[33] When Nguyen Van Tao returned to Vietnam his activism continued: he ended up, finally, as the labor minister of the government of North Vietnam.

## Communism's Appeal

If we have until now concentrated on what the French Communist party did to attract the Vietnamese, we should now turn our attention to how communism was received in the Vietnamese student community, and suggest some reasons for its relative success. Information on how Vietnamese students saw communism and how they responded to it is fragmentary. For evident reasons, Vietnamese Communists who have published in the West have not been profligate in their political introspection, and the materials from which one can draw inferences about communism and the students are uneven. Nevertheless, it is possible to attempt some speculation.

It is not the case that a large number of the Vietnamese students in France became professional revolutionaries. We have mentioned that the French government had the names of forty students who were channeled by the PCF from France to cadre training school in the Soviet Union, and some journalistic estimates place the figure at more than twice that. The Paris prefect of police's report, in 1929, named only ten Vietnamese students who regularly participated in PCF activities.[34] Probably most of these were included in the dozen who met with PCF activist Henri Lozeray at

Saint Denis in 1928 to discuss the foundations of an independent Communist party and to start sending the newspaper *Lao Nong* to Indochina. In a well-informed report, the *commissaire spécial* of Toulouse reported that the number of full-time Communist activists there was also no more than a dozen.[35] Perhaps there were another dozen Vietnamese students who attended Communist training schools in France not included in these figures. We might include the dozen or so students who followed Ta Thu Thau's path from the PAI into Trotskyism, for they would play a historically significant role as *pro-Communists* in Cochinchina during the mid 1930s.[36] Thus out of a total of between two-and three thousand Vietnamese students, it can be estimated that there were perhaps seventy committed and politically active Communists. While this is not a large figure, it does not really reflect the extent of Communist influence on the Vietnamese student movement.

For it can be maintained that just as important as the winning of full-time cadres was the fact that within a mere six-year period from 1925 to 1931, Communists succeeded in changing the very language in which French-educated Vietnamese talked about the liberation of their country. One internal PCF document obtained by French police officials in 1929 described the Party's aim as demonstrating to the students that they were the only political party committed to the independence of Indochina.[37] If the PCF did not completely fulfill this mission it did manage to create a sense of identity, in Vietnamese student rhetoric, and, perhaps in consciousness as well, between the cause of Vietnamese national liberation and the world Communist movement.

The evidence of this is scattered, but rather persuasive. The French official at Toulouse whose report minimized the number of actual Communists among the Vietnamese students, nevertheless pointed out that Communist doctrine had left its traces in the nationalist style of the students there.[38] He pointed to the fact that by late 1928, Vietnamese political rhetoric characteristically included social demands, couched in Marxist (or Leninist) language, in conjunction with nationalist slogans. As one example he cited the Vietnamese student newspaper *L'Annam de Demain* as stating, in its editorial, that Vietnamese independence could not be achieved without breaking the "feudal" hold of Vietnam's large landowners, and raising the cry of "land to the peasants!" A later edition of the same journal argued that Vietnamese would not only have to win independence from "the French oppressor" but also triumph over the "national exploiter," and that Vietnamese would have to win the right to "enjoy the nation's wealth" as well as political independence. The French official's conclusion was that Vietnamese had come to view communism as a "means" to win their independence.

This linking of nationalistic rhetoric to the language of class struggle was also evident in the slogans and pamphlets of the young Vietnamese who succeeded in gaining power in the largest Vietnamese student organization, the AGEI, in 1930. In the spring of that year, the new nationalist board wished to attack the Vietnamese student club at Bourdeaux. The Paris AGEI struck in a style which owed everything to Communist polemics. In a handbill the group proclaimed "You fear that the exploitation of the masses will end only to your detriment, and to the detriment of your families and masters." The identification of the colonial bourgeoisie with the interests of the occupying power was, the Bourdeaux students were reminded, an "inevitable process" which the AGEI was hardly indignant about, because it was "futile to be indignant against the march of history."[39] Such a polemic is noteworthy not because of its depth or originality but because it is indicative of how Marxist concepts flourished in the rhetoric of students who were in the mainstream of Vietnamese student activism and were not considered by the French police to have any particular relationship with the Communist party.

Moreover, there are indications that broader circles of Vietnamese students considered French Communists to be their only allies in the cause of Vietnamese independence. Several Vietnamese students tried to send issues of *Humanité* home to their friends in Saigon. One student, writing in February 1928, commented that the Communist daily was the "only paper to defend us" and added a lengthy digression on the Parisian bourgeois press, all of which, he noted, was hostile to Vietnamese nationalism.[40] The Socialist *Le Populaire* was not even mentioned. Another student wrote of a conference of Vietnamese speakers he attended, and of the French Communist who came by afterwards with offers of assistance.[41] Another quite falsely reported that "all the Vietnamese students are close to the Communist party."[42] Yet the fact that it was possible for a Vietnamese, even mistakenly, to perceive communism as the decisive force within the Vietnamese student community is revealing of the PCF's influence.

Moreover, there were few signs within the Vietnamese student community of an explicitly non-Communist nationalism, the kind of political tendency known in later generations as a "Third Force." There was of course some resistance to a Communist style of politics and analysis among Vietnamese students. Tran Van Giau, a Vietnamese student at the *lycée* at Toulouse who was closely involved with the PCF, wrote a short polemical tract in 1930 rebuking those students who claimed that a "national union" was necessary to achieve victory over the French. Tran Van Giau's argument was that talk of collaboration with the Vietnamese bourgeoisie would deprive the Vietnamese national movement of mass support, because the Vietnamese masses knew there were two classes—the exploiting and the exploited, and wouldn't participate in any national movement to which the Vietnamese "bourgeoisie" belonged.[43] Evidently, then, there were some students who needed to be convinced that the Vietnamese national liberation movement should be fused with internal class warfare. But perhaps Tran Van Giau's analysis can be taken as an indication of the Communist strength within the student community. For no Vietnamese who favored independence for his country suggested that the independence movement be purged of Communists; in France at least, no Vietnamese student could conceive of a nationalist movement in which Communists did not play an influential role. This in itself is a striking indication of the progress Communists had made within the Vietnamese student community from 1925 to 1930.

Why was the Vietnamese student movement so receptive to communism? Two explanations seem possible. One involves speculation about the special fit between the Vietnamese political culture, particularly its Confucian aspects, and Marxist-Leninism. Another focuses on the fact that when the Vietnamese arrived in France they were already in a state of radical agitation, which French Communists exploited more readily than any other group. Though this latter explanation seems more persuasive to me, the outlines of the Confucian-cultural argument should be noted.

Vietnamese were exposed to Marxism at roughly the same time that the last Confucian institutions were receding from the life of the colony. The mandarinal examinations at Hue were terminated in 1915, two years before the Russian Revolution. Marxism, which first began to surface in Vietnam in the mid-1920s, arrived at a time when most Vietnamese nationalists were vigorously rejecting Confucianism as having contributed to Vietnam's weakness. In most realms the doctrines are antithetical. Confucianism is hierarchical, accepts the existence of enduring differences in human status, and is supportive of a static conception of society. On each of these counts, the Marxist conception is opposed. Nevertheless some scholars of Vietnam have noted that many of Vietnam's first Communists, especially those from the northern province of Tonkin, came from the families of former mandarins. Moreover, there are some significant similarities between the doctrines. Both Marxism and Confucianism place stress on an elite whose mission is to indoctrinate the popular classes in correct thought and behavior. Both believe that human nature is malleable, and both stress an ethos of selflessness and service to society. Both doctrines are concerned with man and society, and neither has anything to do with speculation about other states of consciousness or an afterlife. Thus, it has been suggested, Marxism might have contained certain comfortable similarities with the dominant cultural tradition inherited from the past, which made it more attractive to Vietnamese nationalists.[44]

This might explain a good deal about those early Vietnamese revolutionaries from Tonkin, like the members of Thanh Nhien, the Canton-based Marxist group of the early 1920s. In Tonkin, after all, Chinese character schools and other elements of the Confucian tradition persisted well into the twentieth century. It would seem to explain much less about the political consciousness of students from Cochinchina, where the great majority of the Vietnamese students in France came from. Chinese characters—the medium through which Confucian learning could be transmitted—had been absent from the schools in the southern province since the first years of the French conquest, in the 1870s. The Vietnamese in the generation who came to France in the 1920s were not only severed from the Confucian tradition themselves, but few of them had parents who could read Chinese characters, or who had serious links with the Confucian world. As we have pointed out earlier, the absence of Confucian spirit was lamented by French conservatives. In short, Confucianism seems unpersuasive as an explanation for the receptivity of Vietnamese students in France to communism.[45]

A more likely explanation about the Vietnamese willingness to accept communism was that it seemed to satisfy the aspirations of a great many Vietnamese who arrived in France in the years 1926-1928, in the aftermath of the student strikes, the Phan Chu Trinh funeral demonstration, and the French represssion that followed. Many of the Vietnamese who had gone through these experiences arrived in France more interested in working for the independence of their country and fighting the French than they were in abstract and academic learning. They came to France with more contentious spirits than did the Algerians, Tunisians, Senegalese, and others who followed after them. They knew, viscerally, that their ancestors had failed to stand up to the French. Communism seemed to promise the possibility of success. It provided a whole curriculum for the study of rebellion—Party schools, schooling in language theory and agit-prop tactics, and the possibility of higher training—in Moscow! In the Soviet Union, a young Vietnamese could sense the international power of the movement, and could feel that he had allies from China, Japan, Italy, Germany, and elsewhere.[46]

But even if a Vietnamese passed up the opportunity to attend the Stalin school, there were many levels on which the practice of communism in France and the French revolutionary tradition could appeal to him. In particular, communism legitimated the animus many Vietnamese felt against the French, provided a strategy for overcoming the French, useful allies, and more support waiting in reserve. When the dominant experience most Vietnamese rebels had with the colonial power was a sense of powerlessness, these elements represented a considerable attraction.

In assessing the impact of the PCF's activities on France's internal debates about colonialism, the historian Raoul Girardet has suggested that the net result of Communist activity was to impede independence for the colonies. Girardet argues that by placing the cause of colonial freedom in the context of a global Communist revolution that a vast majority of Frenchmen rejected, the PCF only managed to give the various movements for national independence a bad name. According to Girardet

> The constant assimilation of colonial demands with the cause of proletarian revolution could not fail to lead a poorly informed public opinion to systematically confuse the imperatives of imperial defense with the "anti-Bolshevik struggle." This assimilation produced a veritable turning of the tables which gave the good colonial conscience of the masses a superb alibi permitting it to consolidate its prejudices and preserve its intellectual and moral comfort.[47]

## Socialist Timidity

Girardet's assessment raises another question. Why was the PCF the only French major party that supported Vietnamese national demands? The question leads logically to the next focus of our inquiry: what was the stance of the French Socialist party regarding colonial issues in general and, more specifically, what did it do about the political education of the Vietnamese students who had come to France? For if any political party in interwar France could be considered a logical candidate to play the role of a persuasive non-Communist tribune for colonial independence, and if any party could be considered capable of taking young Vietnamese under its wing and inculcating them with the spirit of French Republicanism, it was the party of Léon Blum.

For even though the Socialist minority at Tours had rejected the Communist International's call for "support for colonial independence movements," Blum's speech at Tours clearly affirmed that Socialists would "act for the benefit" of the colonized peoples who were victimized by "capitalist exploitation" in the colonies. He objected however, to the idea that the Socialists should give indiscriminate support to all anticolonial movements, which, Blum claimed, would amount to the instigation of "racial war." The policy that evolved from these strictures was, like so much else in interwar French socialism, a balancing between radicalism and reform that satisfied the imperatives of neither. Socialists supported the emancipation of the colonies at some undetermined time in the future. They regularly and incisively criticized colonial abuses. The party paper, *Le Populaire*, printed lengthy excerpts from André Gide's condemnation of French rule in Africa, *Voyage Au Congo*, and focused attention on French exploitation of native labor and administrative failures. But Socialists supported the government's defense of French prerogatives in Morocco against Abd El Krim's rebellion, and proclaimed that colonial independence without greater economic and social progress would be of no benefit to the natives. This kind of rationale became an excuse for Socialist immobility on the decisive political questions, because it was applicable to all situations in which native political demands clashed with French rule.[48]

Several times in the 1920s the Socialists sought to clarify their position, and to make it plain that they supported colonial independence, at least in principle. In a statement before the Chamber of Deputies in 1927, Léon Blum proclaimed

> We do not admit that there exists a right of conquest, a right of the first occupant, that benefits the European nations . . . We do not allow colonization by force. We believe that the aim to be pursued for the peoples who at this moment, in effect, find themselves, as is the case of France, in possession of colonial territories, must be to grant them independence as soon as possible. We shall achieve what you call our civilising mission the day we shall have been able to give the peoples whose territories we occupy liberty and sovereignty.

Blum softened his stance by adding that the Socialists would not preach insurrection and racial war, and he did not advocate an immediate evacuation of the colonies. But his thrust was clear enough, and in a number of instances throughout the 1920s other mainstream Socialist spokesmen like Marius Moutet and Alexandre Varenne also made clear that for Vietnam at least, the future pointed towards independence.[49]

With these expressions of principle in mind, we can examine what posture the Socialists took towards the Vietnamese students who streamed into France in the latter half of the 1920s. The record is not extensive. In an individual capacity, several Socialists were active in the anticolonial milieu. Marius Moutet, who would serve as colonial minister in the Popular Front government, became acquainted with several Vietnamese on an individual basis. Moutet had given the Vietnamese dissident intellectual Phan Chu Trinh personal and legal advice when he had been exiled in Paris in the early 1920s. When the Yen-Bay crisis broke out in Annam in 1930, Moutet gave a moving account before the Chamber of Deputies of the anguish of a student he knew who was seized by the Paris police and rudely abused, simply because he was Vietnamese.[50]

These were not isolated examples. Many Socialists were active as well in the influential League of Rights of Man. This organization took a regular interest in colonial issues starting in the early 1920s. One of its members, the prolific author and *lycée* professor Félicien Challaye often spoke before small groups of Vietnamese students in the provinces. League members attended the Vietnamese student conference held at Aix in 1927 as observers and made several appeals to the colonial ministry and the goverment in Hanoi to accede to some of the students' requests. The League also protested vigorously when the French government deported students in the aftermath of the 1930 demonstrations. But no more than the Socialist party did the League speak with one clear voice on the transcendant issue of colonial independence; it was divided between a majority who wanted to make French rule more humane and progressive and those, like Challaye, who wanted to end it entirely.[51]

Actions of this nature did not give the Socialists anything close to a comprehensive policy. When one compares the Socialist record with that of the Communists, this becomes clearer. Unlike the PCF, the Socialists never tried to organize the Vietnamese into their own Socialist party and did not finance or arrange for the printing of Vietnamese student newspapers. Nor did they establish training schools in France or anywhere else, where young Vietnamese could combine the study of political theory with the learning of organizational and agitational tactics. No Socialist-inspired anticolonial propaganda was circulated in the colony itself. No young Vietnamese was given a regular column in the Socialist paper *Le Populaire*.

Instead Socialists bemoaned the fact that the government was making insufficient progress in creating a Vietnamese elite. When Moutet summed up his criticisms of the government's policies in the 1930 Indochina debate in the Chamber of Deputies, he made much of this point:

> What are the elements of the population which you can call on to participate in the government? Where are they? . . . It is necessary to create an elite, and then develop it. It would assure the permanence of your civilising work. The greatest reproach I can make to your policy is to not have created this elite, and to have always been suspicious of that elite which was trying to establish itself.[52]

This was a typical Socialist performance: astute and well-informed criticism of governmental policy. One must note however that nothing stood in the way of the Socialists themselves trying to plant the seeds of a future elite among the Vietnamese in France. The idea of undertaking a political education program as serious as that of the Communists would probably have seemed shocking, even treasonous to the majority of France's interwar Socialists. The same party that chose to spend much of its energy in hairsplitting theoretical debate about whether socialism could be brought about in France by legal means or would require an "absence of legality," abstained from quite legal methods of organizing and educating an estranged and available Vietnamese constituency.

Such lack of imagination was all the more regrettable because of the indications that a more active policy might have succeeded. When the French Communist party adopted its "class against class" line in the aftermath of the sixth Comintern conference, its sectarian approach made enemies. Ta Thu Thau, suddenly a target of Communist polemics, was probably the most politically able young Vietnamese in France, and the party he led, the PAI, was Vietnamese nationalism's largest French organisation. But when the French government seized the offices of the PAI in 1929 and disbanded the party the Socialists raised no objections. Their criticism of government colonial policy was always moderate and responsible, and Ta Thu Thau, they must have reasoned, was every bit as intransigent in his demand for Vietnamese independence as the Communists were. Ta Thu Thau did find friends in French Trotskyist circles, and with a handful of Vietnamese followers began to hone his own eclectic and ultimately sterile brand of Trotskyist revolutionary internationalism. But it is interesting to speculate whether he might have grown to fill that huge void in Vietnamese nationalist politics—that of democratic socialism—had he received some encouragement from its influential French proponents. As it happened, when Ta Thu Thau returned to Saigon in the early 1930s, he emerged again as a dynamic figure in the Vietnamese anticolonial movement. But then he could be politically effective only through alliance with the better-organized Vietnamese Communists—and this singular Vietnamese version of the Popular Front lasted only so long as the Communists found it useful. Ta Thu Thau was executed by the Viet Minh in 1945.[53]

Ta Thu Thau's case does serve to illustrate that there were Socialists on the left wing of the SFIO whose anticolonialism was categorical. More orthodox Marxists like Daniel Guérin and Jean Zyromski, as well as the *gauche révolutionnaire* faction led by Marceau Pivert were every bit as anticolonial as the PCF. But the influence of these groups on SFIO policy was never great. As individuals or as factions, moreover, none of the Left Socialists had the resources to do significant work among the Vietnamese students on their own. Nor is it particularly evident that the SFIO's far Left had political values to transmit to the Vietnamese that differed very much from what could be learned from the Communists; they were simply less powerful.[54]

The consequences of the Socialists' failure to develop their own policy towards Vietnam's future elites became clear in 1936. Then the advent of the Popular Front government put Socialist Marius Moutet in charge of the Ministry of Colonies. He would find that there were only two significant groups of politicized Vietnamese: the crumbling remnants of Vietnam's collaborating royal and mandarin elites, and the Communists, by then already entrenched as a powerful force. For Léon Blum's party, this was a lamentable choice, but one it had done almost nothing to forestall.[55]

It is not difficult to speculate on why the Socialists did so little. A partial explanation surely lies in the ambivalence with which they approached the colonial question in general. Socialist anticolonialism, such as it was, was in great part a heritage of the party's Marxism. This might have influenced them to underestimate the role of nationalism as a moving force in world affairs. The legacy of World War I enhanced this tendency; Socialists could not avoid viewing nationalist passions, including those of France's own colonial subjects, as an atavistic, unprogressive sentiment that bred war. Perhaps even more decisive was the fact that Socialists, perhaps even more than other Frenchmen, were touched by the idea that France had its own unique "civilizing mission" to perform in her colonies; this was one of the curious legacies of the French revolutionary tradition, where France conquered people to make them free. One can mention other factors as well: there was among Socialists a lingering technocratic tendency, derived from Saint Simon but not foreign to Marx, that commanded men to do their best at the rational exploitation of the earth's resources. It could easily be argued that Vietnam's resources could be better put to productive use with French knowledge and capital than without it.[56]

Such ideological roots of the Socialist ambiguity towards the French colonies were reinforced by factors pertaining the SFIO's essence as a political organization. Throughout the 1920s and 1930s it remained a party traumatized by the Bolshevik Revolution and the Communist challenge, which had effectively stripped it of its former stature as the most dynamic force on the French Left. No longer a revolutionary party in practice, the SFIO enshrined its commitment to revolution in principle. Debates over whether it was legitimate for Socialists to enter into bourgeois coalitions, or the painstaking distinctions Léon Blum made between the "exercise" of power in a bourgeois regime as against the "conquest" of power leading towards "socialism" took up much of the SFIO's time. These issues were divisive enough for Socialists, who had suffered schisms and feared them. By the time it was apparent that Vietnamese students in France were increasing in number and escaping the government's moral control, the SFIO had settled into its interwar pattern. It had become a party that could do well in elections by picking up former radical voters in France's rural districts, and it could exercise influence through its parliamentary presence, and through several provincial newspapers. But it was losing support in Paris, where the Vietnamese students were most concentrated, and losing clout in French unions, where organizational power counted for more. A more forceful confrontation of colonial problems would simply have placed another divisive issue on the SFIO's plate, for the party contained under its wide umbrella, both militant anticolonialists like Guérin and Zyromski, and men who actually worked in colonial administrations, like Varenne.[57]

Furthermore, the SFIO may have seemed too firmly entrenched in French life to appeal to young Vietnamese who were hostile and estranged from France. The SFIO's leading members were middle-aged, or, in the case of Blum, already old; one finds no parallel in the SFIO of the energetic men in their twenties who came out of the *Jeunesses Communistes*. As Annie Kriegel has pointed out, during this period the Communists seemed to embody the idea of youth and of another world struggling to be born; the Socialists seemed quite well integrated in a world that many Communists, and many Vietnamese, were eager to see destroyed.[58]

For all these reasons then, the SFIO proved incapable of bold efforts to compete with the Communists for the allegiance of the Vietnamese. This might be seen as a regrettable missed opportunity; the party that entertained the idea of one day achieving socialism through an "absence of legality" abstained from measures that were altogether legal under the Third Republic. If some French Socialists noted with regret that the Communists were not equally passive, they did not publicize their feelings.

No less than the Socialists, the French Communists were capable of finding reasons to support French colonialism. The Comintern, it will be remembered, had criticized the PCF regularly for its lack of dynamism on colonial issues, and it was not until the PCF was "Bolshevised" in 1925 that it could be persuaded to carry out a vigorous anticolonial policy. Nor did such policies necessarily reflect the deepest impulses of its members. When the Communist International adopted the strategy of a popular front against fascism in the mid- 1930s, the PCF suddenly found the colonies to be an important bastion of the anti-Fascist defense network. Maurice Thorez found justification for the new policy in a formulation of Lenin: the right of the colonial peoples to obtain a divorce from France did not, Thorez explained, constitute an obligation to do so. There were few objections to this in the Party.[59] By this date, however, the question of the effect of such a turnabout on young Vietnamese nationalists in France was moot: the politically decisive contingent of Vietnamese had passed through France between 1925 and 1932, when the PCF anticolonial posture was most militant, and the number of Vietnamese able to come to France diminished steadily from 1931 onward.

When the policies of France's two principal parties of the Left towards the colonial question are compared, it seems that the most salient difference between them was that one carried out policies ordered by the Communist International. The fact that the PCF's most militantly anticolonial posture happened to coincide with the period of greatest influx of

Vietnamese students into France was a great stroke of fortune for the international Communist movement, and of transcendant importance for the history of Vietnam.

## Notes

1. *L'Ami du Peuple*, 20 January 1929.
2. Gustave Gautherot, an author often cited by French deputies of the Right and Center in debates on Indochina, explicitly made the point of tarring even the most tame Vietnamese nationalists with the Bolshevik brush. "There is scarcely a frontier between nationalists and 'constitutionalists' and communists," he wrote. "All of them work towards the same goals, use the same resources, the same gangs, without one being able to distinguish their respective organizations." *Le Bolchévisme aux Colonies et l'Impérialisme Rouge* (Paris: Librarie de la Revue Française, 1930), 219.
3. *Monde*, 14 June 1930.
4. See chapter 7, below, for a discussion of students from elsewhere in the French empire. I have not found any information pertaining to links between left-wing Catholics and Vietnamese students, probably because the Vietnamese student migration had peaked and was declining by the time left-wing Catholicism was making a mark in French political life.
5. Manuela Semidei, "Les Socialistes Français et le Probleme Colonial Entre les Deux Guerres," *Revue Française de Science Politique* (December 1968).
6. Quoted in Charles-Robert Ageron, "Les Communistes Français Devant la Question Algérienne (de 1921 à 1924)" in Ageron, *Politiques Coloniales au Maghreb* (Paris: Presses Universitaires de France, 1972), 181.
7. Se Branko Lazitch and Milorad Drachkovitch, *Lenin and the Comintern* 2 vols. (Stanford: Hoover Institution Press, 1972), 1: 365-395 and Hélène Carrère d'Encausse and Stuart Schram, *Marxism and Asia* (London: Allen Lane/The Penguin Press, 1969), 16-39 for discussion of the various Communist attitudes at the first two conferences of the International. For Lenin's "theses" see d'Encausse and Schram, 152-159.
8. Ageron, "Les Communistes Français."
9. *Bulletin Communiste*, 14 February 1922. This and other documents tracing the PCF's perspective on colonial issues during this period are included in Jacob Moneta, *La Politique du Parti Communiste Français dans la Question Coloniale, 1920-1963* (Paris: François Maspero, 1971), 18-38.
10. quoted in Huynh Kim Khanh, *Vietnamese Communism 1925-1945* (Ithaca: Cornell University Press, 1982), 62.
11. Trotsky's criticism cited in Moneta, *La Politique du Parti Communiste Français*, 28-29. Ho Chi Minh's recommendations are summarized by Milton Sacks, "Marxism in Vietnam," in Frank Trager *Marxism in Southeast Asia* (Stanford: Stanford University Press, 1959), 109.
12. The PCF's Bolshevization is discussed in Robert Wohl, *French Communism in the Making, 1914-1924* (Stanford: Stanford University Press, 1966), 396-432. Doriot left the PCF in 1933, and three years later founded his own fascist French Popular party.
13. Ibid., 409-410.
14. There were about 1500 Vietnamese workers in France in 1930, less than the

number of students. They were generally either lacquerers or house servants. Not surprisingly, the lacquerers were more likely to be involved in politics, and many were members of the PAI. But no workers played leadership roles in the Vietnamese organizations. See Daniel Hémery, "L'Immigration Vietnamienne en France de 1925 à 1930," *Le Mouvement Social*, Jan.-March 1975, and the Paris prefect of police report in Slotfom, III, 32. The radicalization of the Vietnamese in comparison with other colonials is discussed in chapter 7.

15. Daniel Hémery, "Ta Thu Thau: l'Itinéraire Politique d'un Revolutionnaire Vietnamien pendant les années 1930" in Pierre Brocheux, ed., *Histoire de l'Asie du Sud-Est, Révoltes, Réformes, Révolutions* (Lille: Presses Universitaires de Lille, 1981), contains a useful description of the PAI. For some information about PCF-PAI ties, see also Hémery, "L'Immigration Vietnamienne."

16. *La Nation Annamite*, June 1927, cited in Hémery, "L'Immigration Vietnamienne."

17. Slotfom III, 44. This file contains the lengthy confession of Nguyen The Vinh, the nephew of Nguyen The Truyen, and a former student at the École Supérieure de Commerce at Marseilles. In July, 1931 he confessed before the French *sûreté*, shortly after his return to Vietnam. He attended the University of the Toilers of the East in Moscow from 1926-1927, and accompanied the PCF delegation to the sixth conference of the Communist International in 1928.

18. Slotfom XIII, 2 (letter of Michel Viet).

19. Slotfom III, 44. Jean Dorsenne, in his well-informed "Le Péril Rouge en Indochine," *Revue des Deux Mondes*, 1 April 1932, claims that there were 100 Vietnamese students at the Stalin school.

20. Franz Borkenau, *World Communism* (Ann Arbor: University of Michigan Press, 1971), 291-293.

21. Theodore Draper, *American Communism and Soviet Russia* (New York: Viking, 1960), 302-306. Most works dealing more directly with the Soviet party and the Comintern are reticent about explaining the change in line, undoubtedly because Soviet and Comintern archives are not available. See for example Kermit McKenzie, *Comintern and World Revolution* (New York: Columbia University Press, 1964) and Fernando Claudin, *The Communist Movement: from Comintern to Cominform*, trans. Brian Pearce (New York: Monthly Review Press, 1975).

22. Hémery, "Ta Thu Thau."

23. Slotfom, III, 44. According to Huynh Kim Kanh in *Vietnamese Communism*, 176-177, workers recruited in this manner were much less likely than students to be politically reliable revolutionaries and were far more likely to cooperate with the French authorities.

24. Slotfom III, 44.

25. Hémery, "Ta Thu Thau."

26. Ibid. for Daniel Hémery's sympathetic assessment of Ta Thu Thau. See his *Révolutionnaires Vietnamiens et Pouvoir Colonial en Indochine: Communistes, Trotskyistes, Nationalistes à Saigon de 1932 à 1937* (Paris: François Maspero, 1975) for a detailed account of the vicissitudes of the Trotskyite-Stalinist relationship in Saigon during the 1930s.

27. Slotfom XIII,2 contains a letter of Nguyen Van Tao written from Aix-en-Provence to a friend still in Saigon. The nineteen-year-old wrote: "You are alive, so therefore you must suffer. It makes you a man. I myself have suffered

all of the injustices committed by our oppressors . . . and I know all the degrees of their absolutism which we must shatter. I fear neither the suffering nor the dangers . . ."

28. Slotfom III,44.
29. Daniel Hémery, *Révolutionnaires Vietnamiens et Pouvoir Colonial en Indochine: Communistes, Trotskyistes, Nationalistes à Saigon de 1932 à 1937* (Paris: François Maspero, 1975), 69-70.
30. For diverse reports on Tao's activities with the UFE, see Slotfom III, 150, Slotfom III,32 Slotfom III,5 and ANF7-13470.
31. Claude Liauzu, *Aux Origines des Tiers-Mondismes: Colonisés at Anti-Colonialistes en France 1919-1939* (Paris: Editions L'Harmattan, 1982), 22.
32. Slotfom, III,5.
33. Slotfom III,120. This was the estimate of the Ministry of Colonies in January, 1932. French officials reported that the Comintern was unimpressed with these schools, which were attended by some Negroes and North Africans as well as Vietnamese.Their mandate was to send the most promising students to Moscow. French official information on these schools seems to be regrettably sparse.
34. Slotfom III, 32.
35. AN: F7-13410.
36. Hémery, "Ta Thu Thau."
37. Slotfom III, 7.
38. AN: F7-13410.
39. Slotfom III, 25.
40. Slotfom XIII, 2. (letter of Le Quang Dang)
41. Ibid. (letter of Lien Van Phuc)
42. Ibid. (letter of Michel Viet)
43. Slotfom, III, 25.
44. Nguyen Khac Vien, "Confucianism and Marxism in Vietnam" in Nguyen Khac Vien, *Tradition and Revolution in Vietnam* (Berkeley: Indochina Resource Center, 1974). See also the discussion in William Duiker, *The Communist Road to Power in Vietnam* (Boulder: Westview Press, 1981), 25-29.
45. For a discussion of how Confucianism might be compared with Islam as a factor in explaining how colonial students responded to Communism, see chapter 7, below.
46. Dorsenne, "Péril Rouge en Indochine."
47. Raoul Girardet, *L'Idée Coloniale en France de 1871 à 1962* (Paris: La Table Ronde, 1972), 222.
48. Rudolf von Albertini, *Decolonization* (Garden City: Doubleday, 1971), 309-319, and Semidei, "Les Socialistes Francais."
49. quoted by Semidie, "Les Socialistes Français."
50. 6 June 1930, *Journal Officiel*, Chambre des Députés. For Phan Chu Trinh's gratitude for Moutet's assistance, see his speech before the League of Rights of Man in February 1925, reported in Slotfom, III,17. For an account of the Yen-Bay rising and its consequences, see chapter 6, below.
51. Slotfom III,2 and AOM- Indochine, 51527. The League of Rights of Man debate on colonialism is described in Albertini, 306 and Girardet, 263-264.
52. 27 June 1930, *Journal Officiel*, Chambre des Deputes.
53. Hémery, "Ta Thu Thau" is the best account in French or English of Ta Thu Thau's life. For an account of Communist-Trotskyite cooperation during the 1930s in Vietnam, see chapter 6, below.

54. The colonial positions of the left wing socialists are described in Semidei, "Les Socialistes Français." See also Daniel Guérin, *Aux Service des Colonisés* (Paris: Les Editions de Minuit,1954).

55. Daniel Hémery, "Aux Origines des Guerres d'Indépendence Vietnamiennes: Pouvoir Colonial et Phénomène Communiste en Indochine avant la Seconde Guerre Mondiale," *Le Mouvement Social* (October-Dec. 1977).

56. Semedie, "Les Socialistes Français."

57. See Nathanael Greene, *Crisis and Decline: The French Socialist Party in the Popular Front Era* (Ithaca: Cornell University Press, 1969), 1-70, passim. and Joel Colton, *Léon Blum: Humanist in Politics* (New York: Knopf, 1966), 55-91 for a discussion of the Socialists and their ideological dilemmas during these years.

58. Annie Kriegel, *Le Pain et les Roses* (Paris: Presses Universitaires de France, 1968), 244.

59. Report to the 9th Congress of the PCF, by Maurice Thorez, Arles, December 1937. Excerpted in Moneta, *Les Communistes Français*, 132.

# 6

# The Return of the Rebels:
# Vietnamese Students in the 1930s

However troubling the political evolution of the Vietnamese students was to officials in the Ministry of Colonies, to the *colons*, and to the less radical elements of Vietnamese opinion, it was nevertheless an extremely obscure issue to the vast majority of Frenchmen. There were about one thousand Vietnamese students in Paris, and perhaps two thousand more in the provincial cities, and no reason for the average Frenchmen to notice them if he didn't want to. Indeed the same could be said about the Indochina colony itself, which after the 1926 strikes and demonstrations had returned to calm once more. Vietnam was far from the forefront of the French public mind. This state of affairs was upset, however, in the first months of 1930, when a fresh outbreak of rebellion in Indochina and its echo in Paris brought all of the various questions about Vietnam's relationship to France closer to the surface of French popular concern than at any time in the interwar period.

## The Yen-Bay Catalyst

The immediate catalyst for the reopening of the Indochina question was the emergence of the small and radical Vietnamese Nationalist party, known as the Viet Nam Quoc Dan Dang, or VNQDD. The party was formed in 1927 in Hanoi by a 23-year-old school teacher named Nguyen Thai Hoc. The party's members were young graduates of the Franco-Vietnamese schools in the colony, who generally worked at lower level white collar professions in Hanoi. But the small intensely nationalistic party gained a rising following from the youth of the protectorate in Tonkin; by 1929 it could count 1500 members in 120 cells. In that year, French authorities moved against it on the pretext of the murder of a Frenchman who recruited Vietnamese labor for rubber plantations in the South. While officials soon discovered the killing was not the VNQDD's doing, they continued to imprison the party's leaders. In near desperation, the young leaders who remained free decided to play all their cards at once, and gambled on sparking an insurrection among various garrisons of Vietnamese troops under French command. But the plans went awry. French police uncovered several caches of weapons; a messenger from the party's headquarters sent to postpone the action was captured. The mutiny, planned for the night of February 9, 1930, was carried out with little coordination. A garrison of Vietnamese troops at Yen-Bay killed their French officers and seized the town. A few bombs were tossed in Hanoi. A barracks at Hung Hoa was attacked. That was all: within days all of the insurgents were overwhelmed.

French revenge was swift. The soldiers who participated in the mutiny were executed. The village of Co-Am, thought to be a place of refuge for the mutinous troops, was bombed. One thousand members of the VNQDD were sentenced by a specially formed criminal commission, and eighty of the more active members of the party were condemned to death.[1]

## Showdown in Paris

This fresh outbreak of violence on the part of France's Vietnamese subjects, and the severe French repression that followed, raised passions in Paris among all those who gave a thought to Indochina. As it happened, the Yen-Bay mutiny turned out to be only the beginning of a wave of rebellion that would spill out over the length of Vietnam during the next two years: in 1931 the newly formed Indochinese Communist party would lead a long-lasting and violent peasant rebellion in the province of Nghe-Tinh, which the colonial authorities found much more difficult to contain. But the chaotic effort by the VNQDD at Yen-Bay was the first outbreak of organized violence by anticolonial rebels in Vietnam since World War I. Not surprisingly the trials of the Yen-Bay rebels, the death sentences, and the subsequent executions had an electrifying effect on the already radicalized Vietnamese student community in France, and produced, finally, a showdown between the young radical Vietnamese and the French authorities.

The Yen-Bay episode sharpened even further the conflicts between radicals and moderates within the Vietnamese student community in France. Henceforth these conflicts were carried on in a language that fully anticipated the civil war which would engulf Vietnam in future decades. The largest Vietnamese student association, the *Association Générale des Etudiants Indochinois*, which had passed into the hands of radical nationalists in 1929, embarked, in February 1930, on a campaign against the newly opened government-sponsored Indochina House. It also sought to exercise authority over federations of Vietnamese students outside of Paris. The Vietnamese student organization at Bordeaux was a particular target. The *Association Mutuelle Indochinoise* at Bordeaux had sent a letter to French president Doumergue asking for clemency for the Yen-Bay rebels who were facing execution. In an "open letter" to the Bordeaux organization, the AGEI accused it of the "perfidy of holding out their hands to French imperialism" and warned them that they would never be forgiven. The AGEI logic was that in asking for clemency the Bordeaux students were in fact affirming their loyalty to French rule. The AGEI professed not to be surprised by this, arguing that the "Annamite bourgeoisie" from which the Bordeaux students came was inevitably driven to align itself with French imperialism.[2] Like many revolutionary groups, the young members of the AGEI thought martyrs would be useful to the cause of Vietnamese revolution, and advised all Vietnamese student groups from the provincial cities that clemency would calm the revolt in Vietnam, while the blood of the condemned men would fertilize the soil for revolution.[3] Perhaps the AGEI members took this view because the VNQDD members who were going to lay their heads across the French guillotine were not Communists, and indeed were potential rivals to the Communists for leadership of the resistance to French rule.

Those Vietnamese in France who belonged to groups more directly controlled by the PCF tried to capitalize on Yen-Bay by winning more converts. At several meetings following the mutiny, Nguyen Van Tao made the false claim that the Yen-Bay uprising was carried out under Communist leadership.[4] Within a month after the insurrection, the Vietnamese student community in Paris was awash in political leaflets full of invective, vehemently denouncing the few dozen students who had signed up for rooms in the Indochina House at the *Cité Universitaire*, the Vietnamese student group from Bordeaux, or those few Vietnamese "traitors" who attended social functions hosted by French officials in Paris.[5]

This fresh wave of militancy and emotion soon led Vietnamese students into their first overt clashes with French authority in Paris. In March of 1930, French President Doumergue, the young Vietnamese emperor Bao Dai, and several French cabinet officials attended the ceremony of the opening of Indochina House, the newly constructed residence for Vietnamese students. The French police, anticipating trouble at the event because of the ongoing campaign against the residence, arrested nine Vietnamese students, including both the Communist Nguyen Van Tao and Ta Thu Thau, on the day before the ceremony. On the day of the inauguration of the residence, another fifty Vietnamese students were detained outside the grounds of the *Cité Universitaire*. But these measures were not enough to ensure tranquility. As soon as a Vietnamese resident of Indo-china House took the podium, the president of the AGEI, Le Ba Cang, rose from the audience and accused the speaker of treason. A half-dozen other Vietnamese threw out leaflets calling for the liberation of those arrested after the Yen-Bay rebellion.[6]

This outburst resulted in a half-dozen arrests. Those detained were re-leased the next day, and the matter might have rested there had the Viet-namese not, less than two months later, mounted a more embarrassing action against the symbols of the French state. On the evening of May 21, some fifty Vietnamese students, including members of the AGEI, followers of the Trotskyist leader Ta Thu Thau, and the Communist Nguyen Van Tao held a dinner at a Left Bank brasserie. According to informers' reports, much of the evening was taken up with squabbles between the "Trotskyists" and the "Stalinists" among the students, which nearly re-sulted in a brawl. Nevertheless, at the evening's end, Ta Thu Thau circu-lated and took down the names and addresses of many of the students. What the police informers did not know was that the Trotskyist leader visited each of the students later that night and during the next day, to organize a surprise and illegal demonstration in front of the Elysée palace.

At 3 o'clock the following afternoon, nearly 150 Vietnamese students arrived in taxis in front of the French presidential residence, and handed out leaflets demanding the liberation of the "Yen-Bay comrades." One of the demonstrators filmed the goings-on with a movie camera. While the cameraman escaped with his film, twelve of the Vietnamese were arrested. *Humanité* mockingly reported that some of the bourgeoisie who lived in the neighborhood joined with the police in attacking the students.[7]

These events—scarcely ripples in the perspective of what Paris had seen in its history—nevertheless shocked the bourgeois press, which suddenly found itself face to face with unmistakable evidence of the state of mind of France's most avid colonial pupils. The journal of the right-wing *Jeunesses Patriotes* exclaimed that the French should forget about Yen-Bay, because the real preparations for Vietnamese revolution were being made in Paris. The *Jeunesses Patriotes* complained that the government, despite good intentions, had repeatedly ignored its warnings about the revolutionary activity going on in Paris, and claimed that the police, who wanted to act, were restrained from doing so.[8] The French colonial press struck the pos-ture of a wounded, unappreciated parent who had finally lost patience. *La Presse Coloniale* reported the disturbance at Indochina House under the headline, "We've had enough!" and pointed out that these young men "would be nothing without France" and were doing a poor job of repaying France's efforts on their behalf by insulting its head of state.[9] The *Econo-miste Colonial* echoed that sentiment.[10] The conservative *Le Figaro* used the occasion to launch a broad polemic on French educational methods in the colony. In a vulgarized version of the arguments used by French conservative theorists like Jules Harmand and Louis Vignon a generation before, *Le Figaro's* correspondent Gaetan Sanvoisin claimed that French methods of education were unsuited to Vietnamese because they corresponded "neither to their history, nor to their nature, nor even to their climate." Sanvoisin quoted an unnamed former minister to claim that even scientific knowledge could not be assimilated by "Asiatic brains" and reminded readers that the archbishop of Saigon had predicted thirty years earlier that educating Vietnamese with French concepts would lead to trouble. Such warnings, lamented Sanvoisin, had not stopped the French from trying to stuff the Vietnamese full of Western social science and philosophy.[11]

The two Vietnamese demonstrations transformed the popular image of the Vietnamese student in the French press: the quiet, shy, diligent Oriental gratefully drinking at the fount of French culture became the revolutionary ingrate. The common popular perception of Vietnamese in France thus matched the portrait painted by the most pessimistic of specialist observers.

The demonstrations also served to break the policy stalemate between the various French ministries over what to do with the Vietnamese student radicals; those within the French government who had long favored expelling them from the French capital were finally able to prevail. Because the Vietnamese were not foreigners, but French subjects, the government had no obvious legal justification to repatriate them for demonstrating. After the disruption of the Indochina House ceremony, the first recourse of the Ministry of Colonies was to try to convince the Vietnamese student who had been shouted down by the rebels to press criminal charges. He refused. Next the colonial ministry tried to determine whether the students could be tried before a university disciplinary tribunal and either suspended or expelled from school. University officials however thought that stern disciplinary action was unlikely.[12]

The demonstration in front of the Elysée palace finally pushed the government's hand. Prior to the Elysée action, the Ministry of Colonies had resisted a long stream of requests from the Paris prefecture of police to expel rebellious students from the country, but after the Elysée affair such resistance ceased. The day after the arrests the Parisian police prefect demanded that the Ministry of Colonies withdraw the "carte de séjour" which permitted Vietnamese to study in France. Soon after, the minister of colonies, the minister of interior, the prefect of police and several officials from the two ministries met and decided to deport those Vietnamese who had been arrested at both demonstrations. They decided as well to jail the

Communist organizer Nguyen Van Tao for an undetermined time on the charge of engaging in a Communist plot against the security of the state.[13]

The arrests were only the beginning of broad campaign against the Vietnamese student movement. On May 30, the nineteen students who were arrested at the two demonstrations were taken to the steamer *Athos II* and shipped back to Vietnam. Nguyen Van Tao was placed in a Paris jail for inciting sedition. On June 4, a Parisian court formally dissolved the AGEI because its members had contradicted its charter by participating in politics. Later that month the Parisian *Association Mutuelle Indochinoise* was dissolved; the following month its sister organization in Toulouse was shut down by French police.[14] That summer, Pierre Pasquier, the Governor General of Indochina, stepped up efforts to persuade Vietnamese parents not to allow their children to travel to France. Pasquier circulated a document warning Vietnamese parents that young Vietnamese students in France were "an easy prey" for dishonest people who would play on their scruples and naïveté, that French families were unlikely to take on Vietnamese students as boarders, and that there were numerous examples of Vietnamese families whose children were spiritually lost to them after they had been exposed to a French regime of lewd pleasure, gambling, laziness, and irregular work habits.[15]

### Debate in the Chamber of Deputies

Perhaps the most striking reflection of the effect of Yen-Bay and the student demonstrations on the French polity took place in the French Chamber of Deputies over four days in June 1930: there the Indochina problem received its fullest airing of the interwar period. The student problem was discussed as an integral part of the broader issue. It was the Communist deputy André Berthon who first raised the issue of student deportations. He claimed that the Vietnamese had every right to demonstrate in Paris, and infuriated the *colon* deputies and many others by exulting over the fact that most Vietnamese students returned to the colony as Communists. Before the assembled deputies Berthon read a militant manifesto from the "group of young Vietnamese at Toulouse"—probably drafted by Tran Van Giau, who was soon to depart for Moscow—and lamented that the expelled students, described as the best of their generation, had been deprived of their individual rights.[16]

Berthon might have found more supporters if outrage about the Yen-Bay mutiny and those who glorified it was not still fresh in the minds of the deputies. One member of the chamber set the scene by reminding those assembled of the gory details of the rebellion: in one example a French officer was reportedly disemboweled in front of his wife and children.[17]

When the minister of colonies François Piétri replied to Berthon's charges he had little trouble winning over his audience. Paris was not a "refuge for amateur troublemakers," Pietri told the assembly, and the government had every right to withdraw the rights of the Vietnamese to reside there. The students would be released once their boat returned to Indochina. A condescending and bland rendition of the government's position had been prepared for Piétri by his staff:

> The Indochinese who come to Europe are very young people who sometimes undergo a rapid transformation because of the propaganda which is directed at their milieu. When they are not content to absorb the . . . education which is given them and make themselves guilty of acts against public order, it is in their interest that they be returned to their natural milieu, where familial influence and the influence of their ancestral tradition can aid them to emerge from a crisis which will most probably be temporary.[18]

But when he spoke, Piétri spontaneously expressed a much sharper anger. "My indignation," the minister of colonies exclaimed, "extends towards the conduct of these students, who solicit and receive the hospitality of our laws, our customs, and our ideas, who take advantage of our intellectual and social life, and who have the audacity to insult our chief of state and to proclaim, in France, that those who assassinated French officers and soldiers are heroes."[19] It was a feeling shared by most of those who sat in the French chamber that day.

In addition to the voices of officials who made policy, and those who criticized it in the language of the Comintern, the June Indochina debate brought out two additional types of response. One was that of the French Right, which continued to call into question the whole philosophy of the French educational enterprise in the colonies. Pierre Taittinger, the leader of the *Jeunesses Patriotes*, was more familiar with Vietnamese students than most right-wingers; as noted earlier, his group had arranged a forum with some Vietnamese students the previous year, which had been broken up by Vietnamese radicals. Taittinger knew the politics of the Vietnamese student organizations, and was well aware that those who supported "Franco-Annamite collaboration" had been reduced to silence. In his speech he estimated that two-thirds of the Vietnamese in France were Communist or pro- Communist; his response was to propose that the Vietnamese be returned to a mythical and passive ancestral past. "Déclassé" intellectuals, observed Taittinger, would always be a problem for the French empire; the solution was simply not to create them. The right kind of education for the Vietnamese, he asserted, would be a "professional education . . . (which would) safeguard the ethnic originality of our subjects. . . . the Annamite has marvelous gifts as an artisan, as a wood carver.

He has original conceptions of real artistic value. It would be better to encourage this development rather than to make of him a "déclassé" or a philosopher or an intellectual who has nothing more in his mind than bitterness and resentment."[20]

The French Socialists' contribution to the June debate was the most intellectually astute, though it amounted to little in terms of policy choices. Marius Moutet found the correct rejoinder to Taittinger's condescending sallies: if the Vietnamese were not allowed to come to France, they would certainly go elsewhere to study, with consequences that were probably more pernicious to French rule. Moutet recognized that the most recent Vietnamese outbursts, in the colony and in Paris, meant that the center was not holding. He quoted at length an anguished and pathetic letter he had received from a Vietnamese student now returned to the colony. The young man contrasted the way French people had treated him during his studies, where a French family invited him for dinner every Sunday, with his present status of "no more than a native." "As I have kept European habits" the former student continued

> I feel myself surrounded by defiance, a stranger in my own country. A foreigner so far as you French are concerned, I don't know where to turn or what to do. The French spurn us, while our own people speak only of conspiracies. I would so much wish to work for the good of my country, in peace. In the evening, I sometimes weep all alone in my room—everything here disturbs me . . . and I dream only of returning to France.

Moutet commented that he knew many such Vietnamese, and had seen many others "bit by bit escaping the influence that someone like myself was able to exert on them."[21]

Former Governor General Alexandre Varenne shared Moutet's perspective. He criticized the government for having no program of colonial reforms, and thought Pasquier's policy of returning the rebellious students to Vietnam was ridiculous, and not the way he had done things when he was Governor General. There were, Varenne pointed out, quite enough Communists already in Indochina, and the government was now returning to the colony some of the best-educated Communists it could find. "What can one say about such a decision?" Varenne asked. "A certain number of Annamite leaders have paid with their lives for participation in the revolt, which is now perhaps decapitated. And now we have sent to the Annamites other leaders to replace them."[22] Time would show that Varenne was not wide of the mark with this prediction.

There is also evidence that Vietnamese who were nationalist but not Communist felt that the spring's events had produced a lamentable polarization that undercut any compromise solution to the Indochina question.

Ly Binh Hue, a Paris-trained lawyer who had been one of the organizers of the 1927 Vietnamese student conference at Aix and the editor for several years of a Vietnamese student paper was one who regretted the collapse of a middle ground between the peoples of the two nations. Writing to a friend in Saigon about the spring's events, Hue commented bitterly on the Indochina debate in the French Chamber of Deputies. Hue was furious that some of his friends had been ripped away from Paris by measures that seemed altogether illegal. Taittinger's demagogy, he claimed, had enthused the populace at large, while the arguments of Moutet and the other Socialists had passed unnoticed. So far as Hue was concerned, the arguments of Berthon and the other Communist figures were ludicrous. But the pity of it was that there now existed a situation in which "in the eyes of the government we are all Communists." It was, he continued, a state of "being Communist without knowing it, certainly without wishing it. The shame is that Taittinger and Cachin (the French Communist leader) understand each other perfectly . . . from the far Right to the far Left, we are all considered disciples of Russia."[23]

## The Decline of the Student Movement

The government's decision to repatriate the nineteen students, made in a spasm of anger, turned out to be decisive in resolving the brewing controversy over what to do about radical Vietnamese in France. A first and lasting consequence of the government's moves was a sullen calm that descended over the remaining centers of Vietnamese student activism. Police reports after the expulsion became less frequent, and more often than not brought messages about the cooling off of political passions among France's young *protégés*. In the immediate aftermath of the deportations, the Ministry of Colonies' principal undercover agent reported "calm" and "anxiety" among the students who had formerly belonged to the now legally defunct AGEI. The June monthly roundup of Vietnamese activity prepared by the CAI concluded that the repression seemed to be effective.[24] Colonial officials who had watched the growth of the Vietnamese student associations in such cities as Toulouse and Bordeaux reported similar patterns, not merely in the immediate aftermath of the government's action, but over the next several years. By 1932, the commissioner general of Bordeaux was able to report that there was no longer effective Communist propaganda among the students, who had apparently reckoned "they had much to lose and little to gain" by radical activity.[25]

It is surely not coincidental that the 1930 peak of Vietnamese student radicalism in Paris coincided with the highest numerical presence of Vietnamese in French schools. Travel to France dropped off in subsequent years. Governmental efforts to discourage student travel, such as the Pasquier circular, were surely one reason, but the financial pressures resulting from the global depression were probably more important. Fewer Vietnamese families had sufficient surplus income to send either their own or other children to France. Because the main financial base of the student emigration had been the land-owning families of Cochinchina, the collapse of the price of rice was decisive. The first effects of the depression struck Vietnam in the middle of 1930. From $13 a quintal in April 1930, the price of rice fell to $10 in September, to $7 in March 1931 to just over $3 by November 1933. Other economic indicators showed similar declines. The money value of the colony's exports dropped by over 60 percent between 1928 and 1931.[26]

For the first time since 1919, the number of Vietnamese students enrolled in French schools began to drop. The fall-off was first remarked upon by French officials in the provincial cities. In Toulouse, where the future Communist leader Tran Van Giau had held sway, the number of Vietnamese declined from 104 in 1928 to 23 in 1934. The prefect in Bourdeaux noted "an important reduction" in the number of students, which he attributed to the economic crisis in Indochina. The decline in Vietnamese enrollment in higher level French schools came somewhat later, because many had already started in the pipeline by the late 1920s. Nevertheless at the Sorbonne the number of Vietnamese registered peaked at 203 in 1931. By 1935 there were 102, and only 73 by 1937.[27]

By expelling the core of the Vietnamese student activists, the French achieved temporary calm on the home front, if not acquiescence. Yet the renewed resistance in Vietnam contributed to the growth of anticolonial sentiments within France. Prior to Yen-Bay, anticolonial agitation among Frenchmen had been nearly the exclusive property of the Communist party. A front group of the Communist International, the League Against Imperialism, did, after its founding in Brussels in 1927, attract such prominent non-Communist intellectuals as Felicien Challaye and Victor Basch. But the League never became an influential force in French life, and after the Comintern adopted its "class versus class" approach in 1928, the League too pushed a left-sectarian line and lost many of its non-Communist adherents. Independent writers who were critical of colonialism, like André Gide, were exceptional.[28]

But the Yen-Bay uprising, which was the beginning of years of turmoil in Indochina, sparked a flurry of critical French interest in the colonies. Several large Paris newspapers sent their best reporters to Indochina, and the French were soon exposed to a wave of critical writing about the colony. Several writers displayed a certain fascination with the students who had returned from France radicalized. Andrée Viollis, who accompanied colonial minister Paul Reynaud on a fact-finding tour of Indochina in 1931 scandalized local officials when she insisted on spending her days in Saigon in the company of three of the expelled students, and with them visited Nguyen An Ninh and other Saigon dissidents.[29]

If this was not surprising in the case of Viollis, a regular in left-wing Parisian circles, the case of Louis Roubaud was more interesting. Roubaud was the talented and prolific reporter for the *Le Petit Parisien*, who years before had helped shape the first clichés about the Vietnamese in France. Whereas Roubaud once had described Vietnamese students as shy, gentle, somewhat in awe of the power of French knowledge and industry, while still attached to their ancient ancestral customs, he now portrayed the most militant of them in very respectful terms.[30]

In his book on Vietnam, Roubaud included a lengthy interview with one of the recently repatriated students, who arrived well-tailored and driving a new red roadster. The reporter sparred politely with the young man about the rights and wrongs of the Yen-Bay rising, and was impressed by the young man's concern over the lack of civil liberties in the colony. One point Roubaud repeated to his readers was that in France, Vietnamese were permitted to write, speak, assemble, and travel freely—but not smoke opium, while in Indochina the situation was exactly the reverse. Roubaud was particularly intrigued with the contrast between the young man's politics, which were hard-core Communist, and his fine clothes and gentlemanly manners. "I am neither a dupe nor a slave of my luxuries," the ex-student replied, and "when it is necessary for the liberation of my race I will be able to restrain my desires according to the formula of Confucius— simple food, water to drink, and sleeping with only the elbows as a pillow does not prevent one in any way from being happy.' "[31]

Description of the French-educated Vietnamese as idealistic patriots who were playing a mine canary's role in unmasking the hypocricies of French colonialism was in effect the reverse side of the common right-wing perception—which held the Vietnamese student as a "déclassé," intoxicated by Western revolutionary doctrines and perversely ungrateful for all that France had done for him. Both images were prevalent, and both, in their way, were justified. What had been superseded was the Vietnamese student of the early 1920s, invariably depicted as shy and deferential, if he was not simply a rich boy idling away his parent's money. Vietnamese were no longer patronized in the French press.

In any event, the expulsion of the Vietnamese led to a relative calm about colonial issues on the streets of Paris. Between the spring and fall of 1931 the French held a huge colonial exhibition in the Bois de Vincennes, which drew some six million visitors during its run of six months. Visitors saw replicas of the temples of Angkor and of Moroccan palaces, exotic silks, dancers, artwork. To crown it all, the French organizers had pedicab drivers imported from Indochina to transport visitors from pavilion to pavilion. The colonial exhibition followed the centenary of the French conquest of Algeria, which had produced a widely reported visit of French president Gaston Doumergue throughout French North Africa. Describing the impact of these events, Raoul Girardet wrote "never in (French) history were so many voices raised with such force and assurance to celebrate the magnificence of colonial expansion."[32]

This symbolic celebration of the French empire was precisely the kind of event most likely to provide a rallying point for radical Vietnamese in Paris. Indeed, those nationalists left in France after the expulsion of the nineteen students mounted a campaign focusing on the pedicab drivers, whom, they maintained, had been brought over to convince French visitors that the Vietnamese people were inherently servile. One indication that the government's firm hand the previous year had reduced the number of students willing to challenge the French on their home ground was that the antipedicab campaign never took off, and several planned demonstrations against the colonial exhibit were never held.[33]

Somewhat paradoxically, by the time the Vietnamese student movement in France had lost its force, there had grown a broader constituency for anticolonialism among the French populace—particularly among influential intellectuals. French Communists, acting through the League Against Imperialism, organized a counter-exhibit that concentrated on exposing the crimes relative to the accomplishments of French colonialism. Although this initiative was poorly attended, such well-known intellectuals as Louis Aragon, Paul Eluard, and André Breton signed a manifesto supporting it and urging a boycott of the big show in the Bois de Vincennes.[34]

As various forms of anti-French resistance intensified in Vietnam during the 1930s the reduced contingent of left-wing Vietnamese in France found more allies in the *métropole*. In 1933 a broad-based Committee for Amnesty and Defense of the Indochinese was formed in Paris to protest against French repression in Indochina. Apparently initiated by the pro-Communist architect Francois Jourdain, the committee attracted such prominent non-Communist adherents as Marius Moutet and Louis Roubaud to sign their names beside writers like Henri Barbusse and Leon Werth, who generally supported Communist causes. The committee thus became one of the early harbingers of the Popular Front spirit, and played an important role during the 1930s in pressuring the Indochinese government to release jailed Vietnamese Communists. A further indication of the growth of ties between French leftist intellectuals and Vietnamese radicalism was the publication in Paris in 1935 of the bilingual *Anh Sang*, a pro-Communist paper which had André Malraux and Andrée Viollis among its sponsors.[35]

Though there was, by comparison with the 1920s, less political ferment in the Vietnamese student contingent in France, it is appropriate to ask how the Popular Front ideology of the mid 1930s affected student attitudes. Two questions are pertinent: first, how did the Vietnamese view the rise of Hitler in Germany? and second, did the Popular Front lead to easing of antagonism between Vietnamese "bourgeois" nationalists and Communists, analogous to the united front created within the French Left? Generally, the patterns of politics within the Vietnamese migration had been set in the 1920s, and neither the rise of Nazism nor the Popular Front changed them much. Certainly Vietnamese active in Communist-controlled organizations made alterations in their rhetoric. Communist Vietnamese in France described both French bourgeoisie and supporters of French colonialism as fascist, or aspiring to follow the example of Mussolini and Hitler. But these condemnations had an artificial quality: to the Vietnamese, fascism was seen as a remote phenomenon, of little relevance. Few Vietnamese radicals seemed able to grasp the distinction between Hitler and, for example, a French colonial official like René Robin. Both, according to Vietnam's Paris-based Marxists, were fascist. One can easily take this as an indication of how little of French values, or democratic values, were absorbed by the Vietnamese. But it should be remembered that many Frenchmen on the Left made the same kind of error, and many Westerners from across the political spectrum saw Hitler during the 1930s as representing nothing more ominous than resurgent German nationalism. For the French Left in general, the activism of the antiparliamentary Right provided a perceived common enemy: once the Comintern had decreed the Popular Front policy in 1935 it put itself in step with many in the PCF who wished to head as broad a coalition as possible against what was perceived as a newly resurgent, fascist-leaning French Right. But one finds little indication that this sentiment reached the Vietnamese radicals in France.

Vietnamese radicals did not ease their hostility towards those Vietnamese students who were "bourgeois nationalists" or close to the Constitutionalists. The paper *Anh Sang* was full of strident attacks on Vietnamese students who "collaborated" by residing in Indochina House. Nor was there much effort to build ties between the two main Vietnamese oppositional organizations in Paris during the 1930s, the Communist-dominated *Association d'entraide et de culture*, and the more ideologically diverse *Cercle des études sociales*.[36]

What was an issue to the Vietnamese in France was the question of French power in Vietnam. Thus Vietnamese activists viewed the actual French Popular Front coalition with restrained enthusiasm, after it became clear that the new government would include the French Radical Party which had no interest in Vietnamese independence, and the Socialists, who didn't either. But the Popular Front did open up opportunities for political action in Vietnam, and it is there that the generation of French-educated Vietnamese began to make a mark.[37]

### Stalinists and Trotskyists Return to Vietnam

The Yen-Bay mutiny and its aftermath was only the beginning of a tide of insurrection that swept over Vietnam in 1930 and 1931. After Yen-Bay, there rose a series of peasant revolts which, though concentrated in the North, spread throughout the colony. Peasants refused to pay their taxes, seized government buildings, burned tax rolls; in the northern province of Nghe-Tinh they actually took control of the local government, killed local notables, and redistributed their land. In short, Vietnam experienced a rolling wave of revolt throughout the year; local French troops, though they responded aggressively, could not contain it without the aid of reinforcements from the Foreign Legion.

The Indochinese Communist party was officially established in Hong Kong in January 1930. The ICP was a fusion of several Communist factional groupings that had been based in China during the 1920s; Ho Chi Minh, who had gone to China from Moscow as the Comintern's representative, played a crucial role in bringing them together. At its inception the ICP had roughly 1500 members. The ICP had not played a large role in instigating the peasant rebellions that broke out in Annam later in 1930; these were spurred by the ever worsening economic crisis among the Vietnamese peasantry. The party did not stand aside however, and with a striking combination of daring and insouciance, moved into the breach, particularly in the province of Nghe-Tinh, to give the peasant revolt a more disciplined political focus. The movement, although it involved rebellion throughout Vietnam, has passed into history as the Nghe-Tinh Soviet movement. It took the French several months to crush the rebellion, which has become one of the proud traditions of Vietnamese Communist history.[38]

The French reaction very nearly smothered the ICP in its cradle. What was called by the colonial government the "Red Terror" was followed by a powerful "White Terror." In their counter-offensive the French jailed thousands of participants in the rebellion—including many Communists. By 1931, it seemed that not only had the French smashed the radical nationalist VNQDD but the Communists as well. "Communism has disappeared" announced Governor General Pasquier in 1932. Writing of the period some years later a dissident Communist wrote "The first of May,

1931, when the Party made a census of its forces, was only a feeble gasp testifying to the unrelenting agony of the Indochinese Communist party."[39]

It is against this background that the overall significance of the returning students from France may be understood. For within five years of the White Terror, the Communist movement—including a substantial Trotskyite contingent, had reemerged as the most powerful indigenous political force in Vietnam. The work of rebuilding the Party was done in part by cadres who had crossed the border into China to escape the repression, and then returned; in part it was the work of those who were eventually released from prison—for a great deal of organizing was done behind prison walls. But a crucial element in the revitalization of Vietnamese communism was the second wind the movement received from the return of the radical students from France. Indeed, these students soon achieved a hegemonic position in the world of Saigon politics and political journalism. They effectively short-circuited French attempts to strengthen colonial rule through making timely liberal concessions. Their ideological and organizational sophistication, and their skill in the arenas of open politics and intellectual debate seemed to demonstrate to all of Vietnam that communism was destined to be the dominant ideology of the Vietnamese independence movement.[40]

After the suppression of the Nghe-Tinh Soviets, the focal point of Communist anticolonial activity was the Saigon-based *La Lutte*—the name at once of a newspaper, an electoral united front, and a political movement. *La Lutte* brought together Vietnamese Communists, Trotskyites, and some independent left-wing nationalists. This kind of cooperation, even on a temporary basis, between Communists loyal to the Third International and Trotskyites was a phenomenon unique to Vietnam, and deserves some explanation.

Vietnamese Trotskyism was the creation of a handful of Vietnamese students who had returned from France, led by Ta Thu Thau. He was critical of the Vietnamese Stalinists on several counts, especially with respect to their close cooperation with the French Communists. But the Comintern's left turn in 1928 eliminated many of the purely ideological reasons for disagreement. Another factor that made Trotskyite-Stalinist cooperation possible was that none of the Vietnamese Trotskyites had ever been formal members of the Communist party to begin with, and had thus never been expelled from the party—a circumstance that undoubtedly eliminated some of the emotional barriers between the two groups. Ta Thu Thau and the other Vietnamese Trotskyites had participated in joint demonstrations with the Communists in Paris, and had been subject to the same French penalties. Conflict between the two factions, though considerable, was probably less bitter than conflict between Trotskyites and Stalinists elsewhere. Furthermore, in Vietnam, the Comintern apparently sanctioned the cooperation, feeling that Vietnamese communism was so weakened by the post Yen-Bay repression that it needed to use united front tactics to reemerge as a powerful force. As for the Vietnamese Trotskyites, like their cohorts elsewhere, the policy of forming "united fronts" with other revolutionary Communists was an article of faith.[41]

In any case, the young French-educated intellectuals who formed the core group of *La Lutte* turned out to be the beneficiaries of the limited measures of liberalization granted by the French in the wake of the 1930-1931 rebellion. The French concessions were intended to stave off further outbursts, and mollify the Vietnamese desire to play a more active political role in the colony. The principal measure of liberalization was broadening the limited electorate of the colonial council of Cochinchina and the Saigon municipal council. Contrary to French hopes, the Vietnamese who took most advantage of these measures were not the moderate nationalists or those espousing Franco-Vietnamese collaboration, but the young Communists of *La Lutte*. The group was the first radical opposition movement in Vietnam to practice anticolonial politics that were not furtive, clandestine, conspiratorial, or for that matter, illegal. Every bit of liberty the laws of the colony allowed, the members of *La Lutte* took advantage of. The variety of political, organizational, and editorial skills they had acquired in France gave them a decisive edge over their rivals within the Vietnamese national movement.

*La Lutte* was an organization of young men: the twelve singled out as core leaders in Daniel Hémery's study of the movement were, in 1933, between 23-and 33-years-old. All but two of the twelve had studied in France between 1925 and 1930. Four were among the nineteen expelled by the French government in the aftermath of the demonstration in front of the Elysée palace. The best known were Nguyen Van Tao, the leader of the orthodox Communist or "Stalinist" faction of *La Lutte*, who was released from jail in Paris and returned to the colony from France in 1931, and Ta Thu Thau, who had been expelled from Paris in 1930; during the 1930s he built in Saigon one of the strongest Trotskyite movements in the world. Two of the twelve, Nguyen Van Tao, and Duong Bach Mai—who studied in France and then spent two years at the Communist cadre school in Moscow—later became ministers of the North Vietnamese government. Another important former student from France was Tran Van Giau, who attended the Stalin school in Moscow for two years after spending the late 1920s in France. When he returned to Vietnam in 1933 he became the main figure responsible for rebuilding the underground cadre apparatus of the Indochinese Communist party in the South. Tran Van Giau would become one of North Vietnam's principal intellectuals, and the guardian of official Party history.[42]

The newspaper *La Lutte* was published in French, because journals published in that language were not subject to censorship. Its Vietnamese audience was therefore somewhat limited. Nevertheless within two years of beginning publication *La Lutte* became the most widely read French journal written by Vietnamese, reaching three thousand subscribers, and was extensively read aloud and translated. The paper's general fare was a constant and well-documented denunciation of daily life under colonialism, which revolved around ummasking the inequities of French rule, and ridiculing the patriotic pretenses of the more moderate Vietnamese nationalists. The journal also reprinted longer essays from such French writers as Andrée Viollis and others who wrote under the aegis of the Comintern's League Against Imperialism. The principal area in which the journal differed from previous styles of Vietnamese nationalist agitational writing was that each week it gave its readers an analysis of colonial reality in Marxist terms. By linking the goals of the nationalist movements to the needs and demands of Vietnam's popular classes, *La Lutte* transformed the language of Vietnamese patriotism.[43]

While the journal *La Lutte* changed the very language of anticolonial discourse in Saigon and its environs, the electoral tactics pursued by the coalition demonstrated to France and other Vietnamese that the most dynamic and modern political force in the colony was the Communist Left. In 1933 the colonial government was severely embarrassed when two members of *La Lutte*, Nguyen Van Tao and Tran Van Thach, were elected to two of the six Vietnamese seats on the Saigon municipal council. The coalition's initial victory came after a campaign in which they used techniques probably learned in France. Groups organized by *La Lutte* infiltrated the electoral meetings of rival parties, suggested new agendas, and embarrassed their opponents with well-orchestrated challenges from the floor.[44]

Nguyen Van Tao's election to the Saigon municipal council was annulled because he wasn't old enough to hold the office. But in 1935, the Communist coalition did better still: after a tireless campaign, it performed extremely well, without winning, in early spring elections for the colonial council of Indochina. The coalition had a good showing with a Vietnamese electorate that was restricted, by a variety of complex criteria, to an allegedly "responsible" one percent of the population.[45] Later that year *La Lutte* achieved a dramatic political breakthrough, winning four out of the six open seats on the Saigon municipal council. These two elected bodies had been dominated by the moderate Constitutionalists since World War I;

it came as a grievous shock to the French, and to the Constitutionalists, that moderate Vietnamese could no longer prevail in the heretofore tame and elitist realm of the colony's legal politics. The consequence of these elections—described by French officials as "devastating to our prestige"—was to demonstrate that Saigon's younger voters no longer placed any trust in those Vietnamese who advocated "Franco-Annamite" collaboration; it meant that there existed no moderate and modernist bourgeoisie who might benefit from measures that liberalized the political system.[46]

The weakness of the moderate nationalists would become an important point when the French Popular Front came to power the next year, with an ill-defined commitment to reform the mechanisms of French rule. By that time *La Lutte* had taken advantage of its newly won prestige to organize a vast regional effort to convene an "Indochina Congress." This umbrella organization would bring together various constituencies to pressure the French to grant more political concessions. By then the Constitutionalists found themselves faced with a choice of serving either as powerless figureheads of the *La Lutte*-dominated Congress movement or complete political irrelevance. Confronting this reality, the Blum government's Governor General Jules Brévié concluded that the bourgeois elite in Vietnam was so weak that the government's only option, if it did not want to cede power to the Communists, was to buttress such traditional institutions as the Vietnamese mandarinate and monarchy.[47]

It probably cannot be proven that Vietnamese communism could not have achieved the dominance it did by the 1945 revolution without the second wind it received from the infusion of left-wing graduates from French *lycées*. Communism advanced in the northern provinces to a different rhythm, with a social base more rooted in the poor peasantry; Vietnamese Communist cadres were also trained in China, and some went to Moscow by way not of Paris, but Canton. But it is clear that the Communist movement was strengthened considerably, and at a decisive time, by the Vietnamese *retours de France*. It is also clear that it was these men—the core activists of *La Lutte*, clandestine Communist organizers like Tran Van Giau, and the hundreds who worked with them and the thousands who followed them—that stood in the way of any French efforts to preserve something of their position in Indochina by making concessions to moderate nationalists.

What is important here is that Vietnamese communism—in its Stalinist and Trotskyite variants—was the only political tendency in Vietnam that grew demonstrably stronger as a result of the flow of Vietnamese students into France during the interwar period. The Constitutionalist party, for example, though many of its leaders were French-educated and linked to France by ties of temperament, harvested no significant reinforcements from the students returning from France. The Vietnamese who campaigned without success against *La Lutte* during the 1930s were, for the most part, the very same figures who had challenged the *colons* in Saigon's political forums in the early 1920s, and by the 1930s they were middle-aged or aging.[48]

There were, to be sure, many non-Communist Vietnamese who tried to make a mark in Vietnamese politics after returning from France. A government study of the Cochinchinese collaborating "elite" in 1943 mentions that 27 of the 109 figures singled out had a French education—including 11 of the 13 who were born after 1900. The colonial administration, and the professions of law, medicine and engineering, undoubtedly benefited from those with French training. But French-trained non-Communist nationalists made their appearance in Vietnam's decisive period as individuals, or as the leaders of the incredibly fragmented and quarrelsome array of non-Communist nationalist parties—none of which could effectively challenge the Communist movement.[49]

Thus one must conclude that French colonial education of the Vietnamese was, in political terms, a serious failure. The most striking consequence of the intensified educational contact between France and Vietnam in the 1920s was that those Vietnamese most willing to work for good relations with bourgeois France were weakened and later defeated. Those Vietnamese hostile not only to French colonialism, but to the capitalist and democratic regime that created and continued it, succeeded in turning the political skills learned in France against French rule. They also ensured that Vietnam did not inherit from the French a tradition of political liberalism. Such an outcome may have been impossible to prevent. When one entertains the idea that French-Vietnamese contacts might have bequeathed to Vietnam an elite committed to political freedom and a democratic style of politics, what actually happened seems all the more lamentable. What may be most regrettable is the meagerness of French efforts to shape the attitudes of the colony's future rulers, when successful efforts might have had an extraordinary effect on the future course of Vietnam.

## Notes

1. For a discussion of the Yen-Bay rebellion and the French response, see Paul Isoart, *Le Phénomène National Vietnamien* (Paris: Librarie general de Droit et de Jurisprudence, 1961), 286-287 and William Duiker, *The Rise of Nationalism in Vietnam* (Ithaca: Cornell University Press, 1976), 158-165.
2. Slotfom, V, 25.
3. Slotfom, III, 14.
4. CAI monthly report from February 1930, in Slotfom III, 150.

5. Slotfom III, 14 contains several of these leaflets.
6. Slotfom, III, 7.
7. Ibid. See also *Humanité*, 23 May 1930.
8. *Les Étudiants de France*, May 1930.
9. *La Presse Coloniale*, 26 March 1930.
10. *Economiste Colonial*, 25 March 1930.
11. *Le Figaro*, 29 May 1930.
12. Slotfom III, 7.
13. Slotfom III, 33 and AN F7-13410.
14. Slotfom III, 14; Slotfom III,25; Slotfom III,2.
15. Slotfom III, 118.
16. *Journal Officiel*, (hereafter JO), Chambre, 13 June 1930.
17. JO, Chambre, 6 June 1930.
18. Slotfom III,2.
19. JO, Chambre, 13 June 1930.
20. JO, Chambre, 6 June 1930.
21. Ibid.
22. JO, Chambre, 20 June 1930.
23. Slotfom III, 14.
24. Slotfom III, 14; Slotfom III, 150.
25. Slotfom, III, 25.
26. Isoart, *Le Phénomène National Vietnamien*, 280.
27. Slotfom III,25; Archives of the University of Paris, carton 227.
28. For a discussion of the League Against Imperialism in France, see Claude Liauzu, *Aux Origines des Tiers-Mondismes* (Paris: Editions L'Harmattan, 1982), 30-39.
29. Among the notable books about Vietnam to appear after Yen-Bay were Andrée Viollis, *Indochine S.O.S.* (Paris: Gallimard, 1935), Louis Roubaud, *Viet-Nam: La Tragédie Indochinoise* (Paris: Valois, 1931) and Luc Durtain, *Dieux Blancs, Hommes Jaunes* (Paris: Ernest Flammarion, 1930). See Viollis, 25-30 for an account of her days spent in Saigon with the expelled students.
30. For Roubaud's earlier perceptions of Vietnamese students, see his article in *Le Quotidien* 9 July 1924.
31. Roubaud, *Viet-nam*, 207-219.
32. Raoul Girardet, *L'Idée Coloniale en France de 1871 à 1962* (Paris: La Table Ronde, 1972), 176.
33. Slotfom, III,5.
34. Ibid. For a discussion of the rise of anticolonialism among French intellectuals, see Liauzu, *Aux Origines des Tiers-Mondismes*, 69-95.
35. Even during the period when international communism was in its most sectarian phase, and attacked Socialists as "social fascists," the Comintern organizer Willi Muenzenberg was able to organize committees of intellectuals in which Communists and non-Communist writers participated together. Though I have found no indication that Muenzeberg was involved in the creation of the Committee for Amnesty and Defense of the Indochinese, this organization seemed to have the same sort of united-front aura as the Amsterdam-Pleyel movement and the Writer's Organization for the Defense of Culture, both of which were his creations during these months. For a discussion of Muenzenberg's activities, see R.N. Carew Hunt, "Willi Muenzenberg," *International Communism*, St. Anthony's Papers No. 9, David Footman, ed.

(London: Chatto and Windus, Ltd., 1960). See also David Caute, *Communism and the French Intellectuals* (London: Andre Deutsch Ltd., 1964), 106-108. The Committee for Amnesty apparently influenced Paris to force the Indochina government to carry out periodic amnesties, which helped the new Indochinese Communist movement survive during these most difficult years. See William Duiker, "The Comintern and Vietnamese Communism," Ohio University Center for International Studies, Papers in International Studies, Southeast Asia Series no. 37, 1975. For information on the paper *Anh Sang* see Slotfom, V, 33.

36. One must rely mainly on the monthly political summaries of the Ministry of Colonies to trace Vietnamese political activities in Paris after 1932. These are not very detailed summaries of informer reports, focusing chiefly on the *Association d'entraide* as well as the broader based and short lived *Cercles d'études sociales*. See Slotfom III, 43; Slotfom III, 61; and Slotfom III,75.

37. Daniel Hémery, *Révolutionnaires Vietnamiens et Pouvoir Colonial en Indochine: Communistes, Trotskystes, Nationalistes à Saigon de 1932 à 1937* (Paris: François Maspero, 1975), 144-147.

38. See Douglas Pike, *History of Vietnamese Communism* (Stanford: Hoover Institution Press, 1979), 6-23, and Milton Osborne, "Continuity and Motivation in the Vietnamese Revolution: New Light from the 1930's," *Pacific Affairs* 47, 1 (Spring 1974). The name Nghe-Tinh Soviets was not given to the peasant rebellion by the peasants themselves, but was ascribed to the events after the fact by the Indochinese Communist party. See Thomas Hodgkin, *Vietnam: The Revolutionary Path* (London: The Macmillan Press, Ltd., 1981), 253.

39. Pasquier is quoted in Joseph Buttinger, *Vietnam: A Dragon Embattled* (New York: Praeger, 1967), 220. The later quote is from an unidentified Trotskyist, quoted in Milton Sacks, "Marxism in Viet Nam," in Frank Trager, ed., *Marxism in Southeast Asia* (Stanford: Stanford University Press, 1959), 126-127.

40. The effect of the returning students on the revival of Communist fortunes in the colony has not been stressed by scholars until recently. In his study of the growth of the Indochinese Communist party, Huynh Kim Khanh gives the following assessment: "The injection of these lively and articulate young Vietnamese intellectuals soon helped revitalize the Vietnamese anticolonial movement, which had fallen into disarray after the reprisals of 1930 and 1931. Shortly after their repatriation they were playing an important role in reshaping the outlook, style, and substance of Vietnamese anticolonialism. The cooperation, competition, and disputes among them and the groups they created formed an important part of Vietnamese politics during the 1930's." *Vietnamese Communism* (Ithaca: Cornell University Press, 1982), 194.

41. Hémery's *Révolutionnaires Vietnamiens et Pouvoir Colonial en Indochine: Communistes, Trotskystes, Nationalistes à Saigon de 1932 à 1937* is probably a definitive study of the *La Lutte* movement and of Vietnamese Trotskyism during this period. Also valuable is the discussion of Trotskyism in Milton Sacks, "Marxism in Vietnam" in Trager (ed.) *Marxism in Southeast Asia*, 127-143.

42. Hémery's biographical analysis is in *Révolutionnaires Vietnamiens*, 443-446. See also Pike, *History of Vietnamese Communism*, 63-66, and David Marr's comments on Tran van Giau, in *Vietnamese Tradition on Trial* (Berkeley: University of California Press, 1981), 325-326 and 419-420.

43. Hémery, *Révolutionnaires Vietnamiens*, 78-123.

44. Huynh Kim Khanh, *Vietnamese Communism*, 202.
45. Hémery discusses the suffrage requirements in *Révolutionnaires Vietnamiens*, 249-253. The electorate for both the Colonial Council and the Saigon Municipal Council was restricted. In the case of the former, suffrage was limited to provincial officials and landowners who could read and write French. The Saigon suffrage was less restrictive, but complex registration procedures limited those actually registered to less than 4,000 people.
46. Ibid., 258-259.
47. Daniel Hémery, "Aux Origines des Guerres d'Indépendance Vietnamiennes: Pouvoir Colonial et Phénomène Communiste en Indochine avant la Seconde Guerre Mondiale," *Le Mouvement Social* (October 1977).
48. See Megan Cook, *The Constitutionalist Party in Indochina: The Years of Decline, 1930-1942* (Victoria, Australia: Centre of Southeast Asian Studies, 1977), passim.
49. Ralph Smith, "The Vietnamese Elite of French Cochinchina, 1943," *Modern Asia Studies* 6, 4, (1972).

# 7

# Vietnamese Students and
# The Interwar Colonial Generation

The sweeping entry of Vietnamese students into French universities, their embrace of radical doctrines there, and their return to their homeland to take charge of movements against the colonial power was part of a pattern of voyage and return, of education and rebellion that was being enacted all over the colonial world. In the decades between the two world wars, students from India, from the Middle East, and from Africa flocked to London and Paris by the hundreds, absorbed all kinds of experiences in the centers of colonial power, and returned to their societies with a new sense of how to use Western styles of political thought and organization against those colonial powers.

Just as, in London, Indians constituted the leading edge of an anti-colonial movement that would eventually touch students who came from Africa and the Middle East, in the world of French colonialism, the Vietnamese served as the pioneers of a student journey that would later be undertaken by colonial subjects from French North Africa, the French West Indies, and from sub-Saharan Africa. This movement of students to the metropolitan capitals after World War I changed the nature of resistance to colonialism. After the Western-educated colonial generation returned to their societies, no longer was the revolt against foreign rule spearheaded by men immersed in the values of the traditional, precolonial order. Earlier generations of rebels, inspired by the Confucian ethic and loyalty to the emperor, by tribal allegiances, or by Islamic fundamentalism no longer posed the primary threat to colonial rule. Rising in their place were movements such as an Indian Congress party, which had begun to forge links with the Indian rural masses, or the Tunisian Neo-Destour, which excelled in organizing strikes and other forms of urban agitation.[1]

There were common threads running through all of these movements. Most were anticapitalist. In few of the regions of empire had the merchant class ever ranked highly in social prestige. So long as the main thrust of anticolonial activity consisted of elite requests to the ruling power for the granting of expanded political liberties, few anticolonial leaders were inclined to raise social demands, or to criticize the class structure of their societies. But once they sensed that the road to success was opened by the political organization of the masses, a more socialist orientation became manifest. To the extent that they influenced the colonial students, the disposition of the Western intelligentsia enhanced this tendency. Even before the Great Depression, few of the intellectual mentors of the colonial students had much praise for capitalism, which was rarely considered inextricably bound up with those Western scientific and technological accomplishments that were almost universally admired. At the London School of Economics, Professor Harold Laski played a notable role in popularizing socialist thought among young intellectuals from India and Africa. While there was no single socialist figure of Laski's stature in Paris, (Sartre played this role after World War II) capitalism by itself had almost no defenders among the intelligentsia, and by the 1930s the Soviet Union was widely perceived to be an instructive example of how socialist planning could bring about dramatic economic growth.[2]

But if the broader intellectual climate between the wars helps to explain the favorable disposition towards nationalism and socialism which members of the interwar colonial generation had in common, it cannot account for the distinctions that separate the varied elements within the interwar colonial generation. And it may be that these distinctions have an importance that is every bit as compelling as the intra-generational similarities.

In the case of the French empire, the striking fact is that of all the colonies that sent students to Paris in the interwar period, only from Vietnam did a decisive minority become partisans of the Communist Third International. Furthermore, it is likely that the noncommunism among colonial students from French North Africa and sub-Saharan Africa had as much long-term historical impact as communism among the Vietnamese. The political map of today's postcolonial world is prefigured with uncanny precision by the strength of the various political tendencies in the student hostels and cafés of the Parisian Left Bank during the 1920s and 1930s.

To what extent did France determine these outcomes? Can one attribute the relative weakness of Communist ideology among the non-Vietnamese students to differences in the policies pursued by the French government? Is the answer to be found in the political and cultural background of the various protonationalist student movements? Or is the decisive variable found in differences in the way French societal forces beyond the government's realm interacted with the student groups? While a conclusive answer to these questions would require an analysis of anticolonial movements throughout the French empire that is beyond the scope of this study, a tentative analysis leads to a somewhat surprising conclusion: the experience of France during the 1920s was more likely to lead France's colonial students to Communist allegiances than was the case for those who studied in France during the 1930s.

## Education of an Empire

While French educational policy towards the particular colonies and protectorates of the empire was guided neither by a single explicit doctrine nor a common center of authority, administrators in all parts of the empire faced a common dilemma: that the advance of French education seemed to go hand in hand with political restlessness. The empire's geographical and social diversity produced a wide variety of educational programs. Educational policy was made by officials from the Ministry of Foreign Affairs for the Tunisian and Moroccan protectorates, by the Ministry of the Interior for Algeria, and by the Ministry of Colonies for Indochina and sub-Saharan Africa. The French official in charge of each area had considerable autonomy in formulating policy, and responsibility for financing schools from the local colonial budget. The result was many different approches; as one scholar attempting to summarize French colonial education policies put it: "It is difficult to trace any general characteristic of France's policy in the field of education; indeed one is almost tempted to say that there has been no over-all policy."[3]

If there was no officially sanctioned central doctrine, there was a common shape to the policies that emerged from the varied mixture of French imperial attitudes and local situations. It is not difficult to find French expressions of "wanting to make the natives into Frenchmen" in Africa or elsewhere; with some exceptions, instruction, even at the elementary level, was in French, and the hope was often expressed that when "they will learn to think in French they will have been definitively acquired into our culture."[4] But by the interwar period, the general thrust no longer favored assimilation. Budgetary considerations limited the number of schools, and where they were a factor, so did the wishes of the settlers, who rarely saw any gain in educating a colony's indigenous inhabitants. For every expression of the assimilationist impulse, more authoritative voices urged caution. More representative of French attitudes in the early 1920s was a statement like the following, made by Camille Guy, the Governor General of French West Africa in 1922:

> A bit of fresh air! That is what we need. Good curricula are obtained by
> pruning, not by grafting. Education in French, elementary science, voca-

tional work and technical training appropriate for the milieu; that is all we need. Any other policy produces not French citizens but vain and eccentric outcasts who lose their native qualities and acquire only the vices of their teachers.[5]

Two years earlier Louis Brumot, the director of education for the Moroccan protectorate, had spoken in similar terms:

> The school should in no case be the propagator of political ideas, which, from the sole fact of their novelty, will never be anything but pernicious elements of trouble . . . the school limits itself to increasing the productive capacity of the native . . . politics in the European sense, is not suited to the progress being accomplished here. Consequently, let us not think of emancipating the Moroccan citizen, nor of freeing the slave, nor of the liberty of women; when you get to know the situation in Morocco, you will understand that these dogmas, when transplanted here, are dangerous.[6]

When such ideas were not publicly formulated by the colonial administrators, they were expressed in less subtle and more racist fashion by the French settlers, particularly in Algeria and Tunisia. Nevertheless, in all the colonies there were particular circumstances that made it possible for some colonial subjects to get into French schools. In Africa, for example, the French need for indigenous administrative personnel pushed the administration to create an alternative to the "rural schools" which taught a watered down "indigenous" curriculum. In Senegal, the local schools taught a metropolitan curriculum, and there was inevitable pressure from the African political elites to allow good students to continue on in the French *lycée*. An alternative to the *lycée* was the William Ponty school at Gorée, which trained teachers, administrators and "medical assistants"— but by the interwar period the *Lycée Faidherbe* admitted about seventy African students each year, including some scholarship students.[7]

In the protectorate of Tunisia, the French found a society with a more complex indigenous educational structure to contend with: Zitouna, the Islamic university, had trained the Tunisian elite for centuries, and in 1875, six years before the French acquired Tunisia as a protectorate, a modernist Tunisian minister had founded an alternative, Sadiki College, which provided bilingual instruction in French, Arabic and the sciences. Thus before the onset of French rule, there was already a Tunisian constituency wishing access to Western knowledge. This class of men, with its social base in Tunisia's merchant class, was not initially hostile to French rule, and Sadiki, aided with subsidies from the protectorate, prospered. In Morocco, the system of Koranic schools was more entrenched, and the native push for access to French schooling came relatively later. But the educational structure under French rule had a similar shape in every region of the empire. There was always a larger school system for indigenous inhabitants, allegedly adapted to local conditions. This system taught, in the French language, a simplified and professionally oriented curriculum that led to award of a "native certificate." Parallel to the "native" system was a ladder of French schools leading to the French *lycée*, whose primary clientele was the colony's French citizenry. By the end of World War I, the French system admitted a certain number of the empire's "subjects." The number of those colonial students who received the French *baccalauréat* was in the hundreds in the case of Tunisia and Indochina, in the dozens in Morocco and French West Africa—and somewhere between the two in the French West Indies and Algeria. The overall result, which emerged not from a grand design, but from the particular situation of each colony, was that by the interwar period there were hundreds of young men from French territories all over the world with the training and inclination to pursue the next educational step, considered almost universally to be Paris.[8]

## North African Students

After the Vietnamese, the largest contingent of colonial students came from French North Africa, particularly from Tunisia. Compared to the Vietnamese group, which may have numbered as many as 3000 at its peak in 1931, there were not many North Africans. Unlike the Vietnamese, most had acquired the *baccalauréat* before voyaging to France, where they gravitated towards the University of Paris. Statistics at the Sorbonne record 35 Tunisians enrolled in 1925, 101 by 1930, and 183 by 1934. Rougher estimates put their total number at 200 in 1932—a figure that remained fairly constant until the war. Tunisia's population, however, was about one sixth that of Vietnam's, so the relative numbers are comparable. This was not the case for Algerians and Moroccans. There were no more than 30 Moroccan students in Paris during the entire decade from 1923 to 1932; and about 30 registered every year during the 1930s. Algerians who acquired the *baccalauréat* were more likely to attend the University of Algiers—about 100 Algerian Muslims were enrolled there each year from 1929 to 1939. In 1935, 53 Algerian students were registered at the University of Paris, a high point of the interwar period.[9]

In the minds of the French officials who were responsible for political order in the region, the politics of the North African students were every bit as pernicious and destructive to the colonial power rule as were those of the Vietnamese. Later observers have noted that the Maghreb's nationalism owed its genesis to the Paris experience: there the North African students came into contact with the French left-wing parties and doctrines, with Arab students from Egypt and Syria who spread the concept of Pan-Arab nationalism, and eventually with such figures as Chekib Arslan, the pan-Arabic writer and organizer based in Geneva, and whose polemical paper, the French language *La Nation Arabe* touched the spirits of young men from throughout the Arab world.[10]

Marcel Peyrouton, the resident general of Tunisia and a vigorous exponent of the view that France should stem the tide of students, argued repeatedly within the government that the returning students were the spearhead of anti-French agitation in the protectorate. Peyrouton wanted to limit the number of Tunisian *baccalauréats* granted each year to a maximum of twenty. He urged that the government learn from its failure with the Vietnamese students, and sequester the North Africans away from Paris, and from one another. He suggested that Tunisians be allowed to study only at the University of Algiers, while Moroccans be limited to study at Toulouse. As for the Vietnamese, whom he considered spoiled beyond redemption, Peyrouton recommended that they be allowed to study only at the University at Aix-en-Provence. Like all advocates of stern measures, within and without the administration, Peyrouton was hampered by the fact that such authoritarian measures were not in the Third Republic's political character. As he put it, "the shame is that we would have to proceed by legislation, which would require a long delay."[11] Peyrouton's recommendations were never heeded, and a short while later he was transferred from Tunisia to the less sensitive post of Morocco. When the Popular Front came to power, he was demoted to the post of ambassador to Argentina.

Generally, French efforts to mold the North African student flow followed the relatively passive pattern that had emerged in the government response to the Vietnamese. The government subsidized a "Mediterranean Circle" in Paris, which contained some rooms and conference spaces, and began to raise funds to create a residence for the Maghreb students at the University of Paris.

One reason why stricter French tactics were not put into place was that the nationalism of the North African students did not have the hard intransigent edge of their Vietnamese contemporaries. For if Peyrouton was correct in observing that Tunisians who had taken degrees in Paris were the most effective agitators against French rule, few observers could fail to perceive that they were quite unradical compared not just to the Vietnamese but even to the North African migrant workers in Paris. While the number of students coming from the Maghreb was still a trickle, during the 1920s the charismatic Messali Hadj was organizing the *Étoile Nord-Africaine*, a revolutionary movement of Algerian workers. According to French police sources, the French Communist party helped to create the *Étoile*; the two organizations had a very close relationship during the mid

1920s, while the PCF gave the *Étoile* financial assistance and printed its newspaper, *l'Ikdam*. Utilizing Communist and Islamic slogans in combination, uncompromising in its demands for Algerian independence, and possessing a significant mass base, the *Étoile* was a vivid example of the tough revolutionary nationalism the French hoped to avoid. By contrast, the North African students were moderate. This was a reversal of the Vietnamese pattern, where militant students raised national and Marxist demands far before representatives of the Vietnamese working class.[12]

The focal point of North African student activity was the *Association des Étudiants Musulmans Nord-Africains* (AEMNA) which was founded in Paris in 1927, with the expressed purpose of encouraging more North Africans to come to Paris, and to facilitate their stay. At their initial meeting, AEMNA resolved to raise funds for a library, a microscope, and two skeletons for the medical students among its members. By the 1930s, however, AEMNA had turned its attention to more politically charged issues. In 1930, Algerian students who had acquired French citizenship were told they were no longer welcome: they went on to form their own student group. Nevertheless social and political links between the students of the three Maghreb countries continued. AEMNA held annual meetings from 1931 onward, in Paris, Algiers and in Tunisia, where they pressed demands for the teaching of Arabic language and "Islamic history" in the schools of the region so that a national consciousness could be created. In 1933, AEMNA demanded independence for the protectorates, leading to the formation of a single North African Muslim nation.[13]

Still AEMNA was more interested in compromise with the French than the Vietnamese students were. French official observers were always invited to their conferences. *Étoile* leader Messali Hadj complained of the students' lack of militancy. "France has eaten too deeply into their brains for them to take the route of rupture and sacrifice," was his lament. Before 1930, he later recounted, no Algerian student came forward to offer the *Étoile* the benefit of his intellectual skills.[14] While AEMNA served as a training ground for young North Africans who would later contest French rule as members of the Tunisian Neo-Destour, or the various pressure groups created by the "Young Moroccans," the organization kept its distance from the international Communist movement. The Vietnamese student from the Communist-led League Against Imperialism who spoke and passed out leaflets at the AEMNA meeting in Paris in 1932 received a chilly reception, while some French analysts forecast, incorrectly as it turned out, that most of the young French-educated North Africans would probably be content to eschew politics and concentrate on their professions when they returned home.[15]

In any event there is considerable evidence that the North African nationalist students responded to France with more emotional warmth than did their Vietnamese counterparts. French scholars of the Islamic world commented on this frequently. Emile Dermenghem, writing in the North African publication *Maghreb* noted the young Moroccans "love us more than they realize, and become embittered because they feel rebuffed by France." Louis Massignon described the despair of a student who complained that he could never forgive the French for making him lose his hatred for those who had taken over his country. There is an extensive literature, written in French by North Africans, which treats this pattern of attraction and repulsion—a phenomenon that did not exist to the same degree in the Vietnamese case.[16]

### The Sparkle of *Négritude*

The impact of France on the black colonial students also produced a movement that was more an expression of cultural defiance than adherence to a political ideology. *Négritude*, a literary movement born in Paris, would reverberate through French literature and global black culture for decades. It was the product of a small number of students from diverse backgrounds; the contingent of black students in France was both less active and politically organized than either Vietnamese or North Africans.

To begin with, their numbers were smaller. Estimates of how many black students were in France are often contradictory. A dozen or so black students from French West Africa who had graduated from the William Ponty teacher training college were brought to Aix-en-Provence in 1923, but all of them were returned to Africa quickly, because the stay in France contributed what one French official described as a "troublesome influence."[17] Statistics from the University of Paris indicate that two black students from West Africa were registered during the 1930s.[18] In 1926, French statistics at the Ministry of Colonies record no African students at all. By 1932, the same ministry recorded twenty-one blacks from French West Africa, and another nineteen from Madagascar.[19] Considerably more students from the French West Indies (Martinique, Guadeloupe, and the French Antilles) came to Paris in the 1930s. Estimates of how many there were are particularly elusive. The Ministry of Colonies records that seventy students from the West Indies were given some financial aid for study in France in the years 1932 and 1933. By 1935, the University of Paris recorded seventy-two students from the region, registered in diverse faculties.[20]

There had been black political organizations in France since the end of World War I. Several thousand black soldiers who had been drafted during the war managed to remain in France and find jobs in Paris and in the ports of Marseilles and Toulon. Communists working through the *Union Inter-*

*coloniale* attempted to organize them in the early 1920s, and a number of evanescent political groups, with a few hundred members, sprang up in Paris during that decade, advocating syncretic doctrines of Pan-Africanism, communism, and nationalism. Because these men came from the West Indies as well as different parts of Africa, they had difficulties in defining mutually acceptable platforms, and considerable problems in communicating political doctrines forged in France to the people in their native regions.[21]

Black students from the West Indies and Africa, who began to appear in Paris in the 1930s, made a greater mark. The young men who set off the *Négritude* movement by publishing in little journals like *Légitime Défense* and *L'Étudiant Noir* possessed tremendous talents: Léopold Senghor and Aimé Césaire became figures of world literature. Several of those who wrote for *Légitime Défense* were influenced by the Communist party, or more generally by Marxism, but *négritude* was not a movement that could easily be married with communism. It was first of all an assertion of pride in blackness—and a rejection of European standards, and indeed of modernity, as a measure of civilization's success. Its participants were as intent on celebrating black culture against white civilization as they were in lamenting the injustice of their standing as colonial subjects in the white capitalist world. Césaire, the best of the *négritude* poets, remained close to the Communist party until 1956, but *négritude* in general owed more to such antimodernist intellectual traditions as German romanticism than it did to Marxism.[22] One needs only to read lines like the following, composed after Césaire's first return from France, to be persuaded of his ultimate unreliability as a dialectical materialist:

> Hear the white world
> horribly weary from its immense effort
> its stiff joints crack under the hard stars
> hear its blue steel rigidity pierce the mystic
>     flesh
> its deceptive victories tout its defeats
> hear the grandiose alibis of its painful
>     stumblings
>
> Pity for our omniscient and naive
>     conquerors![23]

Geographical diversity, perhaps, inhibited black students from political militancy, as did their paucity of numbers. A dozen or so like-minded students could put together a journal, but not hold conferences, or effectively demonstrate. Also it should be pointed out that the most influential of the blacks, the future Senegalese leader Léopold Senghor and Césaire attended not the University of Paris, but the École Normale. They had, therefore, a much more rigorous academic program to contend with, and a closer network of French peers. This might have influenced the style of their activism. It was not until after World War II that black students from Africa came to France in sufficient numbers to organize themselves politically, and exert a collective weight in the politics of their homelands.

### Variations in Communism's Appeal

This brief description of the black and North African students leads us back to the central problem of explaining the particular radicalism and willingness to embrace communism of the Vietnamese. Several explanations should be considered. Certainly one factor is the greater level of nationalist unrest that existed in Indochina before the student surge during the late 1920s. Resistance to French rule both in North Africa and south of the Sahara tended, in the 1920s, to be either reactionary or tame. The old elites, both tribal and religious, had demonstrated that they could not eliminate French rule. The Westernized classes—one thinks here of the "Young Algerians" and the original Tunisian Destour—were, in the early 1920s, parties of gentlemen whose moderate and modest petitions for change could be safely brushed off by the colonial authority. None of these areas had experienced anything like the youth rebellion that spilled across the schools of Cochinchina in 1925.

The idea that the Confucian tradition was particularly receptive to Marxism—at least by comparison with political traditions influenced by Islam—has been discussed above. There is no necessary antipathy between the Confucian tradition and Marxism; the Vietnamese Communist groups based in China stressed their Confucian virtues, and many scholars have pointed out that Confucianism was a system of thought that, like Marxism, concerned itself with man and society, and not with the spiritual and concerns of the next world. As the Communist writer Nguyen Khac Vien put it, "It was easier for a Confucian country than for a Muslim or a Christian one to adopt Marxism because Confucianism had not speculated for centuries about another world."[24] But one could also point out that Confucianism has legitimated a variety of modern political systems in East Asia—including, in Korea, Hong Kong, and Singapore, some intensely capitalistic ones.[25]

The related idea—that Islam served as a psychic barrier to the infusion of Marxist ideas into the North African students in particular, and the Arab world in general is equally problematic. In an exhaustive study that explores on many levels the relationship between Islam and modern Western ideologies, the French scholar Maxime Rodinson has concluded "the precepts of Islam have not hindered the capitalist orientation taken by the Muslim world during the last hundred years, and nothing in them is really opposed to a socialist orientation either."[26] Both during and after the colonial period, Muslims have cooperated with Communists. In its early years, Messali Hadj's *Étoile Nord-Africaine*, a movement with a membership far more pious than the North African students, marched in Communist demonstrations and publicized Communist slogans. These instances seem to suggest that the indigenous political and religious tradition does not explain particularly well why communism was grafted easily onto the Vietnamese national movement, and met with considerably less success with the North Africans.

An explanation that seems more convincing involves a more precise comparison of the French scene as experienced by the Vietnamese with that encountered by the black and North African colonial students.

When the question is examined historically, one observation jumps out: colonial students in the interwar generation encountered France at quite different times, and really can be best thought of as belonging to different subgenerations. As we have pointed out, the defining period for the Vietnamese student movement in France was 1925 to 1930; it was then that the tone of Vietnamese student politics passed from a tame constitutionalism and insouciant decadence, through radical nationalism, and arrived at a point where Communist attitudes were deeply rooted. In terms of energy and activism, the Vietnamese movement peaked politically with the Elysée demonstrations in 1930, and reached its numerical zenith the following year. It was in those years that the stage was set for the hegemony of Communist allegiance among Vietnam's most educated. This would become a critical factor in the 1930s and thereafter, when the French allowed greater self-expression to the colony's political tendencies.

Movements from the other colonies encountered a France with a different political spirit—that of the 1930s. These were years of intellectual ferment, leading eventually to the Popular Front and a Socialist-Radical government dependent on Communist support. While Habib Bourguiba, the Tunisian founder of the Neo-Destour, attended French schools from 1924 to 1927, most of the students who joined AEMNA, and who would later become the main cadres of the Tunisian movement, came to France later. AEMNA's yearly conferences became political events from 1932 to 1935—roughly corresponding to the numerical peak of Tunisian attendance at the University of Paris, in 1934. By that year there were twice the number of Tunisians enrolled as in 1930. The presence of Moroccan students in France followed the same rhythm. Again 1934 was the peak year, with thirty-three students enrolled at the University of Paris; during the 1920s, by contrast, less than a dozen Moroccans were studying there. The

Algerian Muslim students, too, were entirely absent from the French university scene during the 1920s, but their numbers peaked in 1934. For students from the French West Indies, the peak year was 1935; for Madagascar, 1934. The most likely explanation for the pattern is the general rise in the number of students who could obtain the *baccalauréat* throughout the interwar period—followed by the effect of the global financial crisis, which made travel to France more difficult.[27]

Why would students who studied in France during the early and mid 1930s be less likely to become carriers of the Communist viewpoint into their nationalist movements? In view of the rise to power of the French Left with the Popular Front, and the more general increase in the influence of Socialist ideas in France during the 1930s, such an assertion seems, at first sight, counter-intuitive. But when one examines more closely the factors by which French society actually influenced the political and moral development of the various student groups, this argument becomes easier to understand.

First of all, one must pay attention to the policies of the French Communist party. We have noted that communism made the greatest headway among the Vietnamese in the 1925-1928 period, when the PCF, sharply goaded by the Communist International, began an energetic anticolonial policy using broad united front tactics. In France, the PCF began to give significant support to "bourgeois nationalists" and other groups who shared with the Party no greater common ground than opposition to French colonialism. This was the PCF's most fruitful period for gaining adherents and influence not only with colonial students, but with all colonial subjects resident in France. During these years, the Party developed close ties with the *Étoile Nord-Africaine* of Messali Hadj. It was during this time that the PCF forged a similarly close relationship with the Vietnamese PAI, at the time the strongest Vietnamese political group in France. In 1927 these two groups, along with the *Comité de Défense de la Race Nègre* and a large number of other organizations, participated in the spectacular League Against Imperialism conference at Brussels, which was organized by Willy Muenzenberg. Albert Einstein and Madame Sun Yat Sen served as honorary presidents.[28]

During these years the nationalist colonial subjects in France could convincingly state, just as Ho Chi Minh had done after the Socialist-Communist split at Tours, and just as the PAI's leader Nguyen The Truyen did in 1926, that the Communist party was the only group in France that supported their national demands. But this reality became more complex when the PCF adopted the "class versus class" line after the 1928 conference of the Comintern. Not only did the PCF abruptly turn against the PAI, but it made increasingly onerous demands on the *Étoile* to allow trusted members of the Algerian section of the Communist party to assume influential positions in the organization. Resisting these pressures, Messali Hadj in 1933 passed an edict that forbade *Étoile* members to have dual membership in both the *Étoile* and the Algerian section of the Communist party, and sought ties with both the Tunisian neo-Destour, and the "Young Moroccans" Communist documents have since come to light which demonstrate that by 1932, the PCF had set out to destroy the *Étoile* from within. If Messali Hadj knew this, it is unlikely that he spoke warmly of the Party to his new student collaborators.[29]

Roughly at the time when Communist sectarianism was making its relationship with radical nationalist movements from the colonies problematic, other elements from the broader French Left began to play a more sympathetic and active role with the colonials. While the Communists characterized the Tunisian students and the AEMNA as "petit bourgeois" and made little effort with them, Robert Jean Longuet, a young Socialist militant (and the great grandson of Karl Marx) decided to start a journal with three young Moroccans who had studied in Paris. Moroccan nationalism, though still a narrowly based and elite movement, had been galvanized by the promulgation of the *Dahir* Berbère in 1930. The *Dahir*, which implied an intensified French effort to divide the Moroccan populace by shielding the Berber population from local Islamic authority, had raised Moroccan national feeling to a more intense level. That same year, Longuet's new journal, *Maghreb*, began to publish articles on North Africa from a number of different perspectives—Marxist, non-Marxist, nationalist,and reformist. While the majority view within the Socialist party was still opposed to the independence of Morocco or any other colony in the French empire, several prominent Socialist deputies agreed to join the *Maghreb* publication committee. In this way they gave their indirect sanction to views such as that expressed by one editor: "Proletariat, bourgeoisie, capitalism—for us these are only imported words without any meaning. For us there are not two classes, but two races, one privileged, which possesses all the advantages and the other subservient, carrying all the burdens." Such writing could not have been viewed favorably by the French Communists. While *Maghreb* was only one manifestation of the Moroccan national movement during the 1930s it did emerge as a major vehicle for French-educated North Africans to communicate with France and one another. It was a link of the sort that never existed between the French non-Communist Left and the Vietnamese.[30]

In the realm of simple politics, then, the leading young French-educated advocates of North African nationalism found, unlike the Vietnamese who had preceded them, a somewhat better reception from the French Socialists than they did from the PCF. Antagonism between the French Communists and the colonial movements would intensify when the Communists shifted, in the mid-1930s, to the strategy of the Popular Front. Then the Communists began to argue for the necessity of keeping the colonies from Hitler and asserted that many nationalist colonials were fascists, or at least doing the work of the fascists. Anticolonial activities instigated by the PCF stopped. This was of course damaging to the prestige of the PCF in Algeria, and did not help them in the rest of North Africa. Had the party developed a strong core of supporters earlier, as it had in Vietnam, it is conceivable that its influence would have survived this last turnabout. But it had not, and the policy of the late 1930s proved to be a devastating blow to the PCF's influence in North Africa.[31]

If the essentially procolonialist position taken by the PCF during the Popular Front made certain that it would not be as influential with the North African elite as it had been with the Vietnamese, there had been a host of other unrelated forces that were working towards the same outcome. From 1930 onwards, there was an outpouring of political literature that called into question every certainty and every value supporting the French pretense of bringing progress to the peoples of its empire. The first years of the 1930s saw the emergence of a number of small journals, written and published by a younger generation of writers who had missed the experience of World War I and did not revel in the fruits of the victory and the peace which France had won. In these periodicals—*l'Ordre Nouveau, Espirit, Réaction, Plans* and a number of others—a new generation of young intellectuals attacked the existing Republic from every ideological direction. What their writings had in common was a rejection of, or boredom with, the materialistic bourgeois state; their perspectives were antiparliamentary, anticapitalist, antibourgeois, antirational; they made up what Raoul Girardet described as a general "calling into question of the West."[32]

There is no particular evidence that the young North Africans or those who had traveled to France from Martinique and Madagascar read these journals—which had few readers—but they must have inhaled the change in climate. For them it meant that every aspect of the established order, including the order of French colonial rule, was being challenged, from many directions, in a variety of voices. In the 1930s then, French communism had lost its quasi-monopoly over the realm of radical dissent. If a colonial student recently arrived in France felt himself alienated, deracinated, or simply envious, he had, by 1934, a broad menu of French political literature to reinforce his sentiment and in which to express himself.

Finally, one further means by which France could have had a different effect on her black and Arabic students than on the Vietnamese should be noted. While no single French academic figure played a role of political mentor to the colonial students, as Harold Laski did across the Channel, students from the Maghreb and the blacks did interact with first-rate scholars who could give them a knowledge of their own societies for which they yearned and could acquire nowhere else. While modern French scholarship of Vietnam did not become active until the 1930s, students from the other regions encountered in France established experts on Africa and the Arab world. More often than not, French Africanists and Orientalists were broadly sympathetic to colonial nationalism in its various manifestations. Senghor has related that *négritude* would not have existed were it not for the inspiration of the French ethnologists like Maurice Delafosse and Marcel Griaule, or the French translations of the German scholar Leo Frobenius. In bringing to light the complexity of Africa's prehistory, Senghor has written that these men "saved us from despair by revealing to us our own riches."[33]

North African students too came into contact with Frenchmen who had a deep knowledge of the Arab world. Louis Massignon, a gifted Orientalist, knew many Muslim students, and advised and participated in the Mediterranean Circle, a residence for North African students sponsored by the city of Paris. Charles André Julien, published *l'Histoire de l'Afrique du Nord* in 1931, providing welcome ammunition in refutation of the French *colon* commonplace that North Africa had no meaningful history before the French conquest. Emile Dermenghen wrote for *Maghreb*. The Vietnamese, on the other hand, came into contact with no one who could approach them on a comparable level, which surely made it easier for those who were so inclined to claim that they had nothing to learn from the West beyond the crudely mechanical.[34]

### The Nationalist Age

One simple conclusion that can be drawn from this study is that those Frenchmen who warned from the outset that exposing France's colonial subjects to higher French education would create a class of more skilled rebels were correct. Of course not all those who attended school in France rebelled. French colonial history, during the interwar period and after, is replete with the biographies of intelligent and idealistic men who sought to become more French, or who collaborated with the French in the administration of their countries. But they were the exceptions. This is a difficult point to prove quantitatively. Nevertheless my sense of the material is that a significant majority of those colonial students who chose to use their education in France as a springboard into public life and political engagement, chose to fight against the right of France to dominate their societies.

There were as many styles of anti-French nationalism as there were colonies. For French-educated blacks, the chief weapon against France was the printed word—in French of course; the same may be said for the Moroccans. Students from Tunisia returned home to forge a modern mass political party, the Neo-Destour, which borrowed its structure and its mobilization techniques from all the totalitarian parties of Europe. In the struggle for independence it proved to be tough, disciplined, hierarchical, and expert at inciting the Tunisian masses; in power it ruled as the political scientist's model of the benign "authoritarian" one-party state. The Vietnamese who counted most embraced the international Communist movement, and studied to be Stalinists.

This work, therefore, does not arrive at a comprehensive generalization about the nature of France's cultural imprint on its colonial subjects. The colonial students chose from a varied and changing menu of what France offered, which they digested in their own way. Being the kind of society it was—a bourgeois democracy—France could not restrict the choices on the menu, could not shield the students from influences that inspired their rebellion. Even modest proposals for social control of the students, whether suggested by reformers like Paul Monet, or conservatives like Marcel Peyrouton, never came near to implementation.

This study can serve as a footnote to one of the larger themes of the twentieth century: the rise and durability of nationalism. In the case of the Vietnamese and the other colonial students, France was unable to smother the idea that political communities, bound by common language and a shared historical culture, had the right to political self-determination. No allegiance the French could create proved to be stronger.

Still it would probably be a mistake to take the French experience with her colonial subjects as a conclusive demonstration that the age of empire is forever past. There are other models for empire besides those created by Europe's nineteenth century liberals. Nothing in this study rules out the possibility that other imperialists, unconstrained by democratic parliaments, their peoples impervious to guilt, might succeed where the French failed.

## Notes

1. See the discussion in Geoffrey Barraclough, *An Introduction to Contemporary History* (New York: Penguin, 1978), 170-194.
2. Edward Shils, *The Intellectuals and the Powers and Other Essays* (Chicago: The University of Chicago Press, 1972), 402-404.
3. Michael Debeauvais, "Education in Former French Africa," in *Education and Political Development*, ed. James Coleman (Princeton: Princeton University Press, 1965), 77.
4. The persistence of the idea of using French language to assimilate is discussed in

Rudolph von Albertini, *Decolonization*, trans. Francisca Garvie, (Garden City: Doubleday & Co, 1971), 344.

5. Guy is quoted in Jean Suret-Canale, *French Colonialism in Tropical Africa* (New York: Pica Press, 1971), 382-383.

6. Cited in John Halstead, *Rebirth of a Nation: the Origins and Rise of Moroccan Nationalism* (Cambridge: Harvard University Press, 1967), 101.

7. Prosser Gifford and Timothy Weiskel, "African Education in a Colonial Context: French and British Styles," in *France and Britain in Africa*, ed. Prosser Gifford and William Roger Louis (New Haven: Yale University Press, 1971).

8. For a discussion of French education in Morocco, see Halstead, *Rebirth of a Nation*, 100-109. The Tunisian situation is discussed in Clement Moore, *Tunisia since Independence* (Berkeley: University of California Press, 1965), 22-35. For the Algerian school system under colonialism, see Charles-Robert Ageron, *Histoire de l'Algérie Contemporaine* (Paris: Presses Universitaires de France, 1979) Tome II, 533-541.

9. University of Paris enrollments are found in ARUP 227. Other estimates are found in M'barka Hamed, "Immigration Maghrebine et Activités Politiques en France de la Première Guerre Mondiale à la Veille du Front Populaire," 1979, (Ph.D. diss., University of Paris VII, p. 110), and, for the Moroccans, in Halstead, *Rebirth of a Nation*, 310. The High Mediterranean Committee, a quasi-governmental body established in 1935, estimated that there were between three and four hundred North African students in France in 1935. See ANSOM, Affaires politiques, Carton 920, dossier 1.

10. Charles André Julien, *L'Afrique du Nord en Marche* (Paris: Julliard, 1952), 20-24.

11. Archives du Ministère des Affaires Etrangères, série K, carton 105, dossier 70. In a subsequent post, as the minister of the interior at Vichy, Peyrouton did not have to contend with this kind of restraint.

12. Ageron, *Histoire de l'Algérie Contemporaine*, 349-360.

13. See the discussion of the AEMNA conferences in Guy Pervillé, "Les Étudiants Musulmans Algériens, 1908-1962" (Ph.D. diss., École des Hautes Études en Sciences Sociales, 1980), 127-134 and Archives du Ministère des Affaires Etrangères, Serie K, Carton 105, dossier 70.

14. Ageron, *Histoire de l'Algérie Contemporaine*, 539 and Claude Liauzu, *Aux Origines des Tiers-mondismes: Colonisés et Anticolonialistes en France 1919-1939* (Paris: l'Harmattan, 1982), 163.

15. ANSOM, affairs politiques, carton 907, dossier 7 and Archives du Ministère des Affaires Etrangères, Serie K, carton 105, dossier 15.

16. For a discussion of the North African writers whose lives have been marked by intense and ambivalent feelings toward French culture, see David Gordon, *North Africa's French Legacy: 1954-1962* (Cambridge: Harvard University Press, 1964), 34-64. See also Louis Massignon, "Colonisation et Conscience Chrétienne," *Esprit*, December 1935 and Emile Dermenghem, "La Crise Economique et la Collaboration des Races," *Maghreb* no. 4, (1932).

17. Suret-Canale, *French Colonialism in Tropical Africa*, 388-389.

18. ARUP, 227.

19. Slotfom VI,9.

20. ARUP 227. Also Slotfom, III, 18.

21. See Imanuel Geiss, *The Pan-African Movement* (New York: Africana Publishing Company, 1974), 305-316. Also J. Ayo Langely, *Pan Africanism and Africanism in West Africa* (Oxford: The Clarendon Press, 1973), 286-325.

22. For a short and incisive discussion of négritude, see Geiss, *The Pan African Movement*, 313-321. A literary history of négritude is Lilyan Kesteloot, *Black Writers in French: A Literary History of Négritude* trans. Ellen Conroy Kennedy (Philadelphia: Temple University Press, 1974). Also informative is Jacques Louis Hymans, *Léopold Sédar Senghor: An Intellectual Autobiography* (Edinburgh: Edinburgh University Press, 1971).

23. Aimé Césaire, "Cahier d'un Retour au Pays Natal," in A. James Arnold, *Modernism and Négritude: the Poetry and Poetics of Aimé Césaire* (Cambridge: Harvard University Press, 1981), 22.

24. Nguyen Khac Vien, "Confucianism and Marxism in Vietnam," in Nguyen Khac Vien, *Tradition and Revolution in Vietnam* (Berkeley: Indochina Resource Center, 1974), 47.

25. Richard Critchfield speculates that Confucianism may contain attributes that make its cultures particularly adept at capitalism. See his article "Science and the Villager," *Foreign Affairs* (Fall 1982). For an interesting discussion of the Confucian political tradition in contemporary Asia, see Lucian Pye, *Asian Power and Politics: the Cultural Dimensions of Authority* (Cambridge: Harvard University Press, 1985), 55-90.

26. Maxime Rodinson, *Islam and Capitalism*, trans. Brian Pearce (Austin: University of Texan Press, 1978), 186.

27. University of Paris enrollment statistics, while not providing an indication of all the students in France, do seem to yield the best year by year barometer of the changing numbers of students. Other government estimates are sporadic, and often contradict one another. See Archives of the Rector of the University of Paris, Carton 227.

28. See Liauzu, *Aux Origines des Tiers Mondismes*, 31-39.

29. Liauzu, *Aux Origines des Tiers Mondismes*, 39-40, and Ageron, *Histoire de l'Algérie Contemporaine*, 352-353.

30. Georges Oved, "La Gauche Française et les Jeunes-Marocains (1930-1935)," in *Cahiers du Mouvement Social*, No. 3, 1978.

31. See Maxime Rodinson, "Marxism and Arab Nationalism" in Rodinson, *Marxism and the Muslim World* (New York: Monthly Review Press, 1981), 224-238 and Ageron, *"L'Algérie Algérienne" de Napoléon III à de Gaulle* (Paris: Éditions Sindbad, 1980), 219-238.

32. Jean Touchard, "L'Espirit des Années 1930," in *Tendances Politique de la Vie Française depuis 1789* (Paris, 1960). See also Girardet, *L'Idée Coloniale en France*, 225-251.

33. Hymans, *Senghor*, 68-69.

34. For a discussion of what Julien's book meant to North African readers, see David Gordon, *Self Determination and History in the Third World* (Princeton, Princeton University Press, 1971), 165-167.

# Conclusion:
# Communism's Master Class

The ideological journey of the Vietnamese students on the Left Bank and elsewhere in France closed the curtain on the concept of *franco-an-namite* collaboration. During the late 1920s, when there was more educational and cross-cultural contact between France and Vietnam than there had been in the previous sixty years of French rule, the idea that attachment to France was worthwhile to the Vietnamese became, for much of the younger generation, discredited beyond redemption. Moreover, those Third Republic traditions of liberalism and political liberty ceased to inspire educated Vietnamese. The nascent Vietnamese Communist movement, rather than any competing party of bourgeois nationalists or collaborators, gained ideological initiative from the students who returned from France to Vietnam during the 1930s.

## Power to the Intellectuals

While these developments were rooted within the specific context of Vietnam's colonial situation, they also form part of a larger pattern of communism's attraction to intellectuals. Communist success with students was not a phenomenon unique to Vietnam. At the same time followers of Stalin and Trotsky were gaining ground within the Vietnamese student movement and broader intelligentsia, a similar process was taking place in China. It had occurred in Russia a generation before: the Bolsheviks had been a party of intellectuals long before they gained support among other segments of the population. The receptiveness of intellectuals—particularly those from backward nations—to Communist ideology has been one of the key elements in that movement's strength and growth. Soviet leaders were not blind to the fact. As early as the sixth Comintern congress, in 1928, one resolution acknowledged that "an important if not predominant part of the Party ranks in the first stage of the movement is recruited from the petty bourgeoisie, and in particular from the revolutionary inclined intelligentsia, very frequently students."[1]

The Comintern leaders responsible for such analysis may have actually believed that members of the working class would one day replace bourgeois intellectuals in the leadership of the various Communist parties then in formation. But nothing of the sort has happened. Intellectuals, and apprentice intellectuals—students—have time and again surfaced as the vanguard of Marxist revolutionary movements, particularly in underdeveloped countries. In nations where the existing intellectual class is small and the bourgeoisie almost nonexistent, students, serving as an embryonic intelligentsia, can carry tremendous political weight. In underdeveloped nations throughout the globe, the political orientation of students is always important, sometimes decisive; nothing of the sort can be said about the proletariat.[2]

Leftward orientation of the intelligentsia is more likely in countries or colonies in which there is no tradition of political freedom. In such circumstances communism can be experienced by the educated elite as the ideology of "revolution from above" promising the maximum empowerment of an educated "new class." Communism promises the new class more or less unrestrained authority to sweep away any remnants of the traditional cultural pattern that might be perceived as obstacles to development. The values likely to be sacrificed along the way include political freedom, of course; but liberty is less likely to be missed if it has never been enjoyed to begin with. Meanwhile the cultural inheritance of the past, also a likely casualty, is generally seen by the new class as a barrier to modernization, not something to be cherished or even tolerated.[3]

### Vietnam's Path

All of these factors were operating in the case of Vietnam. In that colony, the intelligentsia was probably the only class to which an appeal on revolutionary Marxist lines could be made. The Vietnamese industrial working class amounted, in 1930, to as little as one percent of the population. The vast majority of Vietnamese had no contact with either the technological processes of the industrial revolution or the types of organized work that Marx thought would lead to a proletarian class consciousness. Labor unions were almost nonexistent.[4]

Nor did Marxism appeal particularly to the Vietnamese peasantry. Despite famine in much of the Vietnamese countryside, and despite Communist assistance to the rural rebellions in 1930-1931, Vietnam's peasants were generally more responsive to tradition-based political movements. In the 1930s and after, while French-educated intellectuals were discovering Marxist-Leninism, fundamentalist and neotraditionalist religions were spreading like wildfire among the peasantry, particularly in the South. For Vietnamese in the villages, the old symbols of cultural and political allegiance were far from dead, and could be easily revived.[5]

But the relatively privileged class of Vietnam's urban youth had become deaf or hostile to Confucianism and to the other aspects of the Vietnamese tradition. French rule had, over two generations, gradually broken down the old culture and was almost forcing literate and urban Vietnamese to embrace some aspect of the modern. By the 1920s, there remained three political alternatives for a Vietnamese intellectual looking towards the future, but two were very weak.[6]

The first of these alternatives, Franco-Vietnamese collaboration under the conditions of colonialism, may in fact have been doomed by the time World War I ended. For collaboration to make sense to the Vietnamese, such ideas as Vietnam's need for French "protection" had to ring true; this was unlikely after the "protective" power was forced to enlist 100,000 Vietnamese workers and soldiers to help it fight against Germany. The idea that association with France was Vietnam's passport to becoming a modern industrialized state must have appeared equally dubious; other Asian nations were growing at a faster rate than Vietnam. The widely shared perception of the Soviet Union as a nation forging ahead from economic backwardness to industrial power also undermined collaborationist appeals and served to push Vietnamese students leftward.

A number of factors put the second alternative, that of liberal nationalism, at a disadvantage from the start. The small size and negligible political weight of the Vietnamese middle class was the decisive element, and perhaps the only one necessary. Shrewd observers lamented the complete absence of an entrepreneurial class in Vietnam, and a government bureaucracy overstuffed with French bureaucrats kept the Vietnamese administrative class small as well. In addition, liberalism of a kind was the avowed doctrine of those Frenchmen ruling Vietnam, which could not have enhanced its appeal to the Vietnamese. Business enterprises in the colony were usually owned by the French, which ensured that nationalist appeals had an anticapitalist twinge. Parties stressing the idea of political liberty were similarly disadvantaged. One can understand that nationalist Vietnamese, despite their oft-stated desire for democratic reforms, had reason to be skeptical about the claims of "formal democracy"—a practice forbidden to them in the colony, and practiced in the *métropole* by their colonial rulers. The fact that Vietnamese lived without political freedom themselves surely made them less sensitive to its absence in revolutionary Russia, or anywhere in the Communist value system. Political oppression was still selective in the Soviet Union of the 1920s; in those days before Nazism and Stalinism, it may have been impossible for even the most open-minded of Vietnamese nationalists to imagine a society more oppressive than the one France had created in Vietnam.[7]

None of these factors were mitigated by anything that happened to a

Vietnamese student in France. We have noted the passivity of those institutions that might have helped build other, non-Communist, allegiances within the nascent Vietnamese intelligentsia. We have pointed out that the French government, except for its agencies of political surveillance, left the student migration largely untended. No official French organization sought out the most promising young men of Vietnam to give them scholarships for French study; no official French organization tried to soften the sense of uprootedness and isolation that many Vietnamese felt in France. There was an alternative, expressed most forcefully by the gadfly critic Paul Monet, that challenged France to give more to the students and demand more of them—to make them work harder, to reward them with honors and responsibilities, to make an effort to immerse them in the larger culture of France. Such a policy would have required a network of scholarships, special boarding schools, trained teachers, a great deal of money, and above all a firm sense of what France wanted from its young Vietnamese. But all of these elements, particularly the last, were lacking.

Moreover, Vietnamese could make little political progress through political moderation. By World War I, an earlier and politically tamer generation of French-educated Vietnamese had already begun to agitate for some form of political self-determination. Many of them did not want to fight for this self-determination against France, and many wanted continued association with France. These men feared radicalism and violence, as they later would fear communism. Throughout the 1920s, France shut the door on them, denied them successes. The result of these policies was to make Vietnam's older nationalists appear before the nation's youth as ineffectual sycophants, which served to close off alternatives to Communist dominance of the Vietnamese independence movement.

The relative passivity of the French Socialists also contributed to the weakness of non-Communist conceptions of Vietnamese nationalism. As we have seen, French Socialists were quite alert to the importance of the several thousand Vietnamese students in France to the political future of Vietnam. They complained that successive French governments were not doing enough, either in Vietnam or in France, to mold a pro-French Vietnamese elite. But, unlike their Communist competitors, the Socialists did not view the government's omissions as a Socialist opportunity. Vietnamese students in France lived out their years of study in an institutional vacuum which the Socialists made no effort of their own to fill.

Communist organizations were not shy about stepping into that vacuum. One important reason why more Vietnamese returned from France with allegiance to communism rather than to other ideologies was simply that Communists had made more effort to recruit them. These efforts included integrating Vietnamese into Communist-run student organizations, giving funds and printing assistance to Vietnamese student newspapers, providing the psychologically gratifying opportunity to Vietnamese speakers to speak before French audiences. On top of this, the PCF recruited candidates to attend the training school for revolutionary cadres in the Soviet Union, and ran less intensive Party courses for French colonial subjects in France.

Another kind of explanation for the Vietnamese attraction to Marxism-Leninism also emerges from this study, which is both more elusive and more psychological. Contact with France was, for most Vietnamese students, a troubling, exhilarating experience. Suddenly transplanted to a country that appeared efficient, powerful and boundlessly wealthy, young Vietnamese were made directly aware of their own nation's backwardness and poverty. The relative freedom a student experienced in France served to underscore the many choices that were not open to him in the colony. Moreover, prolonged stay in France had the effect off tearing the young student away from his social identity as a Vietnamese. Vietnamese students in France could interact with the French as equals, even as peers—a dramatic turnbout from the situation at home. Yet the very contrast was unsettling. For those Vietnamese who did not choose communism, the experiences described in the writings of Nguyen Manh Tuong and Pham Quynh, or the feelings of the distressed young man whose letter was quoted by Marius Moutet in the French Chamber of Deputies were all too typical. The lament of deracination was not only a description used against the students by Frenchmen opposed to all higher education for Vietnamese; it was, in many instances, the way returning students described themselves. Young Vietnamese often described their return to Vietnam as anguishing, because their French education rendered them no longer able to communicate with their own people, their own parents.[8]

This kind of estrangement became the special burden of the Vietnamese political moderates who were most attracted to French culture. Their political weakness in future struggles was foreshadowed by the successive defeats they suffered in Paris—where, from 1925 to 1930, one moderate or reformist student organization after another crumbled before Vietnamese radicals. In that five-year period the language of politics within the Vietnamese student migration evolved from a discourse calling for liberty and political rights to one calling for class struggle and revolution.

### The Way Out

Marxism-Leninism, the product of Western minds and Western societies, provided a way out of many of these dilemmas. Marxism appealed to the Vietnamese student's desire for the modernization of his society; it stressed industrial development; it was "scientific"; it was couched in the new language of sociology. Marxist ideology explained the West's industrial power, which educated Vietnamese wanted for their own country. But in its Leninist variant, Marxism also carried with it a potently phrased rejection of the West, and a call for the liberation of the colonized peoples. How could this not strike a chord among the Vietnamese? Marxism-Leninism not only provided a method of understanding the West, but claimed to "unmask" it, and thus was a vehicle by which Vietnamese could presume to understand the French more deeply than the French understood themselves. Communist ideology explained the logic of "imperialism." Perhaps more importantly, the ideology gave a sympathetic explanation of why France was rich and powerful while Vietnam was not. It provided a theory of history that promised an eventual Vietnamese victory over colonialism. More than any competing ideology, Marxism proved to be a necessary bridge between two basic emotions shared by the Vietnamese student community: the desire to embrace the West and the hatred of it.

Finally, Marxism-Leninism provided a key to a problem that Vietnamese non-Communists found perpetually vexing: how the Western-educated Vietnamese could relate to his own people, from whom he had become separated by an ocean of education and experience. Non-Communist Vietnamese felt guilty about the fact that, after years in France, they found the Vietnamese of the village backward, superstitious, and crude. Leninism gave the Western-educated Vietnamese a sharply defined role to play in relation to the Vietnamese whom he had left behind. Communist allegiance challenged the student to make himself part of the revolutionary vanguard with the mission to instill revolutionary consciousness in the Vietnamese masses. Thus the Vietnamese peasantry could be perceived as raw material to be fashioned into the hammer of revolution, a weapon to be used against the French rulers of Vietnam. Through Communist activism, through the use of their French academic skills to understand the economy of the village, and through the process of teaching poor Vietnamese peasants how to think about and express their wants in politically useful ways, the Vietnamese Communist intellectual could create for himself a certain kind of reconciliation with those compatriots he had left behind.

For Vietnamese history the implications of this study are clear enough: the leftward turn of the Vietnamese students gave a momentum to Vietnamese communism within the intelligentsia which it retained throughout the wars against the French and the Americans. Can one say that the events on the Parisian Left Bank during the 1920s foreshadowed the Vietnam war? Certainly they eliminated one historical possibility that would have prevented the Vietnam war from taking place: that Vietnamese nationalism would grow under pro-Western or neutralist leadership, willing to pay at least lip-service to France's liberalism and its global aspirations. Had the Left Bank produced a Vietnamese Nehru or Bourguiba, it is possible that France would have initiated steps towards Vietnamese self-determination during the Popular Front, and highly unlikely that France would have fought to deny Vietnam independence after World War II. And of course the United States would never have fought in Vietnam.

### Beyond Vietnam

This limited study lends itself to broader and more contemporary speculations. What is the political effect of the subsequent migrations of "Third World" students, and how do they weigh on the ideological struggles in the world? The case of the Khmer Rouge comes to mind; they too had leaders who, in the 1950s, studied in Paris, and they too were influenced by the French Communist party—though the linkage between their embrace of Stalinism in the *Quartier Latin* and the genocide they carried out twenty years later may never be satisfactorily understood.[9]

The relationship between the educational experience of foreign students and their enduring political values remains murky. For some time there has circulated a cliché which holds that the way to ensure that a student returns from study abroad without Communist values is to send him to Moscow. Surely there are enough examples of Moscow-educated anti-Marxists to keep the cliché alive. They may be exceptions however; there is no indication that the present day Soviet government believes that exposure to its teachers and training is politically counter-productive.

The number of colonial students in the 1920s and 1930s was far fewer than the number of Third World nationals who are studying abroad today. But it may be that greater numbers actually blunt the impact of student politics; westernization, secularization, and communism may have been making their way around the world long enough not to hit 20-year-olds with the force they once did, and the 25-year-old carrier of borrowed Western ideologies might not achieve political preeminence as easily as was the case fifty years ago.

All Western industrialized nations encourage a degree of Third World student migration. The United States hosts more than 300,000 such students annually, more than any other nation. There is, for all practical purposes, no American national policy towards foreign students; both American educators and government officials appear to assume that America is attractive to Third World students because of its openness, manifested by the separation between the government and the universities, and that good-will will flow to the United States naturally, without undue effort.

Most analysts of the subject agree. Indeed, the only scholars who seem particularly worried about the international student flow come from the Left. There the fear is expressed that the appeal of America to Third World students helps to mold Third World elites into the "cultural superstructure of transnational capitalism."[10]

American officials were not always unconcerned about whether the nation's universities played a role in "exporting democracy." In the decade after World War II, the United States government paid detailed attention to the effects of American education on the thirteen thousand Germans who studied under the Fulbright programs. The Germans were subject to regular questioning designed to reveal their attitudes about authority, leadership, dissent and the like; the results were regularly scrutinized by teams of social scientists. In the end Fulbright program migrations are considered to have had a beneficial effect on the building of democracy in the Federal Republic. Now the United States lets students fend for themselves, assuming that—at least in so far as political values are concerned—hands off is the best policy.[11]

Much less, of course, is known about Soviet policies towards Third World students. It is generally thought that Soviet efforts are more systematic. Soviet educational policies towards Third World students are likely to be far more explicitly political. The CIA estimated that there were eighty thousand foreign students in the Soviet Union in 1980; most of them receive full scholarships. The percentage of these from the Third World has risen to about half and is said to be increasing at 20 percent a year.[12]

These figures do not take into account the Afghans, who are the object of an extraordinary Soviet campaign to mold them into Communists. Beginning in 1984, the Soviets began to take away about two thousand children annually, usually between the ages of 6 and 9—a measure of imperial education that the French, for instance, never really contemplated. Almost nothing is known about what happens to these children inside the Soviet Union, and none have yet returned. Communist ideology is thought not to have the resonance it had during the 1930s, but it seems that Soviet policy takes the role of ideological educations seriously.[13]

What can be inferred is simply that the Soviets consider political education in the Third World a serious matter, devote more government resources to it than do Americans or other Westerners, and that this investment has increased in the last decade. We don't seem to know whether they are investing their money well, or their criteria for success. In short, we understand little about the relationship between political ideology and migrating students in today's world. What we do have is historical reason to believe that the eventual political allegiances of students from societies where education is a scarce luxury can have great importance over the long run.

## Notes

1. *Imprecor* Vol. VIII, No. 88, Dec. 12, 1928, quoted in Morris Wattnick, "The Appeal of Communism to the Peoples of Underdeveloped Areas" in Richard Bendix and Seymour Martin Lipset, eds., *Class, Status, and Power* (New York: The Free Press, 1966).

2. For an excellent discussion of the appeal of communism to Arab intellectuals, see Walter Z. Laqueur, *Communism and Nationalism in the Middle East* (New York: Praeger, 1957), 272-280 and passim. The idea that students and other disaffected intellectuals might be the social class most likely to produce a revolutionary Marxist vanguard, even in industrially advanced countries, was emphasized by several Western Marxists in the 1960s and 1970s. An early statement was C. Wright Mills, *Power, Politics and People* (New York: Ballantine Books, 1963), 256-259. See also Alvin W. Gouldner, *The Future of Intellectuals and the Rise of the New Class* (New York: Oxford University Press, 1979), 53-57 and passim. The subject of the political role of students and intellectuals in the postcolonial Third World has already has been the source of a large literature. A good beginning is Seymour Martin Lipset, "University Students and Politics in Underdeveloped Countries" in Seymour Martin Lipset, ed., *Student Politics* (New York: Basic Books, 1967). See also Donald K. Emmerson, ed., *Students and Politics in Developing Nations* (New York: Praeger, 1968).

3. Orwell has made some sharp comments on how this impulse can grow among intellectuals in a developed country. Reviewing James Burnham's *The Managerial Revolution* he writes: "If one examines the people who, having some idea of what the Russian regime is like, are strongly russophile, one finds that, on the whole, they belong to the "managerial" class of which Burnham writes. That is, they are not managers in the narrow sense, but scientists, technicians, teachers, journalists, broadcasters, bureaucrats, professional politicians: in general, middling people who feel themselves cramped by a system that is still partly aristocratic, and are hungry for more power and prestige. These people look towards the USSR and see in it, or think they see, a system which eliminates the upper class, keeps the working class in its place, and hands unlimited power to people very similar to themselves. It was only *after* the Soviet regime became unmistakably totalitarian that English intellectuals, in large numbers, began to show an interest in it. Burnham, although the English russophile intelligentsia would repudiate him, is really voicing their secret wish: the wish to destroy the old equalitarian version of Socialism and usher in a hierarchical society where the intellectual can at last get his hands on the whip." George Orwell, *The Collected Essays, Journalism and Letters of George Orwell* (New York and London: Harcourt Brace Jovanovich, 1968), 178-179.

4. Alexander Woodside, *Community and Revolution in Modern Vietnam* (Boston: Houghton Mifflin, 1976), 203-206.

5. Woodside suggests that the appeal of the syncretic and neotraditionalist Cao Dai and Hoa Hao sects to Vietnamese peasants demonstrates that the symbols

of Vietnam's classical culture were not as dead for the common people as they were to Vietnam's French-educated intelligentsia. For discussion of these movements, see Woodside, *Community and Revolution*, 182-192.

6. In the 1930s fascism was viewed as a potential alternative to communism and liberal democracy, particularly in the Arab world. Any Vietnamese attraction to the extreme Right was probably dampened by the French Right's fondness for patronizing remarks about Vietnamese intellectual pretensions. Taittinger's *Jeunesses Patriotes* tried to avoid this, and an intellectual like Pham Quynh admired Charles Maurras. Still there is little evidence of sustained Vietnamese interest in European fascism.

7. In no Vietnamese newspaper, leaflet, letter, or other documents emanating from the Vietnamese student community during this period have I seen a reference, positive or negative, to the state of personal liberty under Soviet rule.

8. Edward Shils, in "Intellectuals in the Political Development of the New States" in Shils, *The Intellectuals and the Powers* (Chicago: University of Chicago Press, 1972), 405-406 claims that in many cases the "deracinated" label was a term used by the enemies of returned students, and was often an exaggeration. He points out, in reference to Indian students, that many had personal lives grounded in the traditional, in which the women in their lives—wives and mothers—kept them in touch with their people's traditional culture. Perhaps this kind of solace was experienced more by Indian students than Vietnamese. Among the latter, estrangement from potential Vietnamese wives was one of their principal laments.

9. Elizabeth Becker, *When the War Was Over* (New York: Simon & Schuster, 1987) contains a good summary of what is known about the Khmer Rouge-Paris connection.

10. See, for instance, Hans Weiler, "The Political Dilemmas of Foreign Study," *Comparative Education Review* 28,2 (1984):168-79.

11. See Henry J. Kellerman, *Cultural Relations and U.S. Foreign Policy: The Educational, Exchange Program Between the U.S. and Germany, 1945-1954* (Washington D.C.: Department of State, 1978). For current U.S. policies, see for instance Craufurd D. Goodwin and Michael Nacht, *Absence of Decision: Foreign Students in American Colleges and Universities* (New York: Institute for International Education, 1983).

12. See *Foreign Students and Institutional Policy* (Washington D.C.: American Council on Education, 1982).

13. Jeri Laber, "Afghanistan's Other War," *New York Review of Books*, 18 December 1986.

# Sources

I. Archives

A. Archives Nationales (AN), Paris.
Série F7—13170, 13410, 13412.
Série F17—13594, 13650, 13652, 13790, 13954.
Série AJ 16—2708, 5760, 5807, 6946.

B. Archives Nationales, Section d'outre-mer (ANSOM). (This archive, formerly in Paris, has been relocated to Aix-en-Provence.)
1. Service de liaison entre les originaires de la France d'outre-mer. (Slotfom.)
Série I: Cartons 4, 5, 6, 7, 10.
Série III: Cartons 1, 2, 5, 7, 11, 12, 14, 16, 17, 18, 23, 25, 28, 29, 30, 31, 32,
33, 34, 37, 40, 43, 44, 45, 58, 60, 61, 68, 71, 75, 77, 78, 88, 97, 101, 102, 118,
119, 120, 129, 143, 147, 150.
Série V: Carton 33.
Série VI: Carton 9.
Série XIII: Carton 2.
2. Nouveau Fonds Indochine (NFI):
Cartons 224-1806, 231-1900, 259-2223 (1), 259-2226, 259-2229, 269-2373,
286-2492, 326-2637, 331-2679, 336-2695, 1193.
3. Fonds Guernot, Carton 22 Ba.
4. Affaires Politiques, Cartons 907, 920, 1421.
5. Agence Française d'outre mer, Carton 240, dossier 330.

C. Archives du gouvernement générale de l'Indochine, Aix-en-Provence
(AOM-Indochine).
Série R: Cartons 19090, 47470, 51352, 51353, 51355, 51356, 51358, 51373,
51383, 51404, 51433, 51435, 51436, 51439, 51523, 51524, 51526, 51527,
51528, 51529, 51532, 51533, 51334, 51535, 51536, 51537, 51539.
D. Archives du Ministère des Affaires Etrangères, Paris
Afrique, Série K: Carton 105; dossiers 15, 70, 72.
E. Archives of the Rector of the University of Paris (ARUP).
Cartons 7, 16, 37, 212, 213, 214, 219, 227, 238.

II. Newspapers and Periodicals. (Those consulted over a period of time are listed here. References to individual articles in other journals are given in the notes.)

Académie des sciences coloniales
Clarté
Espirit
Humanité
Journal des étudiants annamites
La Dépêche coloniale
L'Afrique française
L'Annam de demain
L'Asie française

Le Populaire
Le Temps (supplément coloniale)
L'Étudiant catholique
L'Étudiant d'avant garde
Maghreb
Revue universitaire

III. Books and Articles

Ageron, Charles-Robert. "L'Association des étudiants musulmans nord-africains en Franace durant l'entre-deux-guerres." *Revue français d'Histoire d'Outre-Mer*, tome LXX(1983).
_____. *"L'Algérie algérienne" de Napoleon III à de Gaulle*. Paris: Editions Sindbad, 1980.
_____. *Histore de l'Algérie contemporaine*. Tome II. Paris: Presses Universitaires de France, 1979.
_____. *France coloniale ou parti colonial?* Paris: Presses Universitaires de France, 1978.
_____. "Les Communistes français devant la question algérienne (de 1921 à 1924)." *Politiques coloniales au Maghreb*. Paris: Presses Universitaires de France, 1972.
_____. *Les Algériens musulmans et la France, 1871-1919*. Paris: Presses Universitaires de France, 1968.
Albertini, Rudolph von. *Decolonization*. Garden City: Doubleday, 1971.
Altbach, Philip G. and Gail P. Kelly, eds. *Education and the Colonial Experience*. New Brunswick: Transaction, 1984.
American Council on Education. *Foreign Students and Institutional Policy*. Washington, D.C.: American Council on Education, 1982.
Andrew, Christopher and A. S. Kanya-Forstner. *France Overseas: The Great War and the Climax of French Imperial Expansion*. London: Thames & Hudson, Ltd., 1981.
Arnold, James. *Modernism and Negritude: The Poetry and Poetics of Aimé Césaire*. Cambridge: Harvard University Press, 1981.
Aron, Raymond. *Espoir et peur du siecle. Essais non partisans*. Paris: Calmann-Levy, 1957.
Barraclough, Geoffrey. *An Introduction to Contemporary History*. New York: Penguin, 1978.
Becker, Elizabeth. *When the War Was Over*. New York: Simon & Schuster, 1987.
Bendix, Reinhard and Seymour Martin Lipset, eds. *Class, Status and Power*. New York: Free Press, 1966.
Bennabi, Malek. *Vocation d'Islam*. Paris, 1954.

Bernard, Paul. *Nouveaux aspects du probleme économique indochinois*. Paris: Fernand Sorlot, 1937.

Bernstein, Richard. "Remaking Afghanistan in the Soviet Image." *The New York Times*, 24 March 1985.

Berque, Augustin. "Les Intellectuels algériens." *Revue africaine* 91 (1947).

Berque, Jacques. *French North Africa: The Maghrib between Two Wars*. Translated by Jean Stewart. London: Faber and Faber, Ltd., 1962.

Betts, Raymond F. *Tricouleur*. New York: Gordon & Cremonesi, 1978.

———. *Assimilation and Association in French Colonial Theory, 1890-1914*. New York: Columbia University Press, 1961.

Borkenau, Franz. *World Communism*. Ann Arbor: University of Michigan Press, 1971.

Brandt, Conrad. "The French Returned Elite in the Chinese Communist Party." In *Symposium on Economic and Social Problems of the Far East*. Edited by E. F. Szezepanik. Hong Kong, 1961.

Brocheux, Pierre. "Les Grands dien chu de la Cochinchine occidentale pendant la period coloniale." In *Tradition et révolution au Vietnam*. Edited by Jean Chesneaux, Georges Boudarel and Daniel Hémery. Paris: Editions Anthropos, 1971.

Brower, Daniel R. *The New Jacobins, the French Communist Party and the Popular Front*. Ithaca: Cornell University Press, 1968.

Brunschwig, Henri. *French Colonialism, 1871-1914, Myths and Realities*. Translated by William Glanville Brown. London: Pall Mall Press Ltd., 1966.

Buttinger, Joseph. *Vietnam: A Dragon Embattled*. Vols. I & II. New York: Praeger, 1967.

Carrère d'Encausse, Hélène, and Stuart Schram. *Marxism and Asia*. London: Allen Lane, The Penguin Press, 1969.

Catrice, Paul. "Les Etudiants orientaux dans l'enseignement secondaire et supérieur." *La Documentation catholique*, no. 604, March 19, 1932.

———. "Les Étudiants orientaux en France." *La Documentation catholique*, 576, August 15, 1931.

———. "L'Orient à l'école de l'occident." *Documents de la vie intellectuelle*, June 20, 1931.

Caudel, Maurice. *Pour les étudiants étrangers en France, notes, conseils, lectures*. Paris: Librarie Plon, 1925.

Caute, David. *Communism and the French Intellectuals*. London: Andre Deutsch, 1964.

Challaye, Félicien. *Souvenirs sur la colonisation*. Paris: Librarie Picart, 1935.

Chesneaux, Jean. *Contribution à l'histoire de la nation vietnamienne*. Paris: Editions Sociales, 1955.

Claudin, Fernando. *The Communist Movement: From Comintern to Cominform*. Translated by Brian Pearce. New York: Monthly Review Press, 1975.

Cohen, William. *Rulers of Empire: The French Colonial Service in Africa*. Stanford: Hoover Institution Press, 1971.

Colton, Joel. *Léon Blum: Humanist in Politics*. New York: Alfred Knopf, 1966.

Confer, Vincent. *France and Algeria: The Problem of Civil and Political Reform, 1870-1920*. Syracuse: Syracuse University Press, 1966.

*Congrès internationale de l'évolution culturelle des peuples coloniales*. Paris 1938.

Cook, Megan. *The Constitutionalist Party in Indochina: The Years of Decline, 1930-1942*. Victoria, Australia: Center of Southeast Asian Studies, 1977.

Critchfield, Richard. "Science and the Villager." *Foreign Affairs*, Fall 1982.

Debeauvais, Michel. "Education in Former French Africa." In *Education and Political Development*. Edited by James Coleman. Princeton: Princeton University Press, 1965.

Delétie, Henri. "De l'Adaptation de nos programmes d'enseignement au milieu annamite." *Académie des sciences coloniales*. Tome 14. 1929-1930.

_____. "Le Problème universitaire indochinois." *Académie des sciences coloniale*. Tome 8. 1926-1927.

_____. "L'Instruction publique en Indochine." *Académie des sciences coloniales*. Tome 2. 1923-1924.

de Tocqueville, Alexis. *The Old Regime and the French Revolution*. Translated by Stuart Gilbert. Garden City: Doubleday, 1955.

Devillers, Phillipe. *Histoire du Vietnam de 1940 à 1952*. Paris: Editions du Seuil, 1952.

Diep Van Ky. L'Enseignement des indigènes en Indochine." *Académie des sciences coloniales*. Tome 4. 1924-1925.

Dorsenne, Jean. "Le péril rouge en Indochine." *Revue des deux mondes*, April 1, 1932.

Draper, Theodore. *American Communism and Soviet Russia*. New York: Viking, 1960.

Duchêne, Albert. *La Politique coloniale de France*. Paris: Payot, 1928.

Duiker, William T. *The Communist Road to Power in Vietnam*. Boulder: Westview Press, 1981.

_____. *The Rise of Nationalism in Vietnam, 1900-1941*. Ithaca: Cornell University Press, 1976.

_____. "The Comintern and Vietnamese Communism." Ohio Center for International Studies, Southeast Asia Series, No. 37, 1975.

Durtain, Luc. *Dieux blancs, hommes jaunes*. Paris: Ernest Flammarion, 1930.

Emmerson, Donald T., ed. *Students and Politics in Developing Nations*. New York and London: Praeger, 1968.

Ennis, Thomas. *French Policy and Developments in Indochina*. Chicago: University of Chicago Press, 1936.

Fanon, Franz. *The Wretched of the Earth*. Translated by Constance Farrington. New York: Grove Press, 1963.

FitzGerald, Frances. *Fire in the Lake: the Vietnamese and the Americans in Vietnam*. Boston: Little Brown, 1972.

Frederick, William. "Alexandre Varenne and Politics in Indochina." In *Aspects of Vietnamese History*. Edited by Walter Vella. Honolulu: University of Hawaii Asian Studies, 1973.

Furnivall, John S. *Educational Progress in Southeast Asia*. New York: Institute of Pacific Relations, 1943.

Gautherot, Gustave. *Le Bolchévisme aux colonies et l'impérialisme rouge*. Paris: Librarie de la Revue Française, 1930.

Geiss, Imanuel. *The Pan-African Movement*. New York: Africana Publishing Company, 1974.

Gide, André. *Travels in the Congo*. Translated by Dorothy Bussey. New York: Alfred A. Knopf, 1929.

Gifford, Prosser, and Timothy Weiskel. "African Education in a Colonial Context: French and British Styles." In *France and Britain in Africa*. Edited by Prosser Gifford and William Roger Louis. New Haven: Yale University Press, 1971.

Girardet, Raoul. *L'Idée Coloniale en France de 1871 à 1962*. Paris: La Table Ronde, 1972.

Goodwin, Craufurd D., and Michael Nacht. *Absence of Decision: Foreign Students in American Colleges and Universities*. New York: Institute for International Education, 1983.

Gordon, David. *Self-Determination and History in the Third World*. Princeton: Princeton University Press, 1971.

_____. *North Africa's French Legacy: 1954-1962*. Cambridge: Harvard University Press, 1964.

Gouldner, Alvin W. *The Future of Intellectuals and the Rise of the New Class*. New York: Oxford University Press, 1979.

Greene, Nathanael. *Crisis and Decline: The French Socialist Party in the Popular Front Era*. Ithaca: Cornell University Press, 1969.

Grousset, René. *Le Réveil de l'Asie*. Paris: Plon, 1924.

Gruber, Helmut. *Soviet Russia Masters the Comintern*. New York: Anchor Press/Doubleday, 1974.

Guérin, Daniel. *Aux Service des Colonisés*. Paris: Les Editions de Minuit, 1954.

Halberstam, David. *Ho*. New York: Random House, 1971.

Halstead, John. *Rebirth of a Nation: The Origins and Rise of Moroccan Nationalism, 1912-1944*. Cambridge: Harvard University Press, 1967.

Hardy, Georges. *Nos Grandes Problèmes Coloniaux*. Paris: Armand Colin, 1933.

Harmand. *Domination et Colonisation*. Paris: Ernest Flammarion, 1910.

Hémery, Daniel. "Ta Thu Thau: l'Itinéraire politique d'un révolutionaire vietnamien." In *Histoire de l'Asie du sud-est: révoltes, réformes, révolutions*. Edited by Pierre Brocheux. Lille: Presses Universitaire de Lille, 1981.

_____. "Du Patriotisme au Marxisme: l'Immigration Vietnamienne en France de 1926 à 1930." *Le Mouvement Sociale*, January 1975.

_____. "Aux origines des guerres d'indépendance vietnamiennes: pouvoir coloniale et phénomène communiste en Indochine avant la seconde guerre mondiale." *Le Mouvement social*, January-March 1975.

_____. *Révolutionnaires vietnamiens et pouvoir colonial en Indochine: communistes, trotskystes, nationalistes à Saigon de 1932 à 1937*. Paris: François Maspero, 1975.

Hodgkin, Thomas. *Vietnam: The Revolutionary Path*. London: Macmillan, 1981.

Hoffmann, Stanley. "Paradoxes of the French Political Community." In *In Search of France*. New York: Harper and Row, 1965.

Hunt, R. N. Carew. "Willi Muenzenberg." St. Anthony's Papers no. 9. In *International Communism*. Edited by David Footman. London: Chatto and Windus, 1960.

Huynh Kim Khanh. *Vietnamese Communism 1925-1945*. Ithaca: Cornell University Press, 1982.

Hymans, Jacques Louis. *Léopold Sédar Senghor: An Intellectual Autobiography*. Edinburgh: Edinburgh University Press, 1971.

Isoart, Paul. *Le Phénomène National Vietnamien*. Paris: Librarie Générale de Droit et de Jurisprudence, 1961.

Julien, Charles-André. *L'Afrique du Nord en Marche*. Paris: René Julliard, 1952.

Kedourie, Elie. *Nationalism in Asia and Africa*. New York: New American Library, 1970.

Kellerman, Henry J. *Cultural Relations and U.S. Foreign Policy: The Educational Exchange Program Between the U.S. and Germany, 1945-1954*. Washington, D.C.: Department of State, 1978.

Kelly, Gail P. "Schooling and National Integration: The Case of Interwar Vietnam." *Comparative Education* 18, 2 (1982).

_____. "Colonial Schools in Vietnam: Policy and Practice." *Proceedings of the 2nd Annual Meeting of the French Colonial Historical Society* (March 1977).

Kempf, François. "Les Catholiques Français." In Marcel Merle, *Les Eglises chrétiennes et la décolonisation*. Paris: A. Colin, 1967.

Kesteloot, Lilyan. *Black Writers in French: A Literary History of Négritude*. Translated by Ellen Conroy Kennedy. Philadelphia: Temple University Press, 1974.

Khérian, Grégoire. "La Querelle de l'industrialisation." *Revue indochinois juridique et l'économique* IV, 1938.

Kriegel, Annie. "Aux origines françaises du communisme chinois." In *Communismes au miroir français*. Paris: Gallimard, 1974.

_____. *The French Communists*. Translated by Elaine Halperin. Chicago: University of Chicago Press, 1972.

_____. *Le Pain et les roses*. Paris: Presses Universitaires de France, 1968.

Laber, Jeri. "Afghanistan's Other War." *New York Review of Books*, 18 December 1986.

Lacouture, Jean. *Ho Chi Minh: A Political Biography*. Translated by Peter Wiles. New York: Random House, 1968.

Lancaster, Donald. *The Emancipation of French Indochina*. London: Oxford University Press, 1961.

Langely, J. Ayo. *Pan Africanism and Nationalism in West Africa*. Oxford: Clarendon Press, 1973.

Langlois, Walter. *André Malraux: The Indochina Adventure*. New York: Praeger, 1966.

Laqueur, Walter Z. *Communism and Nationalism in the Middle East*. New York: Praeger, 1956.

Lazitch, Branko, and Milorad Drachkovitch. *Lenin and the Comintern*. Volume 1. Stanford: Hoover Institution Press, 1972.

Le Bon, Gustave. "L'Influence de l'éducation et des institutions Européenes sur les populations indigenes des colonies." *Congrès coloniale internationale de Paris*, 1889.

Le Calloc'h, Bernard. "Le role de Pham Quynh dans la promotion de *quoc ngu* et de la littérature vietnamienne moderne," *Revue française d'histoire d'outre-mer*. tome LXXII, 1985.

"Les Étudiants Orientaux en Europe." *Documents de la Vie Intellectuelle*, 20 October 1931.

Levenson, Joseph. *Confucian China and its Modern Fate*. Berkeley: University of California Press, 1958.

Lévi, Sylvain. "L'Enseignement en Indochine." *Académie des Sciences Coloniales*, Tome 4, 1924-1925.

Liauzu, Claude. *Aux origines des tiers mondismes: Colonisés et anti-colonialistes en France, 1919-1939*. Paris: Editions L'Harmattan, 1982.

Lipset, Seymour Martin, editor. *Student Politics*. New York: Basic Books, 1967.

Loubet del Bayle, Jean Louis. *Les Non-conformistes des années 30: une tentative de renouvellement de la pensée politique française*. Paris: Éditions du Seuil, 1969.

Mansur, Fatma. *Process of Independence*. London: Routledge & Kegan Paul, 1962.

Marr, David. *Vietnamese Tradition on Trial*. Berkeley: University of California Press, 1981.

_____. *Vietnamese Anticolonialism: 1885-1925*. Berkeley: University of California Press, 1971.

McAlister, John T., Jr. *Viet Nam: The Origins of Revolution.* New York: Alfred A. Knopf, 1969.

McClane, Charles B. *Soviet Strategies in Southeast Asia.* Princeton: Princeton University Press, 1966.

McKenzie, Kermit. *Comintern and World Revolution.* New York: Columbia University Press, 1964.

Memmi, Albert. *The Colonizer and the Colonized.* Translated by Howard Greenfield. Boston: Beacon Press, 1967.

Mills, C. Wright. *Power, Politics and People.* New York: Ballantine Books, 1963.

Monet, Paul. *Entre Deux Feux.* Paris, 1928.

_____. *Français et Annamites.* Paris, 1925.

Moneta, Jacob. *La Politique du parti communiste français dans la question coloniale, 1920-1963.* Paris: François Maspero, 1971.

Moore, Clement. *Tunisia Since Independence.* Berkeley: University of California Press, 1965.

Mortimer, Edward. *The Rise of the French Communist Party, 1920-1947.* London: Faber and Faber, 1984.

Mus, Paul and John T. McAlister. *The Vietnamese and Their Revolution.* New York: Harper and Row, 1970.

Nam Kim. *Nam et Sylvie.* Paris: Plon, 1957.

Nguyen Ai Quoc (Ho Chi Minh). *Le Procès de la Colonisation Française.* Hanoi: Editions des Langues Etrangères, 1962.

Nguyen An Ninh. "La France et l'Indochine." *Europe,* 15 July 1925.

Nguyen Khac Vien. "Confucianism and Marxism in Vietnam." *Tradition and Revolution in Vietnam.* Berkeley: Indochina Resource Center, 1974.

Nguyen Manh Tuong. *Sourires et Larmes d'une Jeunesse.* Hanoi: Éditions de la Revue Indochinoise, 1937.

Orwell, George. *The Collected Essays, Journalism and Letters of George Orwell.* Vol. 4. New York and London: Harcourt, Brace Jovanovich, 1968.

Osborne, Milton. "Continuity and Motivation in the Vietnamese Revolution: New Light from the 1930s." *Pacific Affairs* 47, 1 (Spring 1974).

_____. "The Faithful Few: The Politics of Collaboration in Cochinchina in the 1920s." In *Aspects of Vietnamese History.* Edited by Walter Vella. Honolulu: University of Hawaii Asian Studies, 1973.

_____. *The French Presence in Cochinchina and Cambodia: Rule and Response (1859-1905).* Ithaca: Cornell University Press, 1969.

Oved, Georges. "La Gauche française et les jeunes marocains (1930-1935)." *Cahiers du mouvement sociale,* 3, 1978.

Pham Quynh. *Essais Franco-annamites.* Hue: Bui Huy Tin, 1938.

_____. Nouveaux *Essais Franco-annamites.* Hue: Bui Huy Tin, 1937.

Pike, Douglas. *History of Vietnamese Communism.* Stanford: Hoover Institution Press, 1979.

Prost, Antoine. *Histoire de l'Enseignement en France, 1800-1967.* Paris: Armand Colin, 1958.

Pye, Lucian. *Asian Power and Politics: The Cultural Dimensions of Authority.* Cambridge: Harvard University Press, 1985.

Robequain, Charles. *The Economic Development of French Indochina.* London: Oxford University Press, 1944.

Rodinson, Maxime. *Marxism and the Muslim World.* Translated by Jean Matthews. New York: Monthly Review Press, 1981.

_____. *Islam and Capitalism.* Translated by Brian Pearce. Austin: University of Texas Press, 1978.

Roubaud, Louis. *Viet-Nam: La Tragédie Indochinois.* Paris: Valois, 1931.

Sacks, Milton. "Marxism in Viet Nam." In Frank Trager, *Marxism in Southeast Asia.* Stanford: Stanford University Press, 1959.

Sarraut, Albert. *Grandeur et Servitudes Coloniales.* Paris: Editions du Sagittaire, 1931.

_____. *La Mise en valeur des colonies françaises.* Paris: Payot, 1923.

*Semaines sociales, Le Problème social aux colonies.* Marseilles, XXII session, 1930.

Semidei, Manuela. "Les socialistes français et le problème colonial entre les deux guerres." *Revue française de science politique,* December 1968.

Shils, Edward. *The Intellectuals and the Powers and Other Essays.* Chicago: The University of Chicago Press, 1972.

_____. *The Intellectual between Tradition and Modernity: The Indian Situation.* The Hague: Mouton, 1961.

Singer, Barnett. "From Patriots to Pacifists: The French Primary School Teachers, 1880-1940." *Journal of Contemporary History* 12 (1977).

Smith, R. B. "The Vietnamese Elite of French Cochinchina, 1943." *Modern Asian Studies* 6, 4 (1972).

_____. "Bui Quang Chieu and the Constitutionalist Party in French Indochina, 1917-30." *Modern Asian Studies* 3, 2 (1969).

_____. "The Development of Opposition to French Rule in Southern Vietnam 1880-1940." *Past and Present* 54 (February 1972).

Soucy, Robert. *French Fascism: The First Wave, 1924-1933.* New Haven: Yale University Press, 1986.

Stern, Fritz. "Visions of Europe from Algiers to Tokyo." *Foreign Affairs,* October 1977.

Stora, Benjamin. *Messali Hadj.* Paris: Le Sycomore, 1982.

Suret-Canale, Jean. *French Colonialism in Tropical Africa.* New York: Pica Press, 1971.

Talbott, John. *Educational Reform in Post War France.* Princeton: Princeton University Press, 1969.

Thompson, Virginia. *French Indochina.* New York: Macmillan, 1937.

Touchard, Jean. "L'Espirit des années 1930." *Tendances politique de la vie française depuis 1789,* Paris, 1960.

Vignon, Louis. *Un Programme de politique coloniale: les questions indigènes.* Paris: Librarie Plon, 1919.

Viollis, Andrée. *Indochine S.O.S.* Paris: Gallimard, 1935.

Wang, Y.C. *Chinese Intellectuals and the West.* Chapel Hill: University of North Carolina Press, 1966.

Weiler, Hans. "The Political Dilemmas of Foreign Study." *Comparative Education Review* 28, 2 (1984): 168-179.

Werth, Léon. *Cochinchine.* Paris: F. Rieder & Co., 1926.

Wohl, Robert. *French Communism in the Making, 1914-1924.* Stanford: Stanford University Press, 1966.

Woodside, Alexander. *Community and Revolution in Modern Vietnam.* Boston: Houghton Mifflin Co., 1976.

_____. *Vietnam and the Chinese Model.* Cambridge: Harvard University Press, 1971.

Zeldin, Theodore. "Higher Education in France, 1848-1940." *Journal of Contemporary History* 2 (1967).

IV. Unpublished Manuscripts

Coyle, Johanne Marie. "Indochinese Administration and Education: French Policy and Practice, 1917-1945." Ph.D. diss., Fletcher School of Law and Diplomacy, Tufts University, 1963.

Hamed, M'barka. "Immigration maghrébine et activités politique en France de la premiere guerre Mondiale à la Veille du Front Populaire." Ph.D. diss., University of Paris, 1979.

Kelly, Gail P. "Conflict in the Classroom: A Case Study from Vietnam." Unpublished Manuscript. (Privately communicated.)

———. "Franco-Vietnamese Schools, 1918-1938." Ph.D. diss., University of Wisconsin, 1975.

Pervillé, Guy. "Les Etudiants musulmans algériens, 1908-1962." Ph.D. diss. Écoles des Hautes Études En Sciences Sociales, 1980.

Schor, Ralph. L'Opinion française et les étrangers en France, 1919-1939." Ph.D. diss., University of Nice, 1980.

# Index